the trip of a lifetime

President & Publisher Mike Richardson

Editor Daniel Chabon

Assistant Editor Chuck Howitt

Digital Art Technician Josie Christensen

Spy Island

Collects issues #1–#4 of the Dark Horse Comics series *Spy Island.*

Library of Congress Cataloging-in-Publication Data

Names: Cain, Chelsea, writer. I Miternique, Lia, designer/artist. I McCall, Elise, artist. I Rosenberg, Rachelle,
    colourist. I Caramagna, Joe, letterer.
Title: Spy island / writer, Chelsea Cain ; cover/designer/supplemental art, Lia Miternique ; artist, Elise McCall ;
    colorist, Rachelle Rosenberg ; letterer, Joe Caramagna.
Description: First edition. I Milwaukie, OR : Dark Horse Books, 2020. I "Creators: Chelsea Cain & Lia Miternique"
Identifiers: LCCN 2020017440 (print) I LCCN 2020017441 (ebook) I ISBN
    9781506721026 (paperback) I ISBN 9781506721033 (ebook other)
Subjects: LCSH: Comic books, strips, etc.
Classification: LCC PN6728.S679 C35 2020 (print) I LCC PN6728.S679 (ebook) I DDC 741.5/973--dc23
LC record available at https://lccn.loc.gov/2020017440
LC ebook record available at https://lccn.loc.gov/2020017441

Published by
Dark Horse Books
A division of Dark Horse Comics LLC
10956 SE Main Street
Milwaukie, OR 97222

DarkHorse.com

To find a comics shop in your area, visit comicshoplocator.com

First edition: March 2021
Ebook ISBN 978-1-50672-103-3
Trade paperback ISBN 978-1-50672-102-6

10 9 8 7 6 5 4 3 2 1
Printed in China

Neil Hankerson **Executive Vice President** • Tom Weddle **Chief Financial Officer** • Randy Stradley **Vice President of Publishing** • Nick McWhorter **Chief Business Development Officer** • Dale LaFountain **Chief Information Officer** • Matt Parkinson **Vice President of Marketing** • Vanessa Todd-Holmes **Vice President of Production and Scheduling** • Mark Bernardi **Vice President of Book Trade and Digital Sales** • Ken Lizzi **General Counsel** • Dave Marshall **Editor in Chief** • Davey Estrada **Editorial Director** • Chris Warner **Senior Books Editor** • Cary Grazzini **Director of Specialty Projects** • Lia Ribacchi **Art Director** • Matt Dryer **Director of Digital Art and Prepress** • Michael Gombos **Senior Director of Licensed Publications** • Kari Yadro **Director of Custom Programs** • Kari Torson **Director of International Licensing** • Sean Brice **Director of Trade Sales**

Spy Island

A Bermuda Triangle Mystery

a 4-day adventure at sea

NORTH
ATLANTIC
OCEAN
BERMUDA
FLORIDA
THE
BERMUDA
TRIANGLE
PUERTO RICO

CREATED BY
CHELSEA CAIN & LIA MITERNIQUE
A MINISTRY OF TROUBLE PRODUCTION

ISLAND LINES
Cruise The Bermuda Triangle

You get all this!

- 4-night cruise + five nights at the fabulous Bermuda Triangle Marriott!

- 5-day car rental, from arrival until departure, including unlimited mileage (you pay only for gas and insurance).

- Detailed map of the Island.

- Exciting Call to the Kraken welcome ceremony at the famed Memorial Beach State Park including cover charge, drink, dancing, tax, tip.

- $1 off all purchases at the Yogurt Hut during your stay.

- Complimentary Cocktail and Show plus dinner at the Lusty Hag Lounge.

Cruise departs from the mainland on Thursdays!

Itinerary MAINLAND/ISLAND/MAINLAND

One unforgettable vacation to revel in the glories of the Bermuda Triangle and the Island. Soak up the sun, ride the surge in a catamaran, and participate in the many activities happening every day, every night, everywhere! All of the Island at your own leisurely pace. Among the many places you will want to visit are the Atlantean Ruins National Park, Ghost Pirate Cove, and the Deadly Marsh Weed Ecological Reserve. You will also enjoy golfing, surfing, and gathering fossilized mermaid teeth along the Island's many off-the-beaten-path beaches. Never was Paradise so accessible and so convenient.

WRITER CHELSEA CAIN **COVER/DESIGNER/SUPPLEMENTAL ART** LIA MITERNIQUE
ARTIST ELISE McCALL **COLORIST** RACHELLE ROSENBERG **LETTERER** JOE CARAMAGNA
SUPPLEMENTAL ART STELLA GREENVOSS **HAIKUS** EMILY POWELL
SUPPLEMENTAL LETTERING ELIZA FANTASTIC MOHAN

All aboard.

Nothing is quite the same in the Bermuda Triangle.
Discovery gaiety, adventure, exotic flora and fauna, beauty salons, and more, on this adventure of a lifetime. Welcome to your dream vacation. You will enjoy sunny, carefree days at sea, interesting friends, tempting foods and sightseeing adventures afloat and ashore. It's everything you've dreamed a cruise should be.
87% rain-free. Air conditioned cabins.
5% off hats in the gift store.

SPORTS DECK
BOAT DECK
RENDEZ-VOUS DECK
SAPPHIRE DECK
EMERALD DECK
CORAL DECK
AMBER DECK

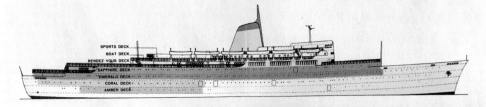

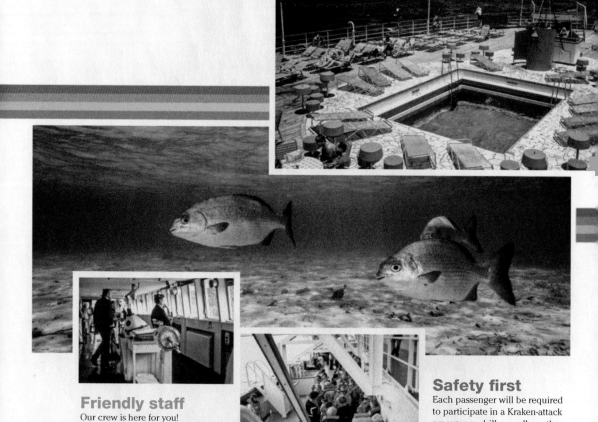

Friendly staff
Our crew is here for you!
Trained in every manner of service.

Safety first
Each passenger will be required to participate in a Kraken-attack emergency drill, as well as other disaster scenarios.

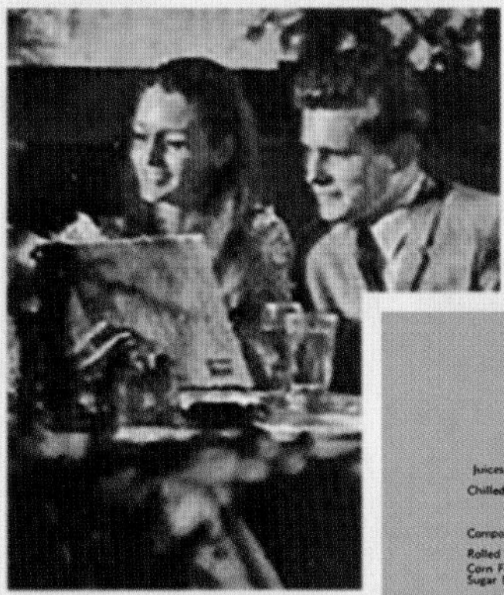

5-star dining

We offer cottage cheese with every meal.

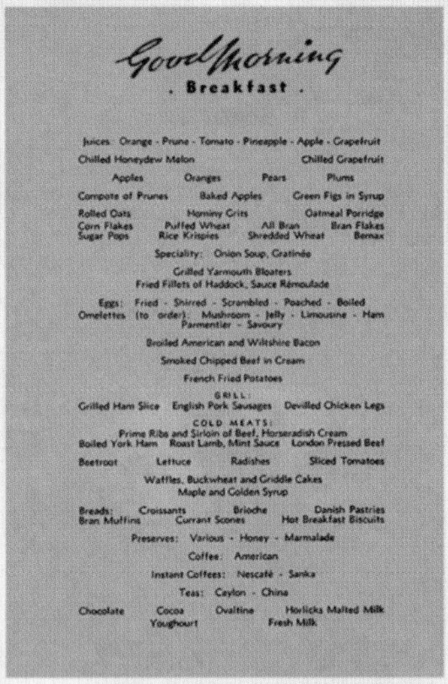

Good Morning
. Breakfast .

Juices: Orange - Prune - Tomato - Pineapple - Apple - Grapefruit
Chilled Honeydew Melon Chilled Grapefruit
Apples Oranges Pears Plums
Compote of Prunes Baked Apples Green Figs in Syrup
Rolled Oats Hominy Grits Oatmeal Porridge
Corn Flakes Puffed Wheat All Bran Bran Flakes
Sugar Pops Rice Krispies Shredded Wheat Bemax
Speciality: Onion Soup, Gratinée
Grilled Yarmouth Bloaters
Fried Fillets of Haddock, Sauce Rémoulade
Eggs: Fried - Shirred - Scrambled - Poached - Boiled
Omelettes (to order): Mushroom - Jelly - Limousine - Ham
Parmentier - Savoury
Broiled American and Wiltshire Bacon
Smoked Chipped Beef in Cream
French Fried Potatoes
GRILL:
Grilled Ham Slice English Pork Sausages Devilled Chicken Legs
COLD MEATS:
Prime Ribs and Sirloin of Beef, Horseradish Cream
Boiled York Ham Roast Lamb, Mint Sauce London Pressed Beef
Beetroot Lettuce Radishes Sliced Tomatoes
Waffles, Buckwheat and Griddle Cakes
Maple and Golden Syrup
Breads: Croissants Brioche Danish Pastries
Bran Muffins Currant Scones Hot Breakfast Biscuits
Preserves: Various - Honey - Marmalade
Coffee: American
Instant Coffees: Nescafé - Sanka
Teas: Ceylon - China
Chocolate Cocoa Ovaltine Horlicks Malted Milk
Youghourt Fresh Milk

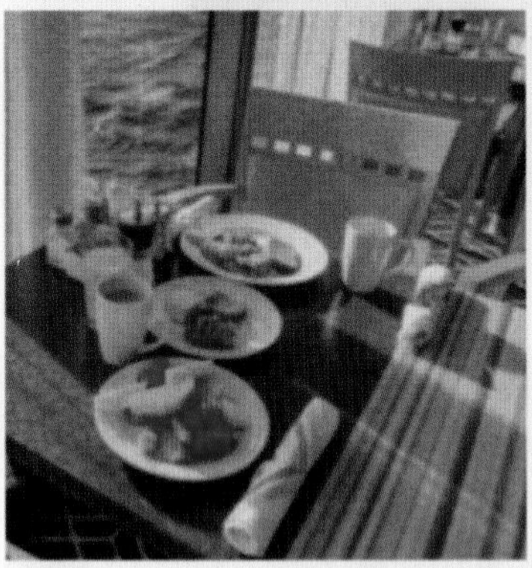

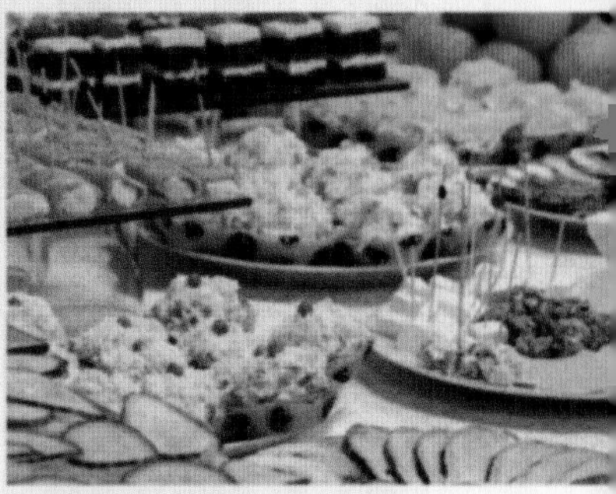

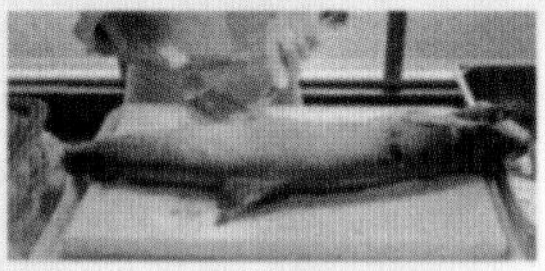

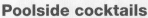

Poolside cocktails

Our daily poolside cocktail specials are free-of-charge, depending on your beverage package.

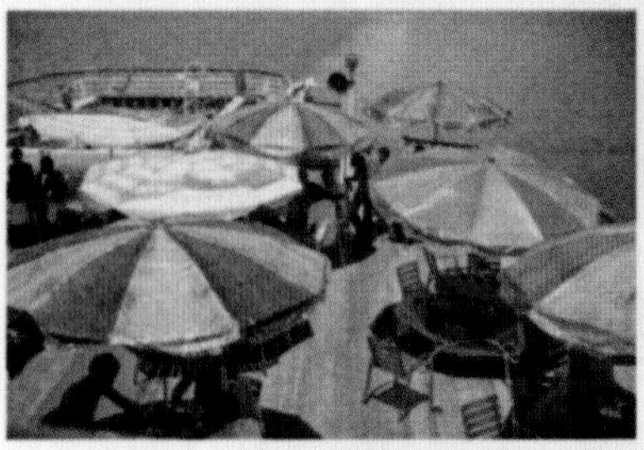

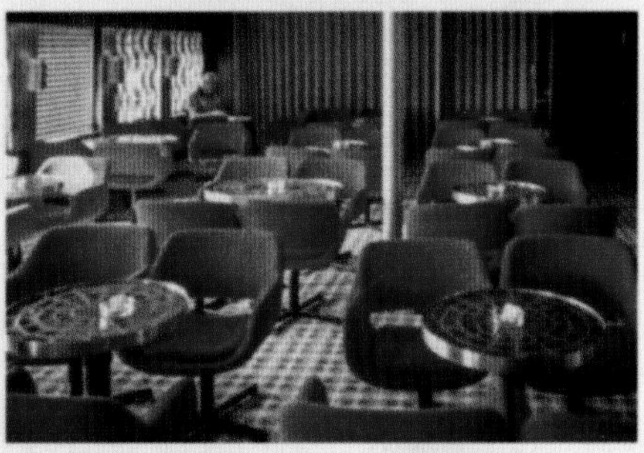

Late night lounge

Karaoke to the cool jams of Jonathan Coulton, Paul and Storm, The Doubleclicks, and Molly Lewis.

Luxury accommodations

Island Lines offers you the best in hospitality suites, including private baths and daily housekeeping. If you don't return to your cabin to find a towel handcrafted in the shape of an animal, your cruise is on us!

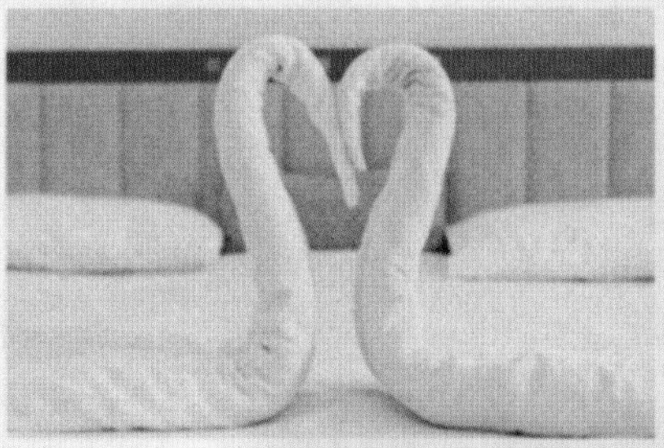

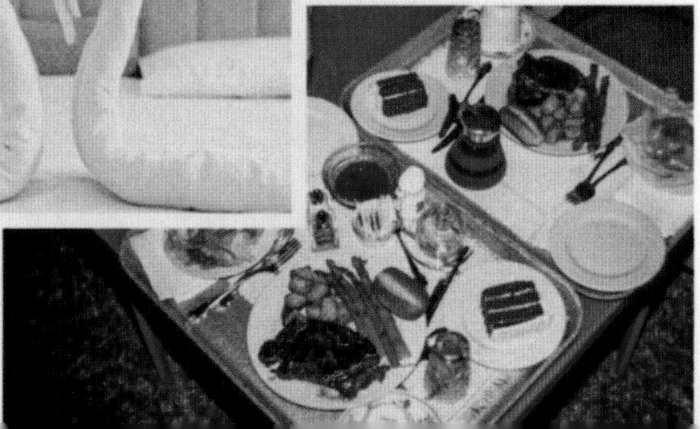

Welcome to the

You've arrived! The Island is everything you've ever wanted. From thrilling excursions to contemplative meditation, you will find what you need when you need it. Embrace the adventure, or consider the psychological implications; you're free to do both, or neither. On the Island, it's up to you. This package is all-inclusive.

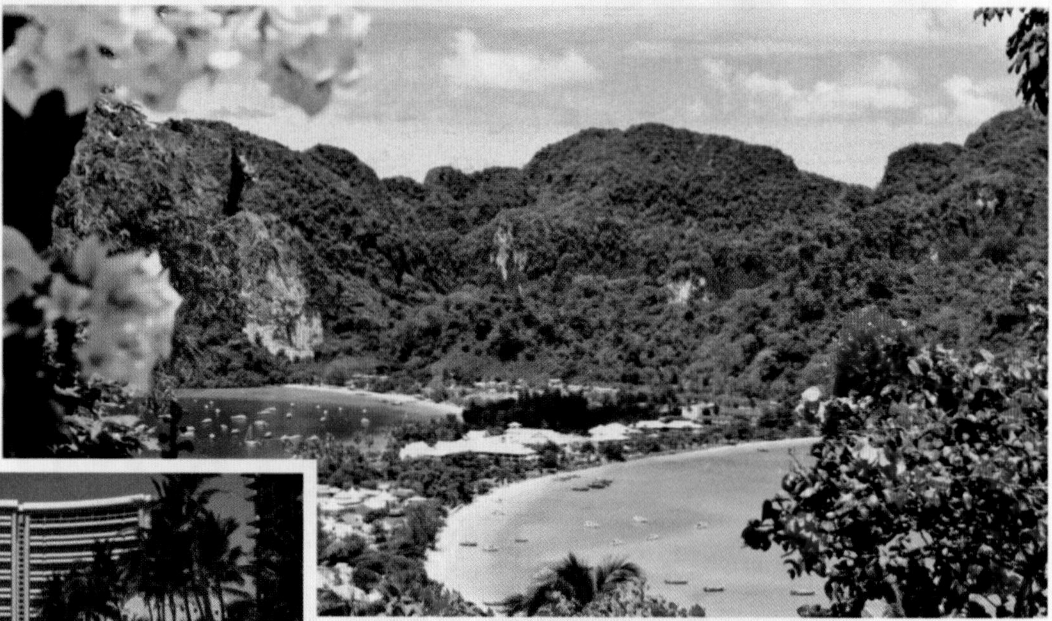

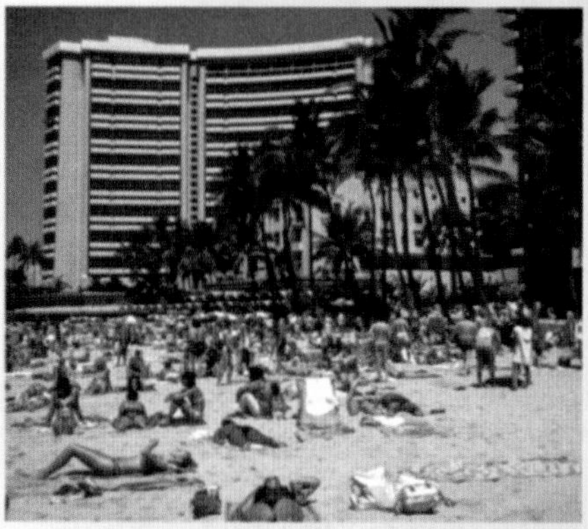

Tranquil Beaches

Enjoy secluded beaches, private coves, and other hidden oceanfront hotspots. These coastal shores are yours to explore.

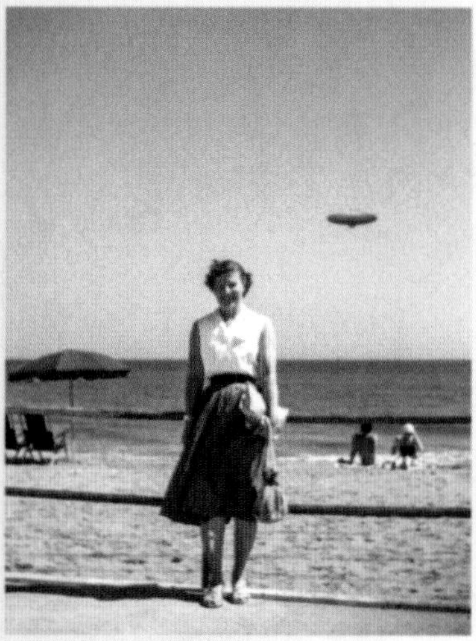

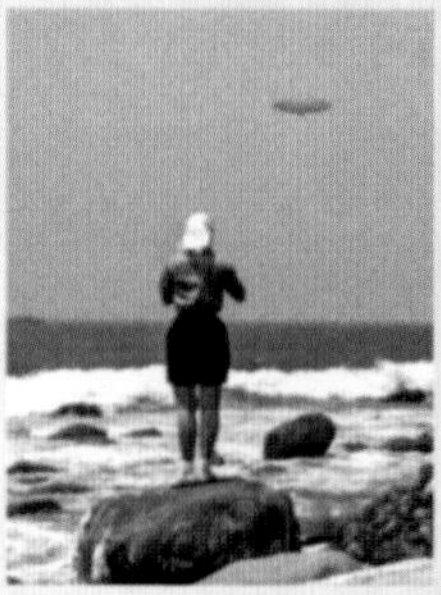

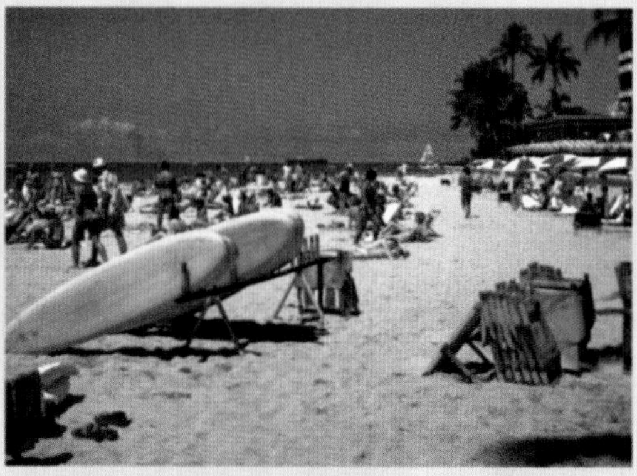

Island

Cultural events

The Call to the Kraken ceremony is a highlight of every Triangle cruise. Embrace the local culture, while celebrating the tentacled monster that lurks just below the surface.

	ECONOMY	LEVEL 2	LEVEL 3	PREMIUM
ISLAND EXCURSIONS				
Mermaid Trail of Tears Tour	•	•	•	•
Weredolphin Wildlife Reserve Snorkeling Day Trip		•	•	•
Underwater Atlantean Ruins National Park Snorkeling Day Trip			•	•
Mud Volcano Hike			•	•
Creatures of the Deep Tour			•	•
Sunset Sail – Danger River		•		
Sunset Sail – Danger Lake			•	
Sunset Sail – Danger Pond (float)	•			
Sunset Sail – Shrieking Phytoplankton Passage				•
Deadly Marsh Weed Ecological Reserve Tour and Lunch				•
Scuba Outing and Ear Eel Encounter		•	•	•
Nude Beach Half-Day Trip (bring sunscreen!)				•
Sand Flea Safari and Quicksand Picnic			•	•
Slime Garden Tea Party				•
Ghost Pirate Sanctuary			•	•
Call to the Kraken	•	•	•	•
ON BOARD ACTIVITIES				
Children's Get-Together, pool side, Upper Deck	•	•	•	•
Young Adults' Get-Together, Discotheque, Main Dec Aft	•	•	•	•
Cocktail Serenade, Marine Veranda and Smoking Room		•	•	•
ALCOHOL PACKAGES				
Wine Only	•			
Well Drinks	•	•		
Top Shelf	•	•	•	
Poolside Cocktails	•	•	•	•

Fun for the whole family

Kids love snorkeling over shipwrecks, followed by a stop for frozen yogurt at the Yogurt Hut. Family friendly excursions include half-day trips to the Lava National Park and the Screaming Coral Wetlands.

Poolside Cocktail

~ *Daily Special* ~

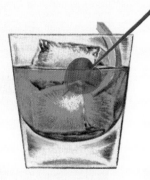

DAY 1

BLUE LAGOON

1 ½ oz Vodka
½ oz Blue Curaçao
Stir well with ice
Pour into highball glass
Add lemon-lime soda and cherry

ISLAND LINES
Cruise The Bermuda Triangle

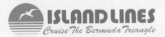

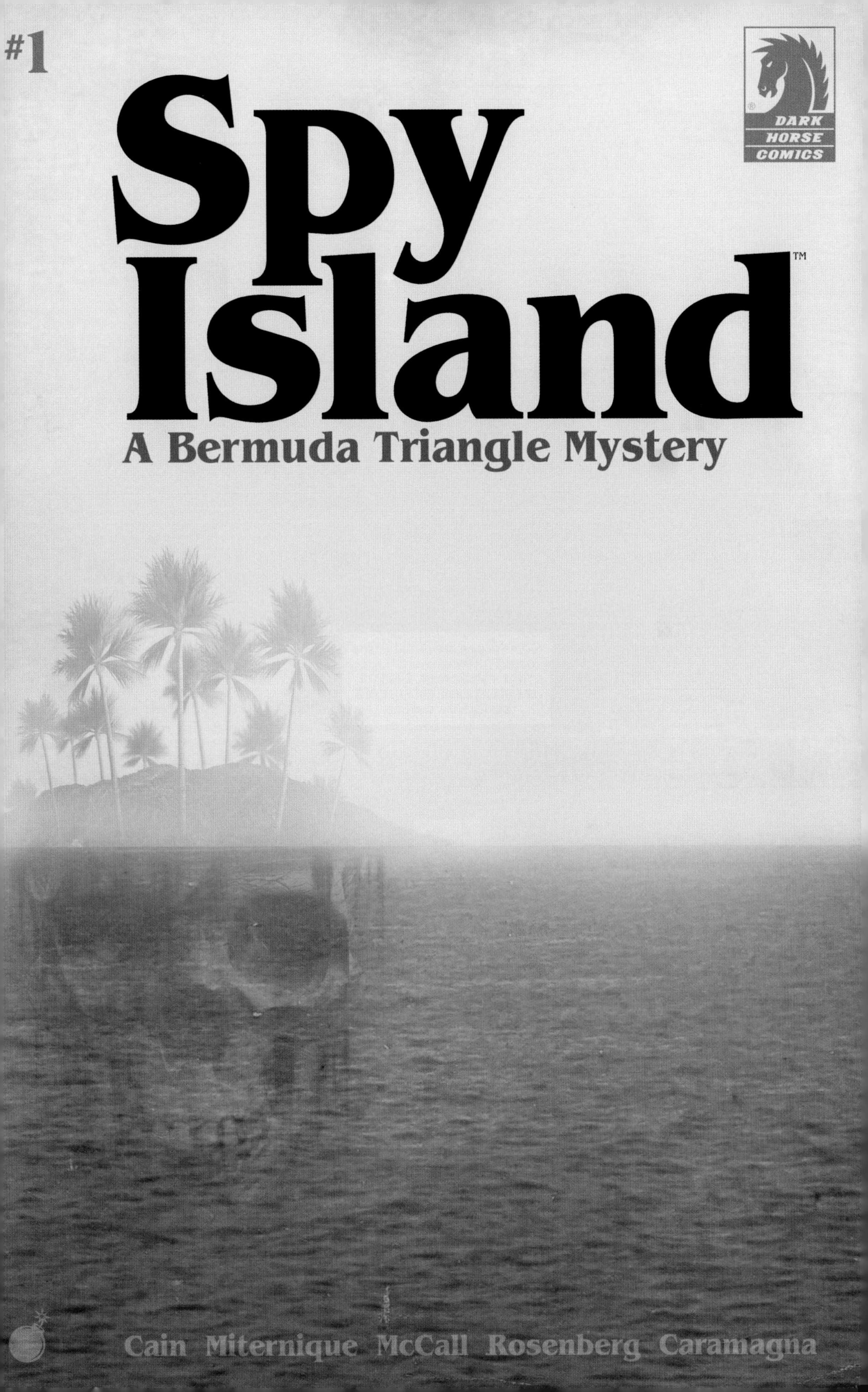
#1
DARK HORSE COMICS
Spy Island™
A Bermuda Triangle Mystery
Cain Miternique McCall Rosenberg Caramagna

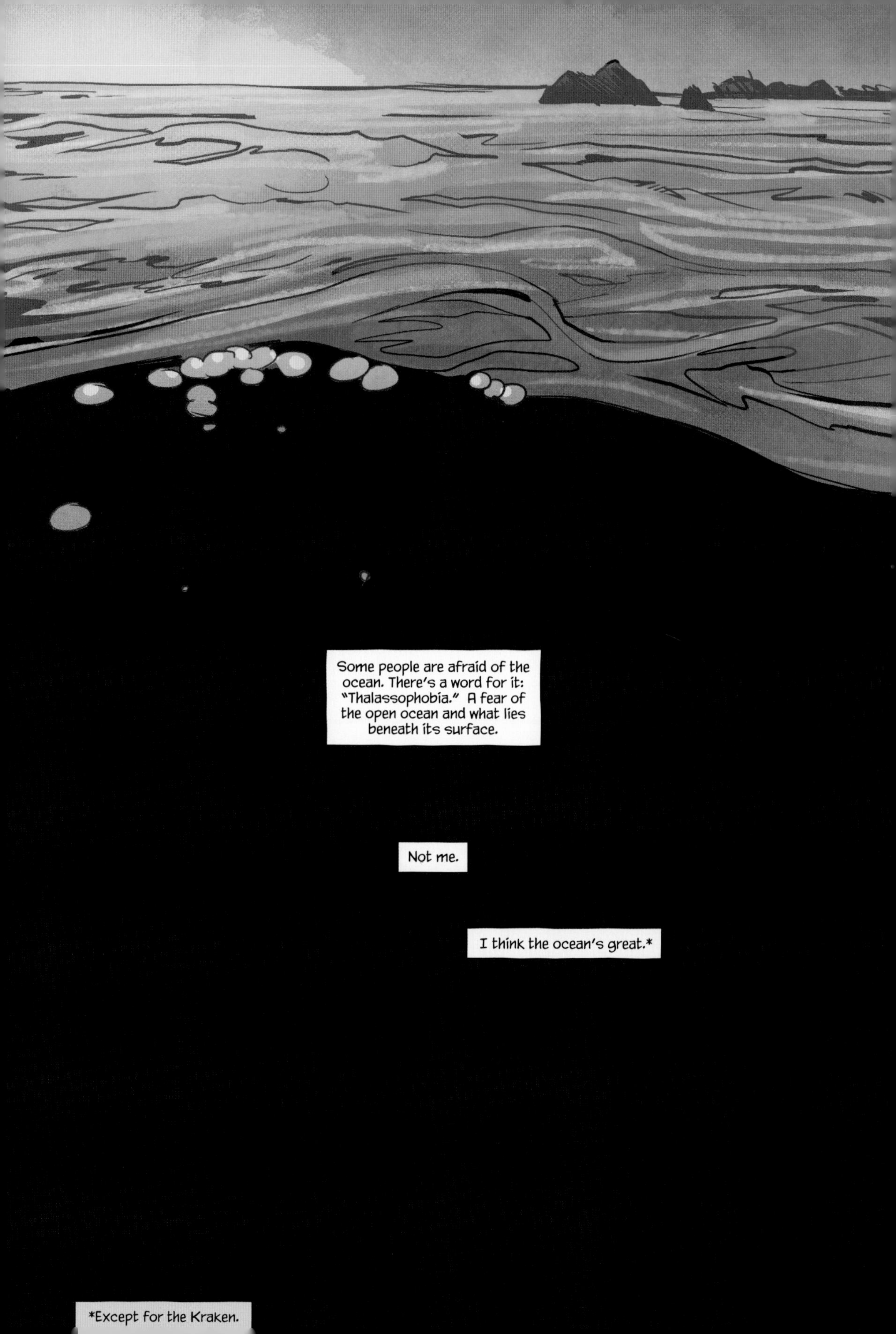
Some people are afraid of the ocean. There's a word for it: "Thalassophobia." A fear of the open ocean and what lies beneath its surface.
Not me.
I think the ocean's great.*
*Except for the Kraken.

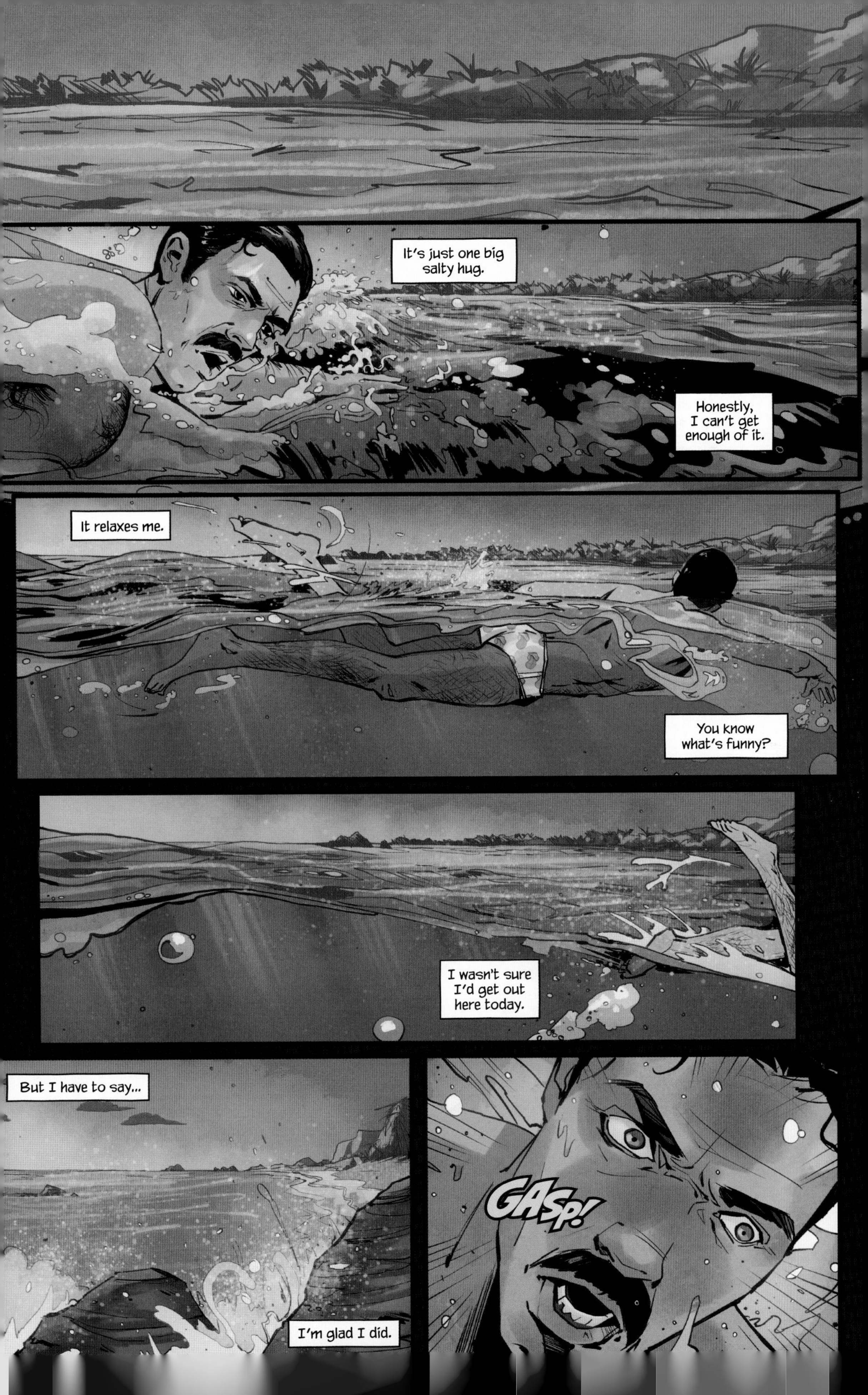
It's just one big salty hug.
Honestly, I can't get enough of it.
It relaxes me.
You know what's funny?
I wasn't sure I'd get out here today.
But I have to say...
I'm glad I did.
GASP!

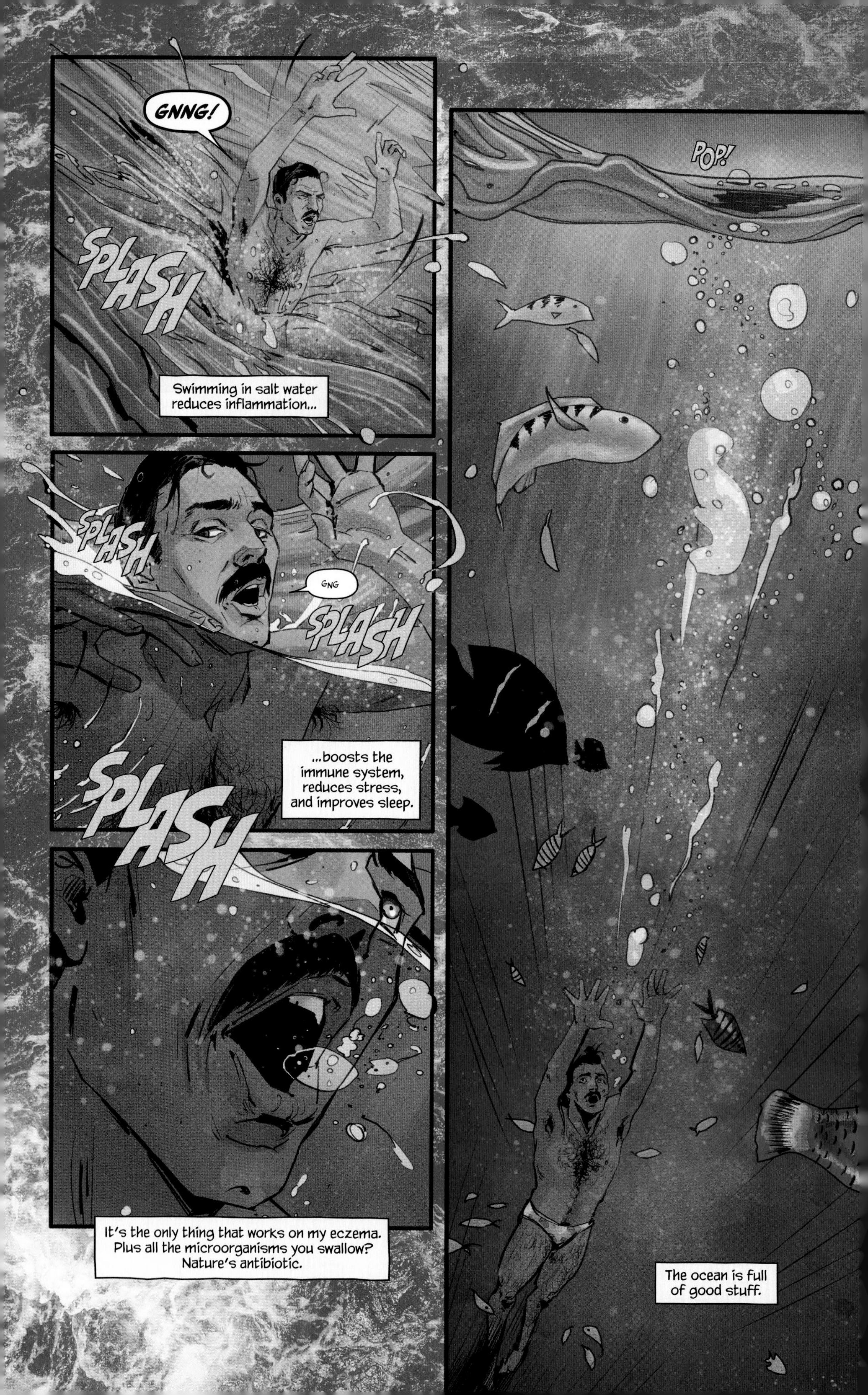
GNNG!
SPLASH
Swimming in salt water reduces inflammation...
SPLASH
GNG
SPLASH
SPLASH
...boosts the immune system, reduces stress, and improves sleep.
It's the only thing that works on my eczema. Plus all the microorganisms you swallow? Nature's antibiotic.
POP!
The ocean is full of good stuff.

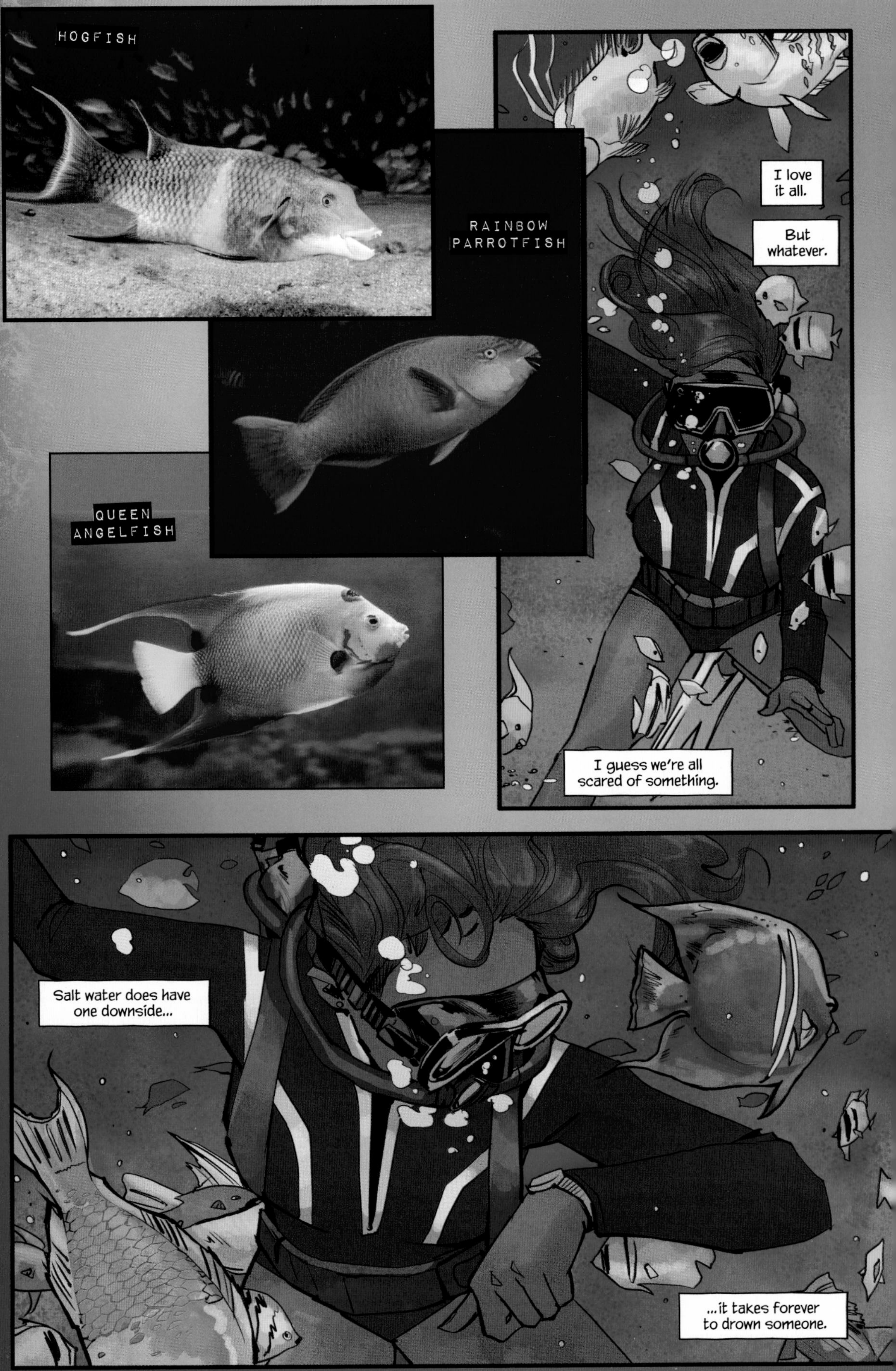
HOGFISH
RAINBOW PARROTFISH
QUEEN ANGELFISH
I love it all.
But whatever.
I guess we're all scared of something.
Salt water does have one downside...
...it takes forever to drown someone.

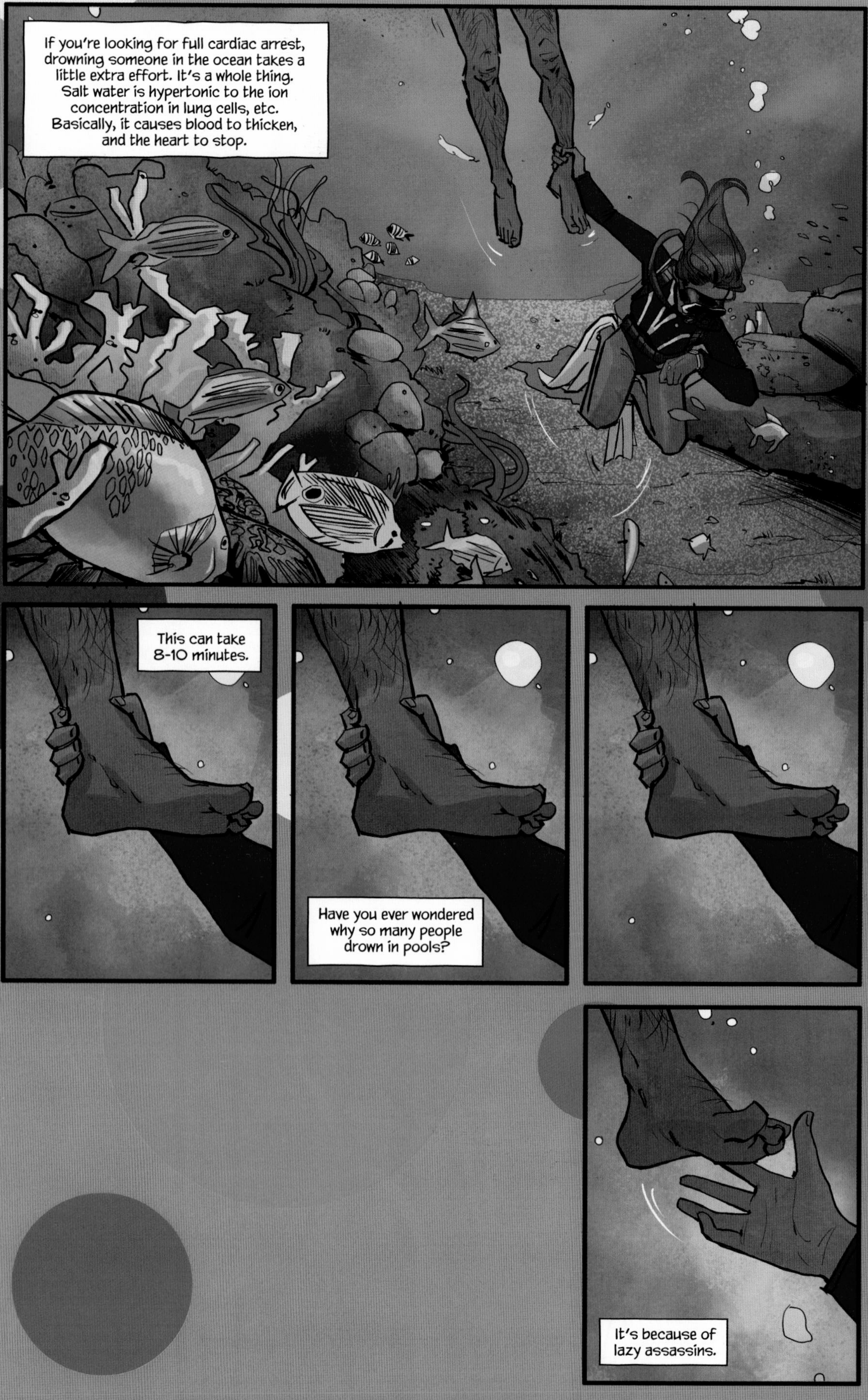
If you're looking for full cardiac arrest, drowning someone in the ocean takes a little extra effort. It's a whole thing. Salt water is hypertonic to the ion concentration in lung cells, etc. Basically, it causes blood to thicken, and the heart to stop.
This can take 8-10 minutes.
Have you ever wondered why so many people drown in pools?
It's because of lazy assassins.

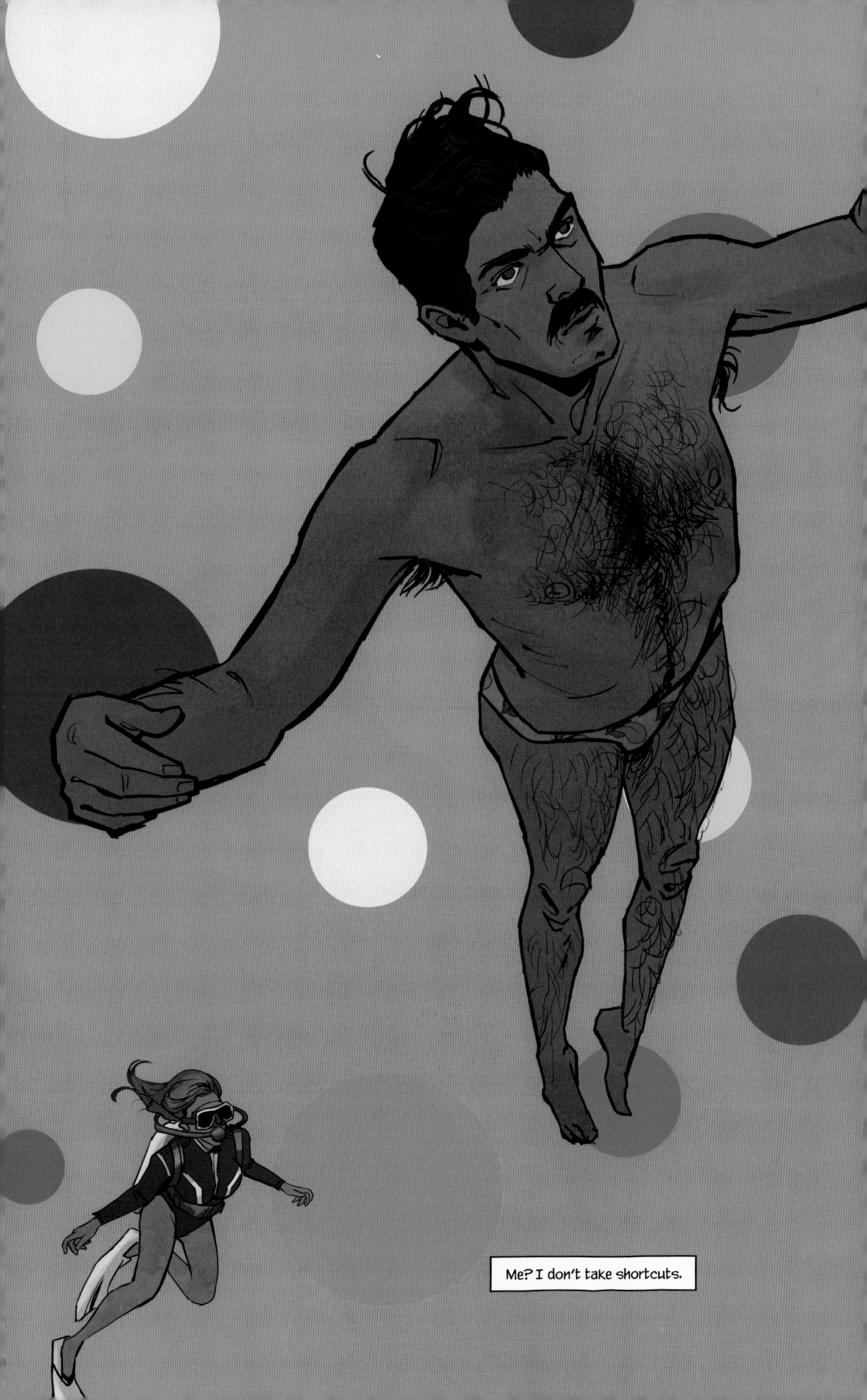
Me? I don't take shortcuts.

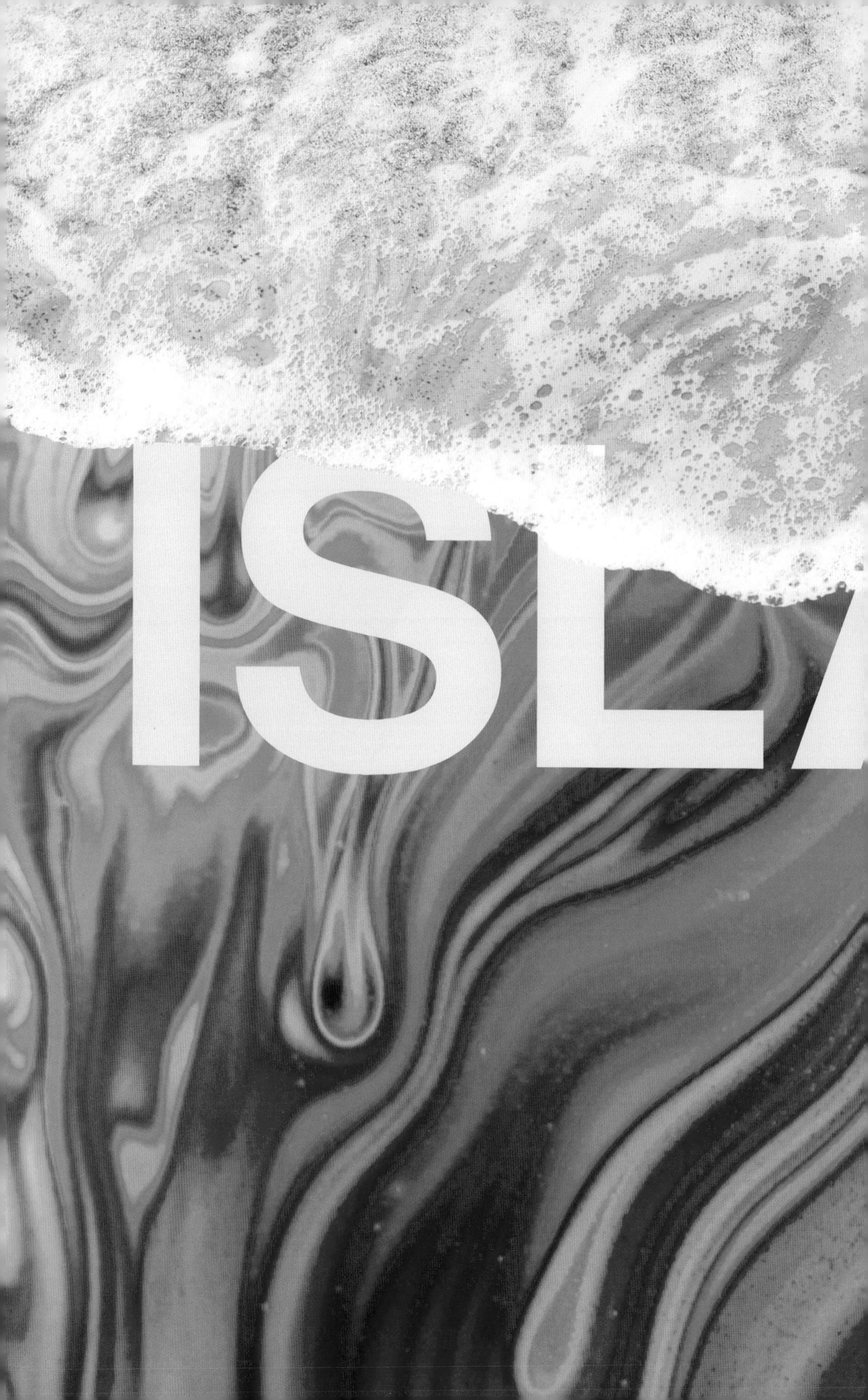
ISL

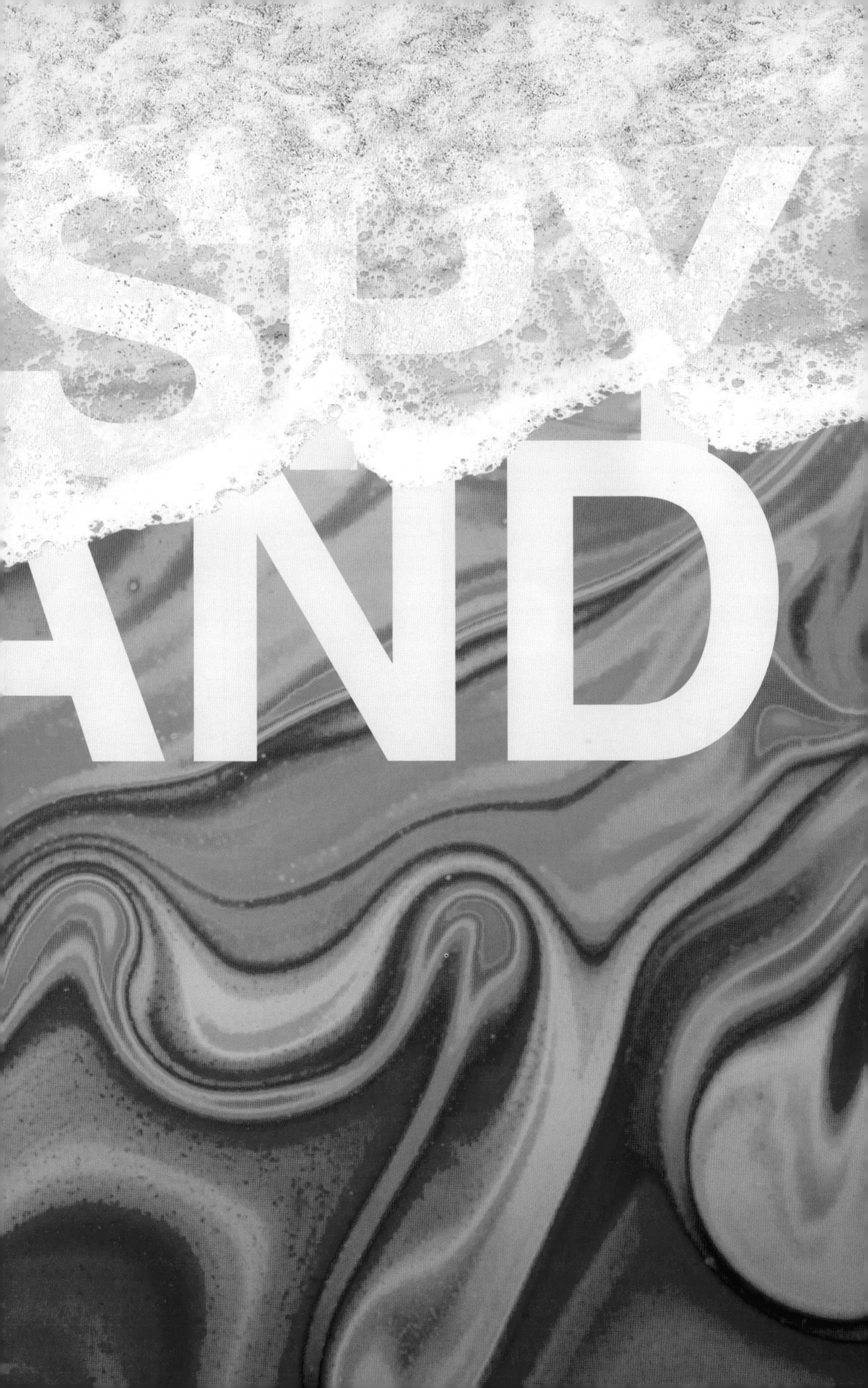

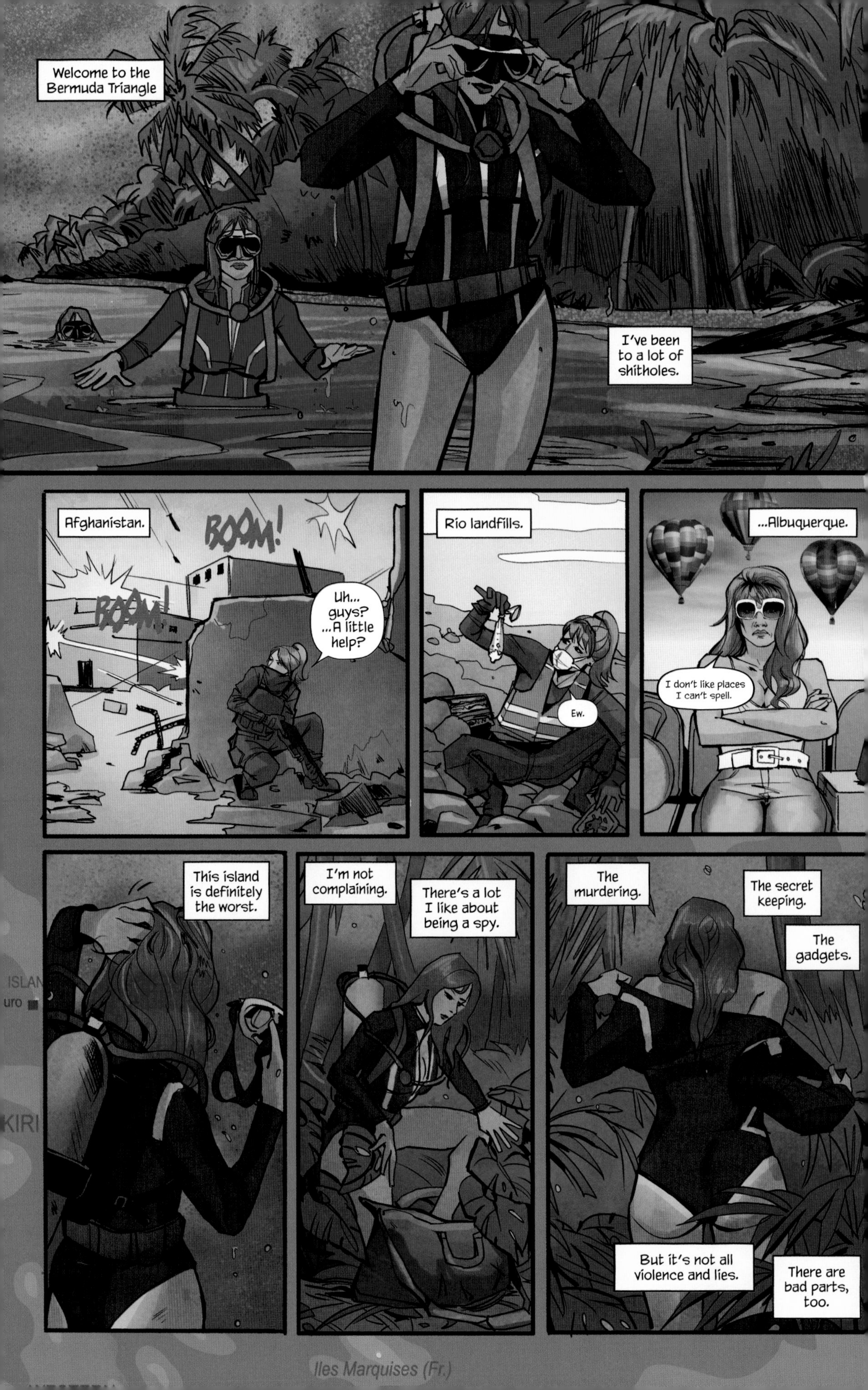
Welcome to the Bermuda Triangle
I've been to a lot of shitholes.
Afghanistan.
BOOM!
BOOM!
Uh... guys? ...A little help?
Rio landfills.
Ew.
...Albuquerque.
I don't like places I can't spell.
This island is definitely the worst.
I'm not complaining.
There's a lot I like about being a spy.
The murdering.
The secret keeping.
The gadgets.
But it's not all violence and lies.
There are bad parts, too.
Iles Marquises (Fr.)

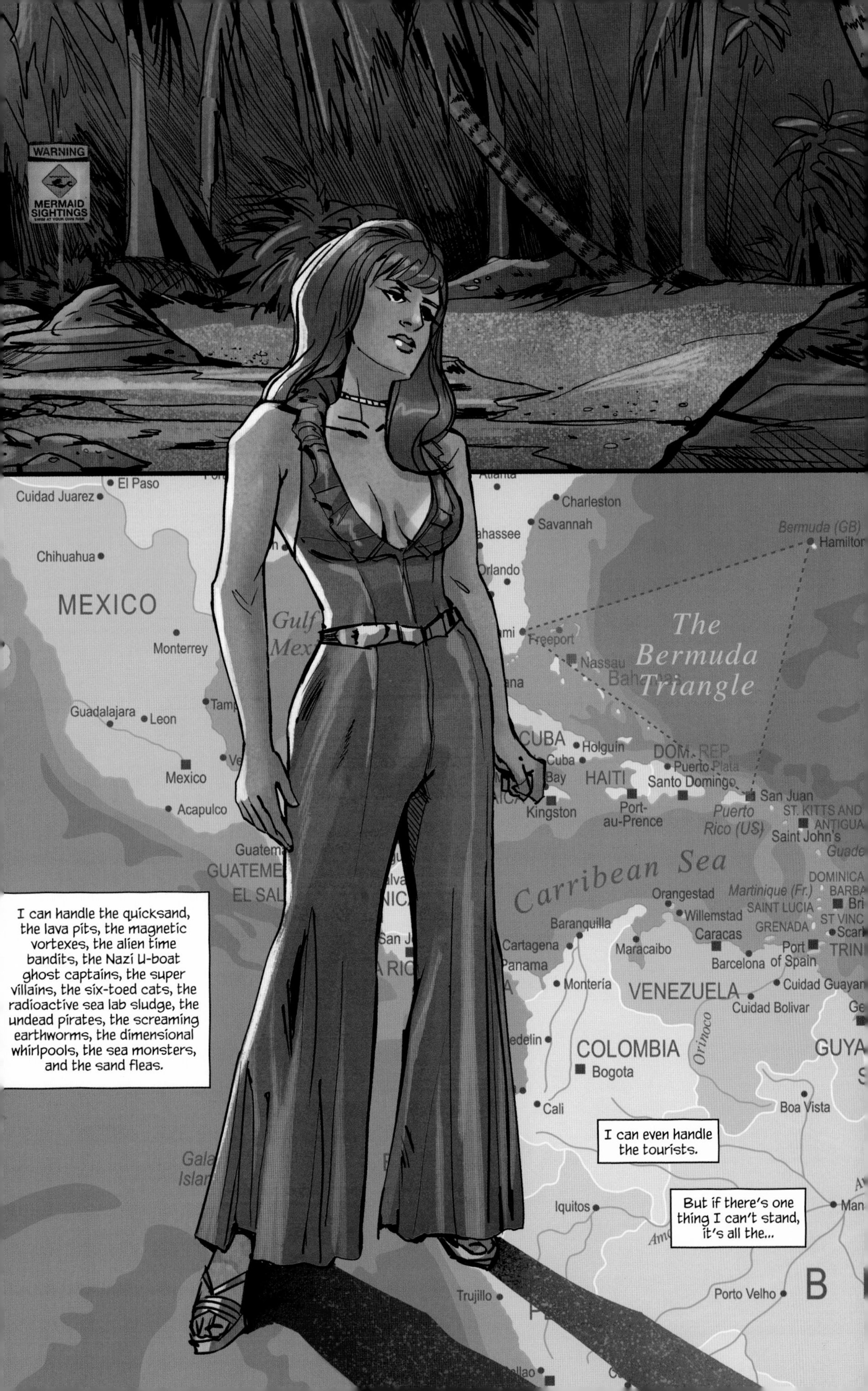
WARNING
MERMAID SIGHTINGS
SWIM AT YOUR OWN RISK
El Paso
Cuidad Juarez
Charleston
Savannah
Chihuahua
Bermuda (GB)
Hamilton
Orlando
MEXICO
The Bermuda Triangle
Monterrey
Freeport
Nassau
Guadalajara
Leon
CUBA
Holguin
DOM. REP.
Puerto Plata
Mexico
HAITI
Santo Domingo
San Juan
Acapulco
Kingston
Port-au-Prence
Puerto Rico (US)
ST. KITTS AND ANTIGUA
Saint John's
Carribean Sea
DOMINICA
Orangestad
Martinique (Fr.)
Willemstad
SAINT LUCIA
Baranquilla
GRENADA
Cartagena
Maracaibo
Caracas
Panama
Barcelona
Port of Spain
Montería
VENEZUELA
Cuidad Bolivar
COLOMBIA
Orinoco
Bogota
Cali
Boa Vista
Iquitos
Trujillo
Porto Velho
I can handle the quicksand, the lava pits, the magnetic vortexes, the alien time bandits, the Nazi U-boat ghost captains, the super villains, the six-toed cats, the radioactive sea lab sludge, the undead pirates, the screaming earthworms, the dimensional whirlpools, the sea monsters, and the sand fleas.
I can even handle the tourists.
But if there's one thing I can't stand, it's all the...

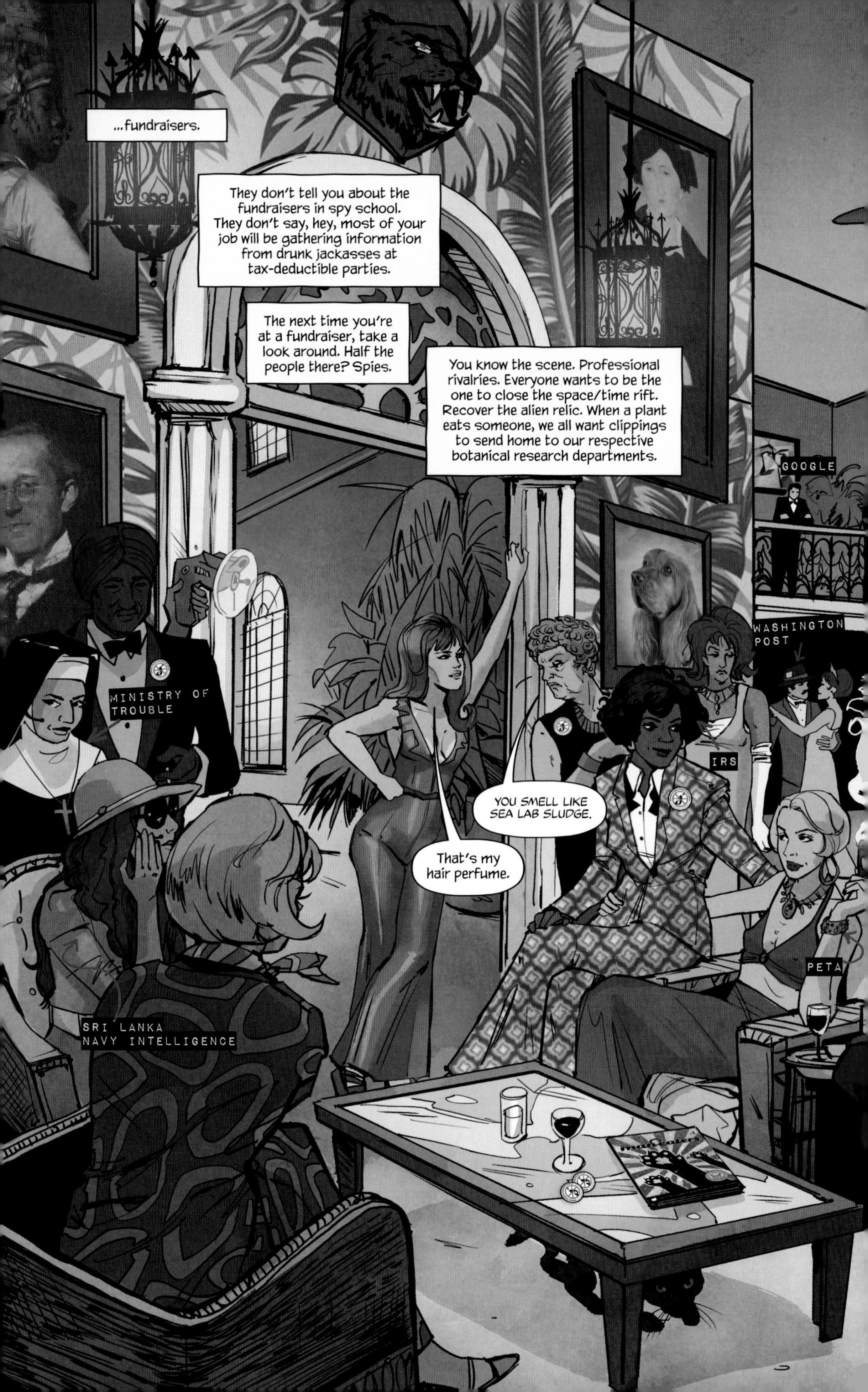
...fundraisers.
They don't tell you about the fundraisers in spy school. They don't say, hey, most of your job will be gathering information from drunk jackasses at tax-deductible parties.
The next time you're at a fundraiser, take a look around. Half the people there? Spies.
You know the scene. Professional rivalries. Everyone wants to be the one to close the space/time rift. Recover the alien relic. When a plant eats someone, we all want clippings to send home to our respective botanical research departments.
GOOGLE
WASHINGTON POST
MINISTRY OF TROUBLE
IRS
YOU SMELL LIKE SEA LAB SLUDGE.
That's my hair perfume.
PETA
SRI LANKA NAVY INTELLIGENCE

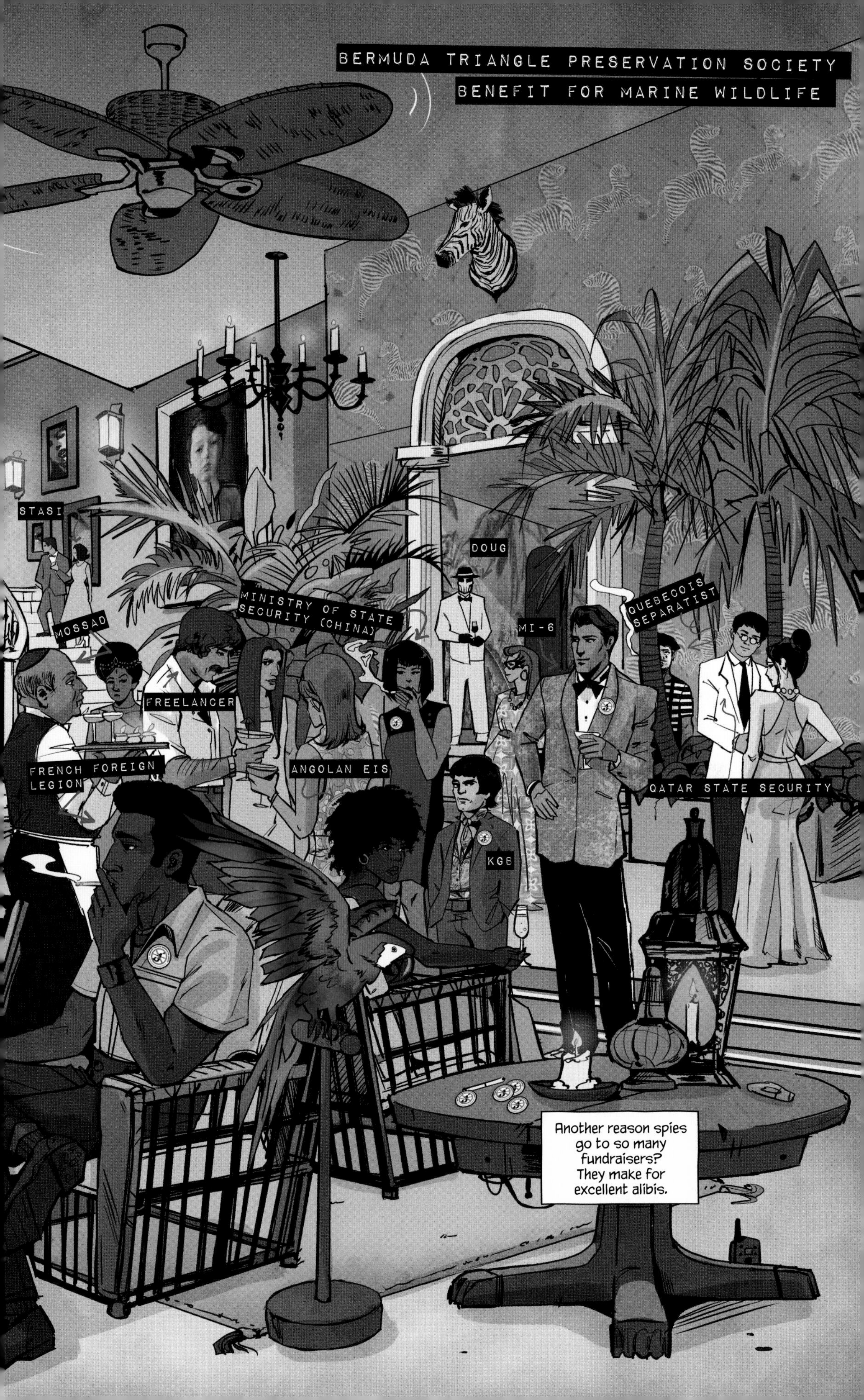

BERMUDA TRIANGLE PRESERVATION SOCIETY
BENEFIT FOR MARINE WILDLIFE
STASI
DOUG
MINISTRY OF STATE SECURITY (CHINA)
QUEBECOIS SEPARATIST
MOSSAD
MI-6
FREELANCER
FRENCH FOREIGN LEGION
ANGOLAN EIS
QATAR STATE SECURITY
KGB
Another reason spies go to so many fundraisers? They make for excellent alibis.

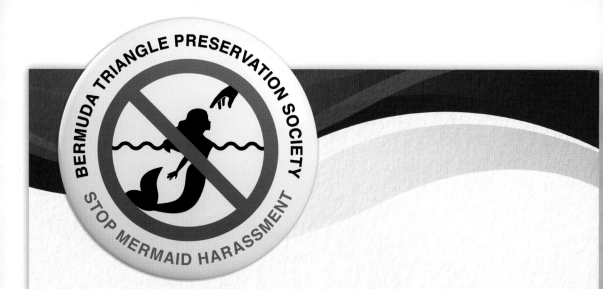

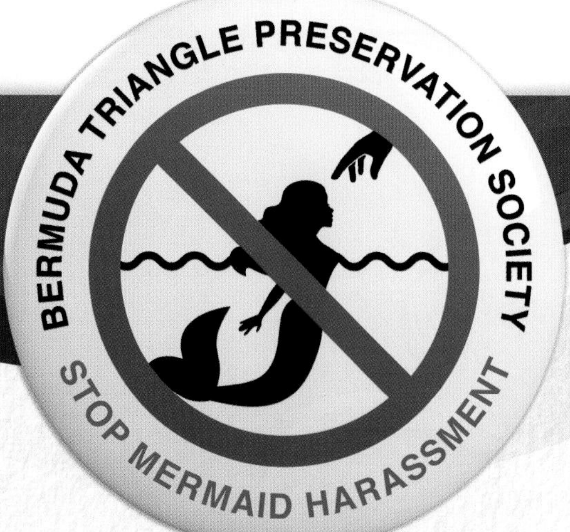
BERMUDA TRIANGLE PRESERVATION SOCIETY
STOP MERMAID HARASSMENT

BERMUDA TRIANGLE PRESERVATION SOCIETY

CONSERVE. PROTECT. RESPECT.

As a member of the Bermuda Triangle Preservation Society, you are most likely familiar with our Stop Mermaid Harassment initiative.

Mermaids inhabit temperate or tropical waters. While they may gather on quiet sandy beaches or offshore rocks during the day, they always retreat to cooler deep waters at night. Although hunted in the past, the current mermaid population has stabilized since the passage of the Mermaid Protection Act of 1961. However, of the five species of mermaids, the Bermuda Triangle mermaid is the only one whose population has decreased. This is due to loss of habitat and human interference.

Your contribution will help!

Our understanding of mermaids continues to evolve.

We now know that it is inappropriate to swim with, feed, tease, ogle, or capture mermaids. Help us educate the public about these new social norms.

For a donation of $100 or more, you'll receive a photograph of a mermaid, adoption papers, and naming rights.

Yours,

Tabitha Caruthers, Countess of Heathcliff
Co-Chair
Bermuda Triangle Preservation Society

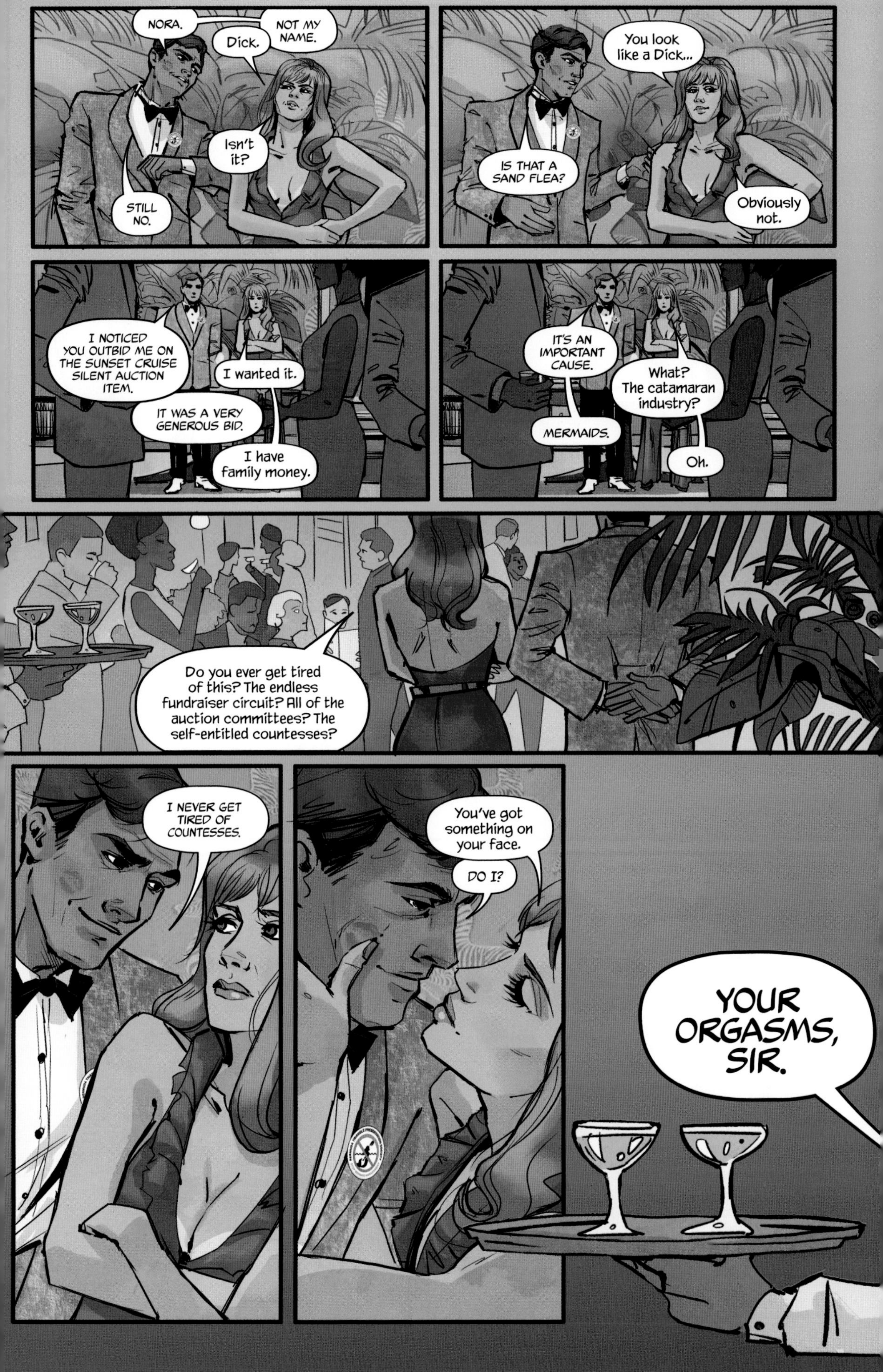
NORA.
NOT MY NAME.
Dick.
Isn't it?
STILL NO.
You look like a Dick...
IS THAT A SAND FLEA?
Obviously not.
I NOTICED YOU OUTBID ME ON THE SUNSET CRUISE SILENT AUCTION ITEM.
I wanted it.
IT WAS A VERY GENEROUS BID.
I have family money.
IT'S AN IMPORTANT CAUSE.
What? The catamaran industry?
MERMAIDS.
Oh.
Do you ever get tired of this? The endless fundraiser circuit? All of the auction committees? The self-entitled countesses?
I NEVER GET TIRED OF COUNTESSES.
You've got something on your face.
DO I?
YOUR ORGASMS, SIR.

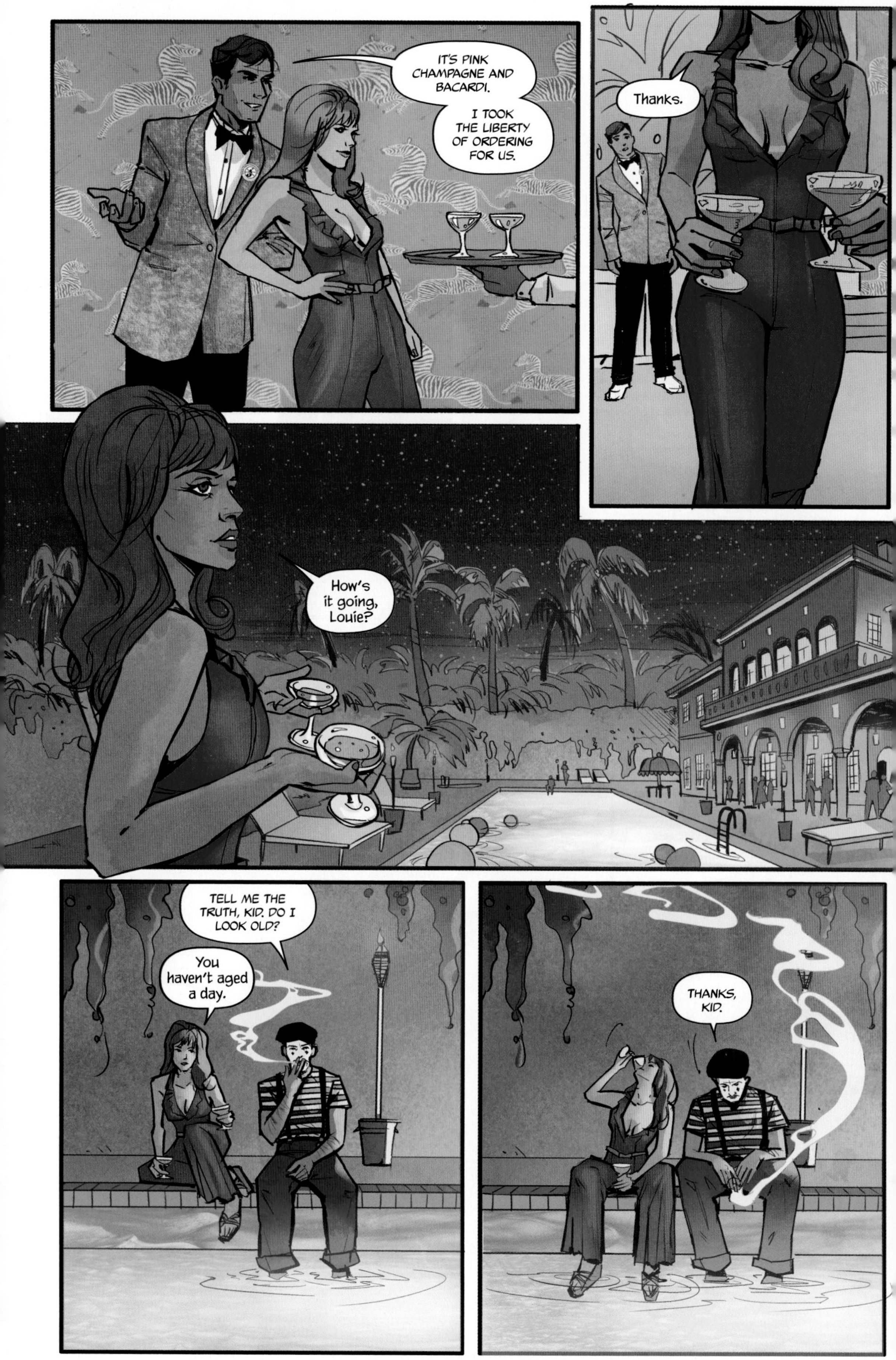
IT'S PINK CHAMPAGNE AND BACARDI.
I TOOK THE LIBERTY OF ORDERING FOR US.
Thanks.
How's it going, Louie?
TELL ME THE TRUTH, KID. DO I LOOK OLD?
You haven't aged a day.
THANKS, KID.

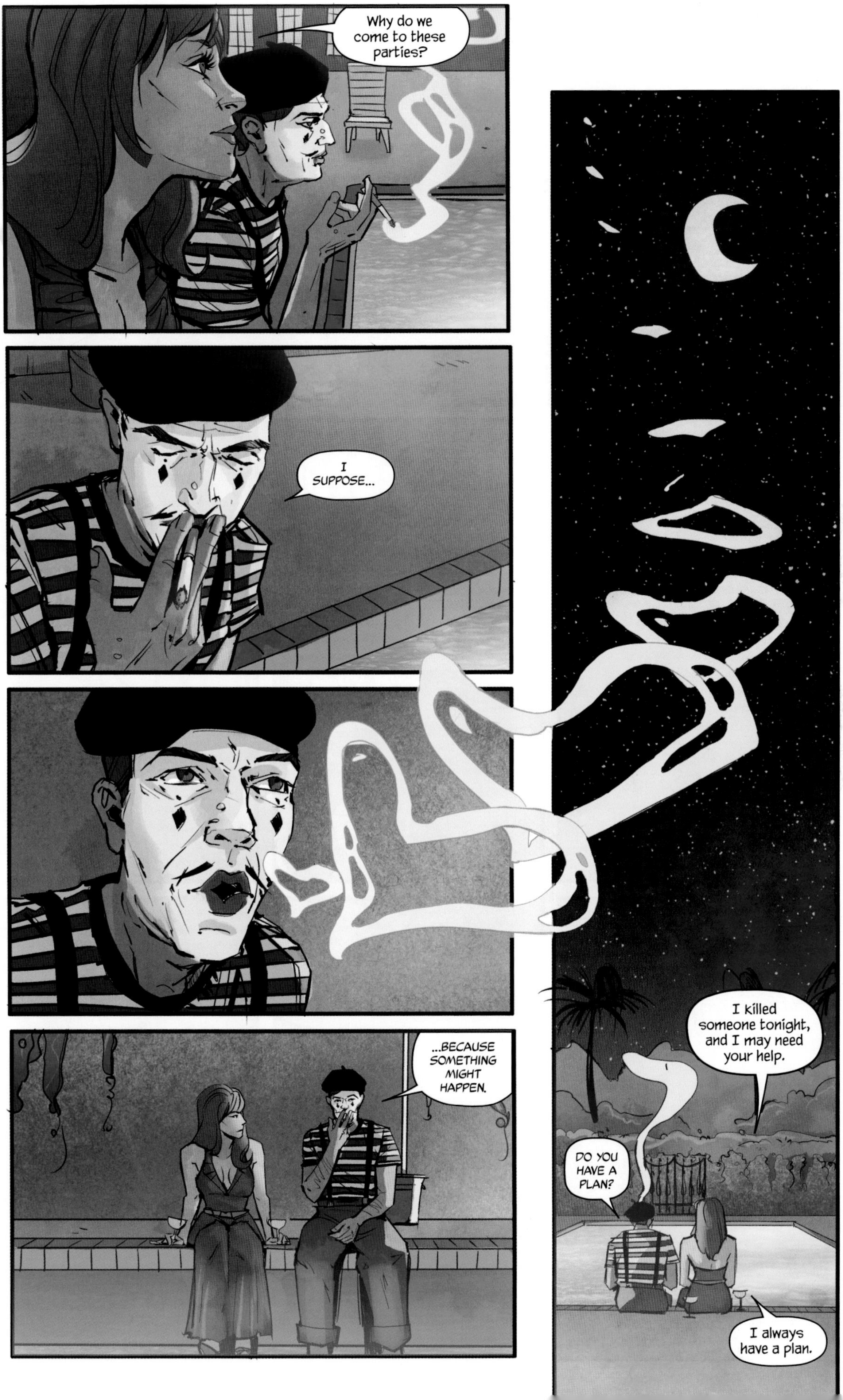
Why do we come to these parties?
I SUPPOSE...
...BECAUSE SOMETHING MIGHT HAPPEN.
I killed someone tonight, and I may need your help.
DO YOU HAVE A PLAN?
I always have a plan.

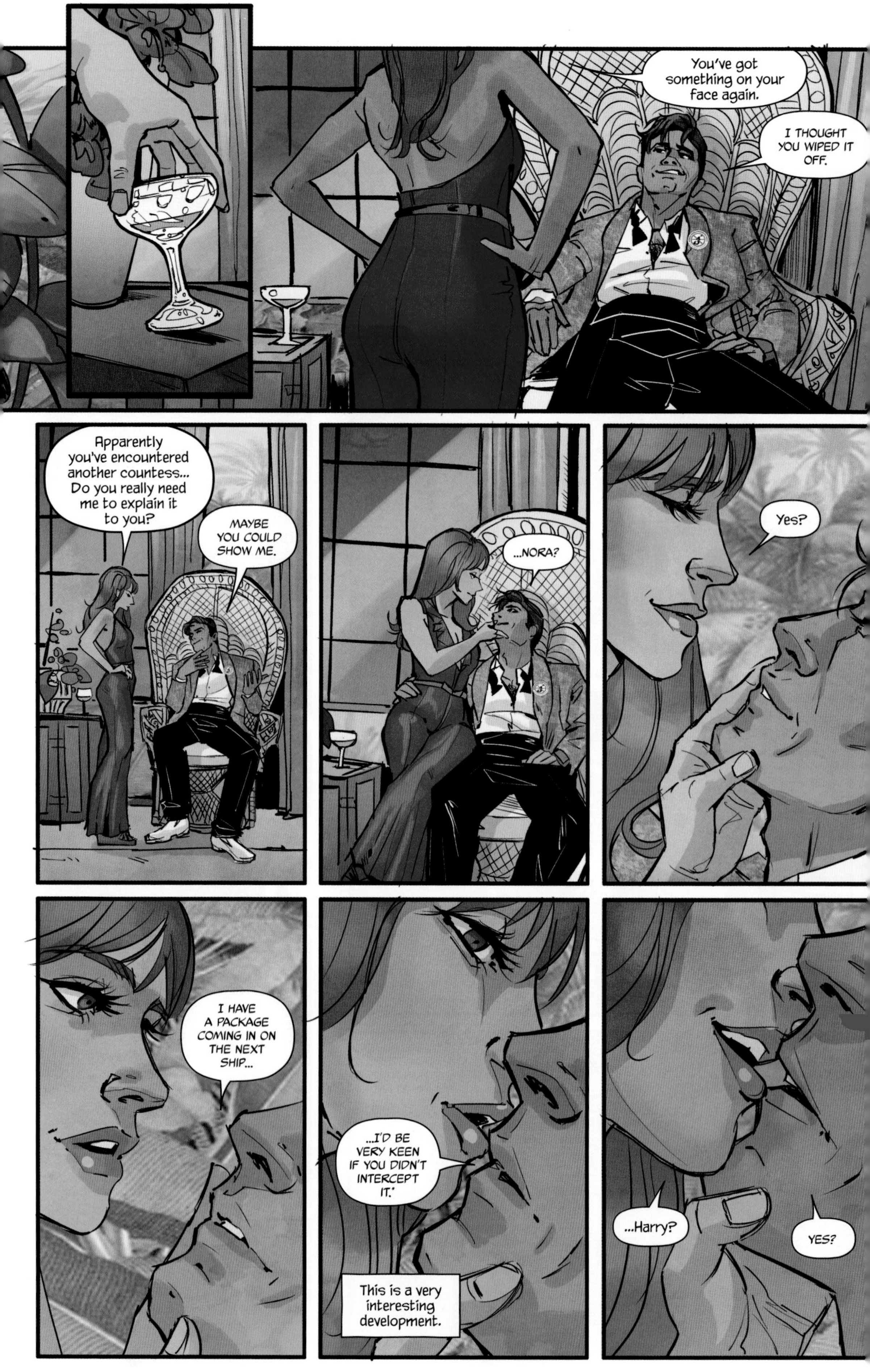
You've got something on your face again.
I THOUGHT YOU WIPED IT OFF.
Apparently you've encountered another countess... Do you really need me to explain it to you?
MAYBE YOU COULD SHOW ME.
...NORA?
Yes?
I HAVE A PACKAGE COMING IN ON THE NEXT SHIP...
...I'D BE VERY KEEN IF YOU DIDN'T INTERCEPT IT.'
This is a very interesting development.
...Harry?
YES?

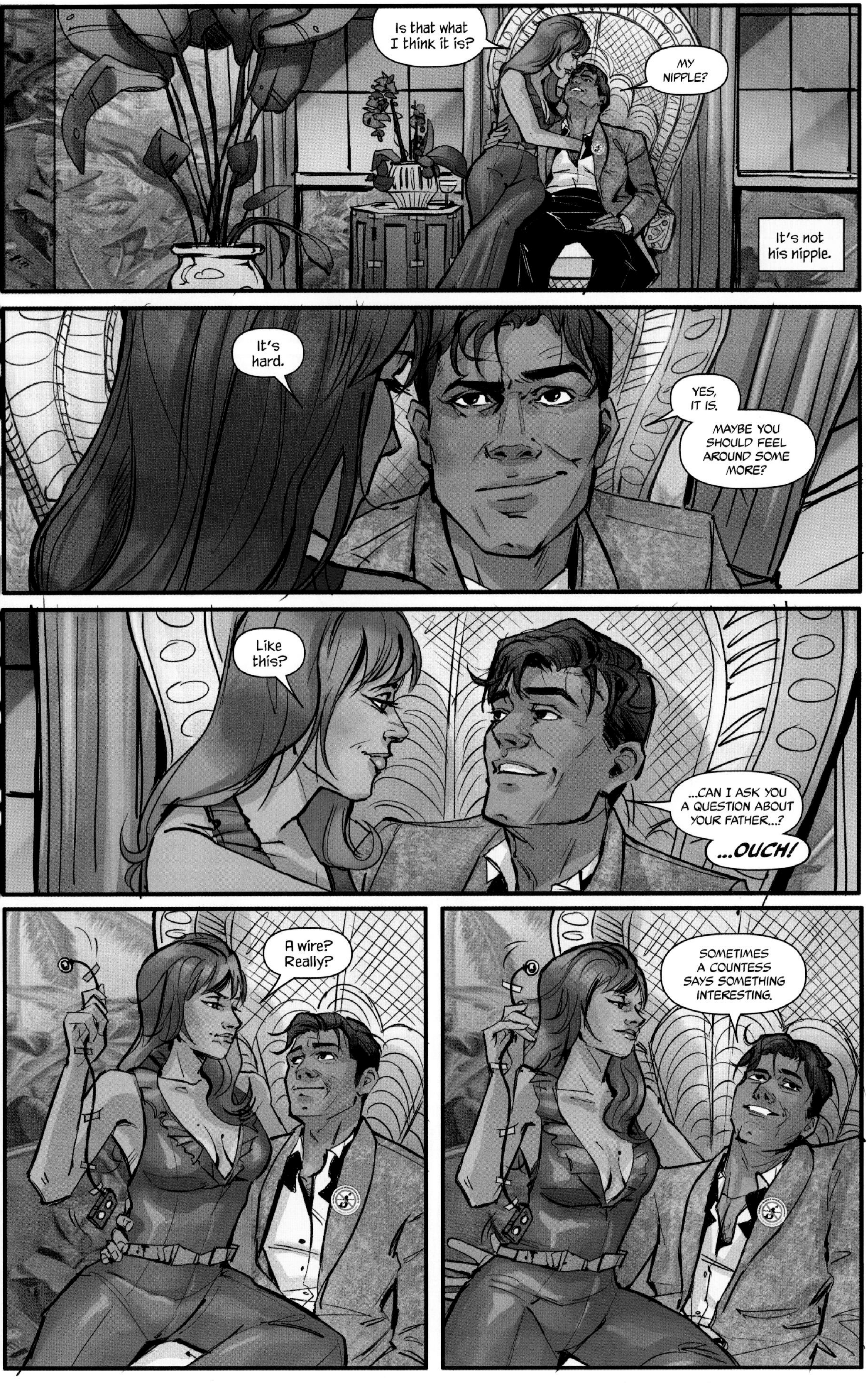
Is that what I think it is?
MY NIPPLE?
It's not his nipple.
It's hard.
YES, IT IS.
MAYBE YOU SHOULD FEEL AROUND SOME MORE?
Like this?
...CAN I ASK YOU A QUESTION ABOUT YOUR FATHER...?
...OUCH!
A wire? Really?
SOMETIMES A COUNTESS SAYS SOMETHING INTERESTING.

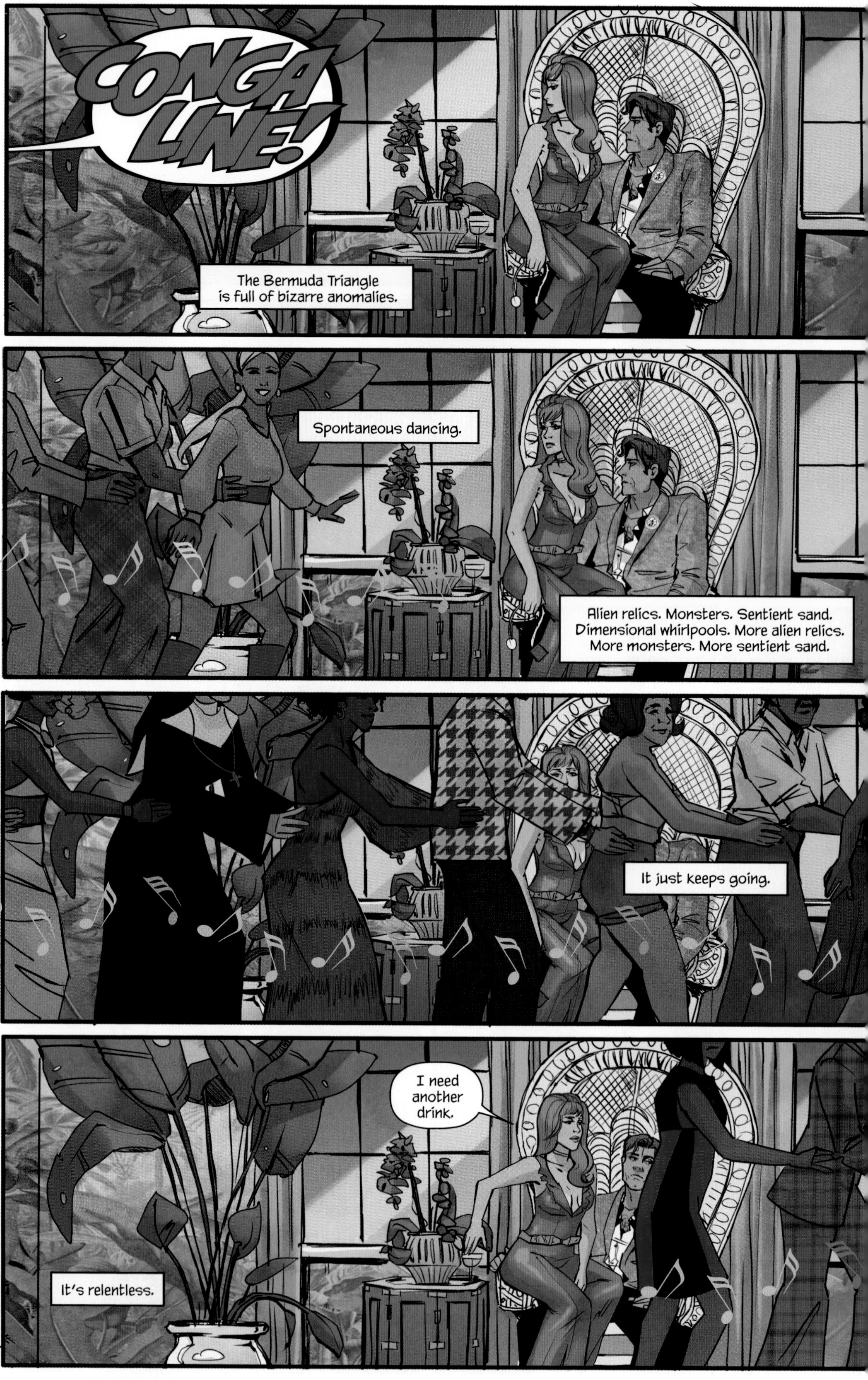
CONGA LINE!
The Bermuda Triangle is full of bizarre anomalies.
Spontaneous dancing.
Alien relics. Monsters. Sentient sand. Dimensional whirlpools. More alien relics. More monsters. More sentient sand.
It just keeps going.
I need another drink.
It's relentless.

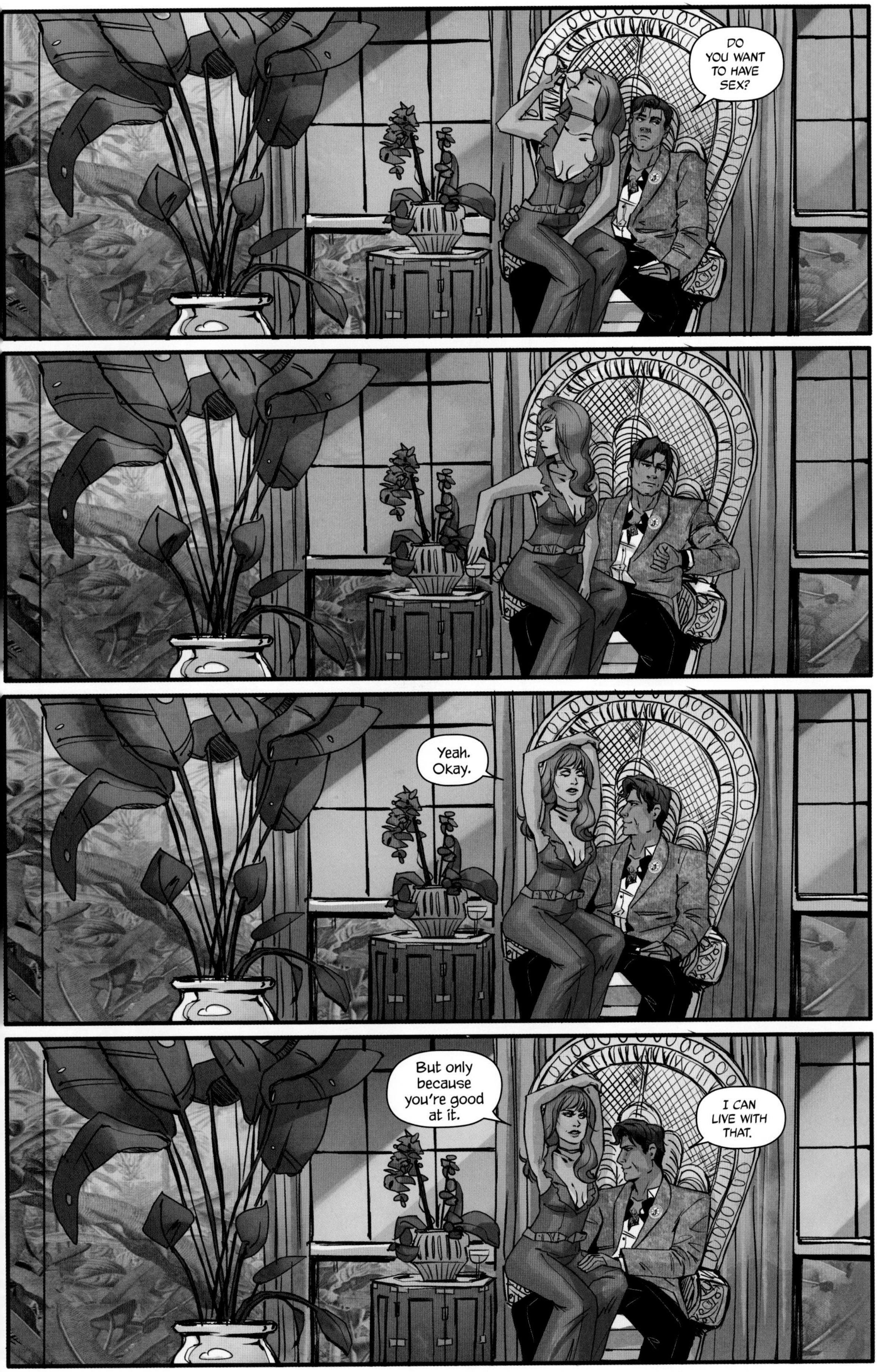
DO YOU WANT TO HAVE SEX?
Yeah. Okay.
But only because you're good at it.
I CAN LIVE WITH THAT.

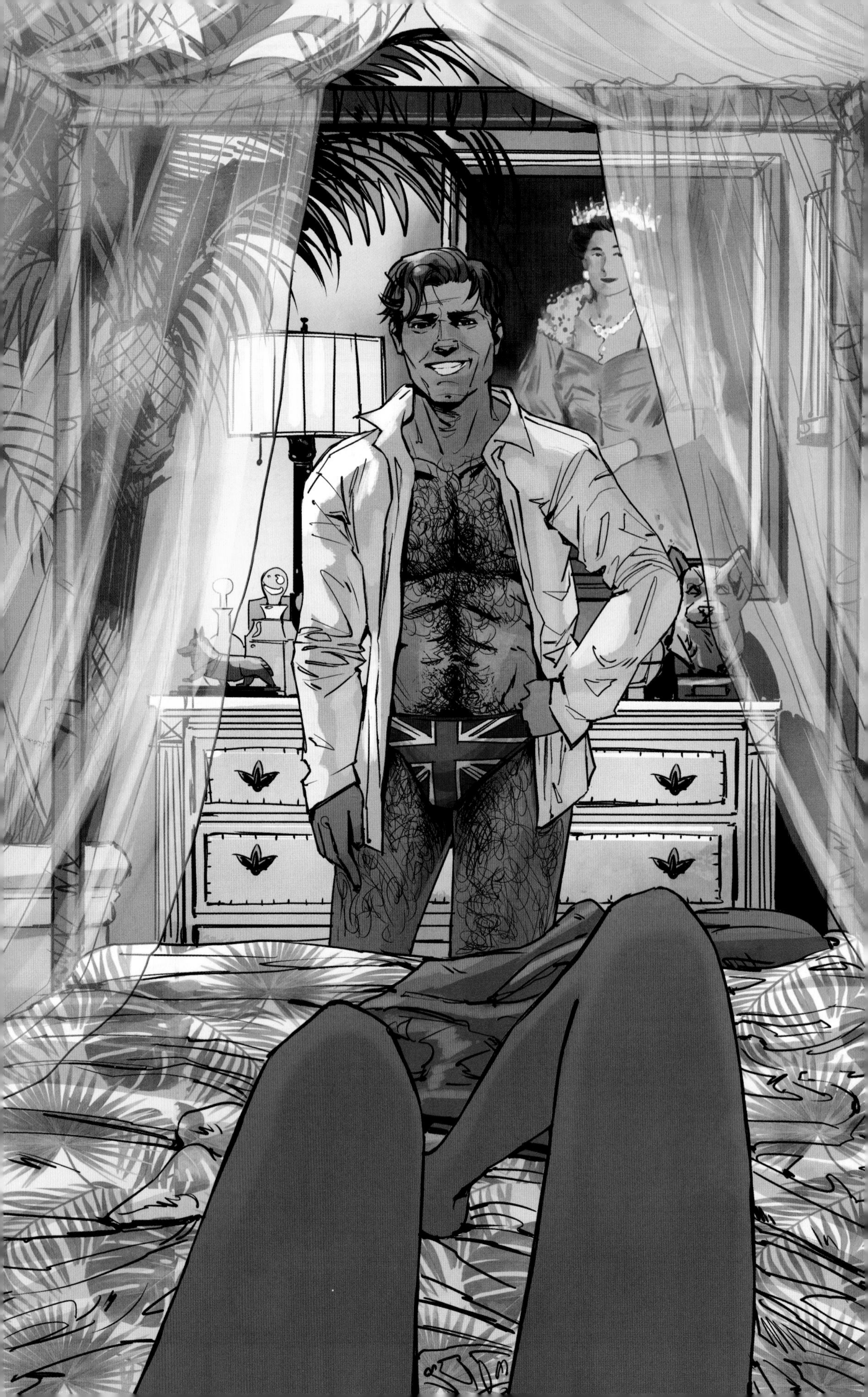

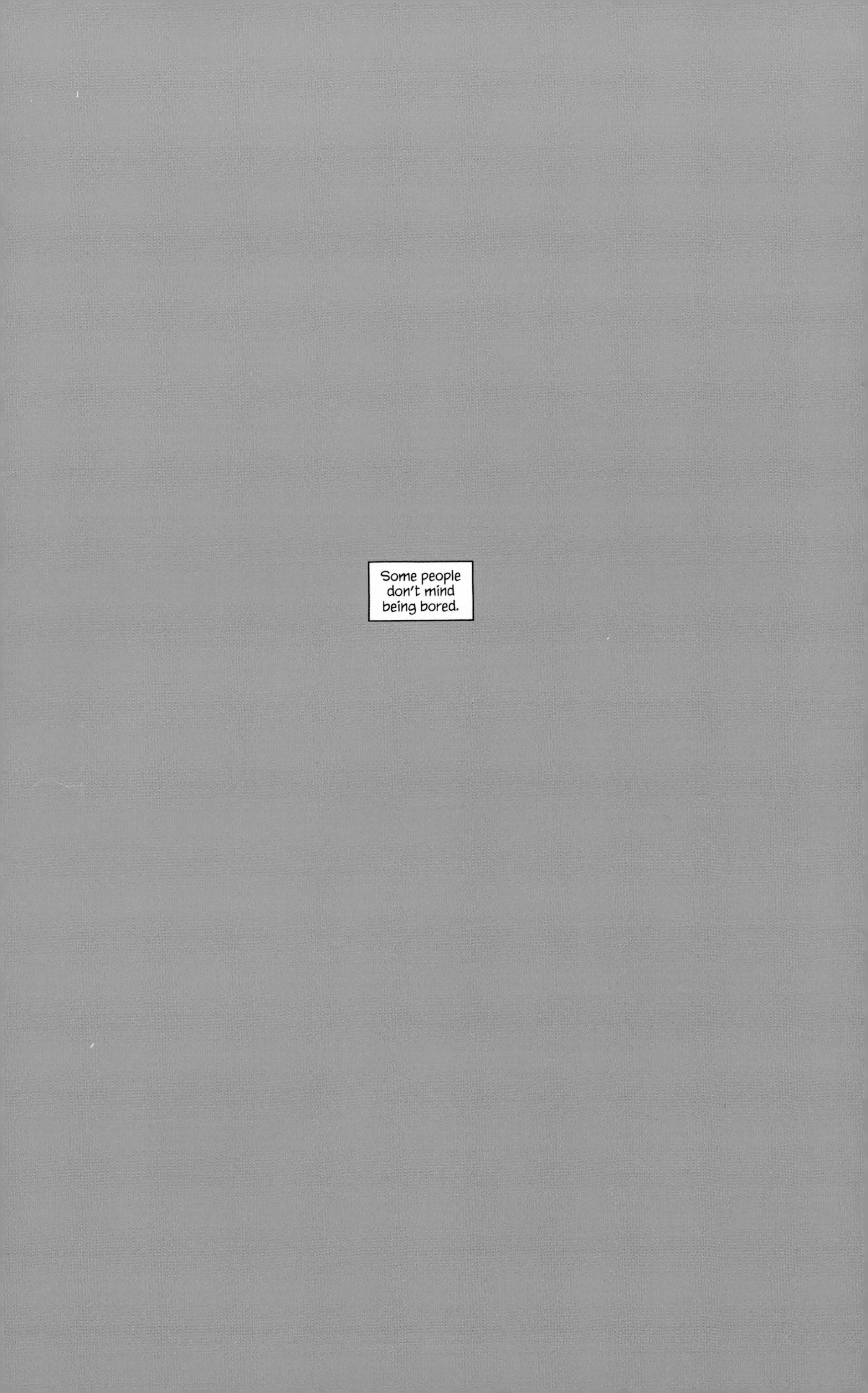
Some people don't mind being bored.

SEX

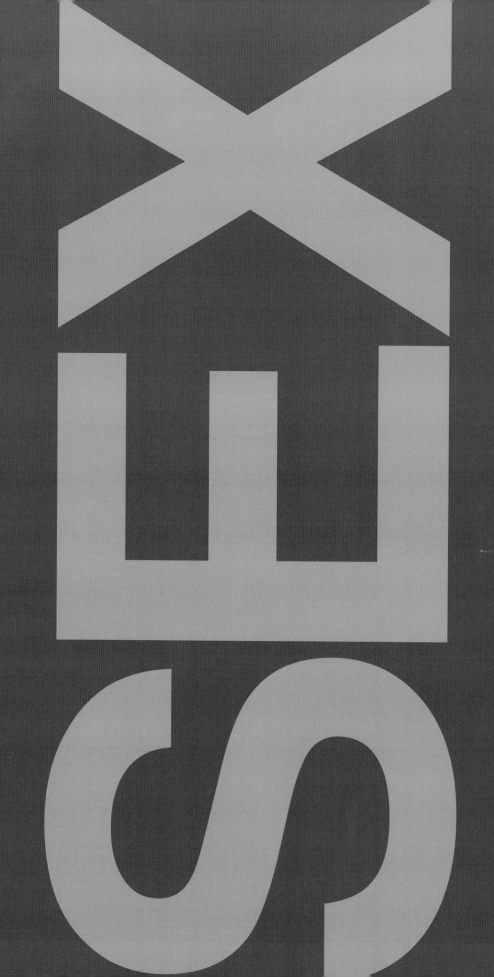

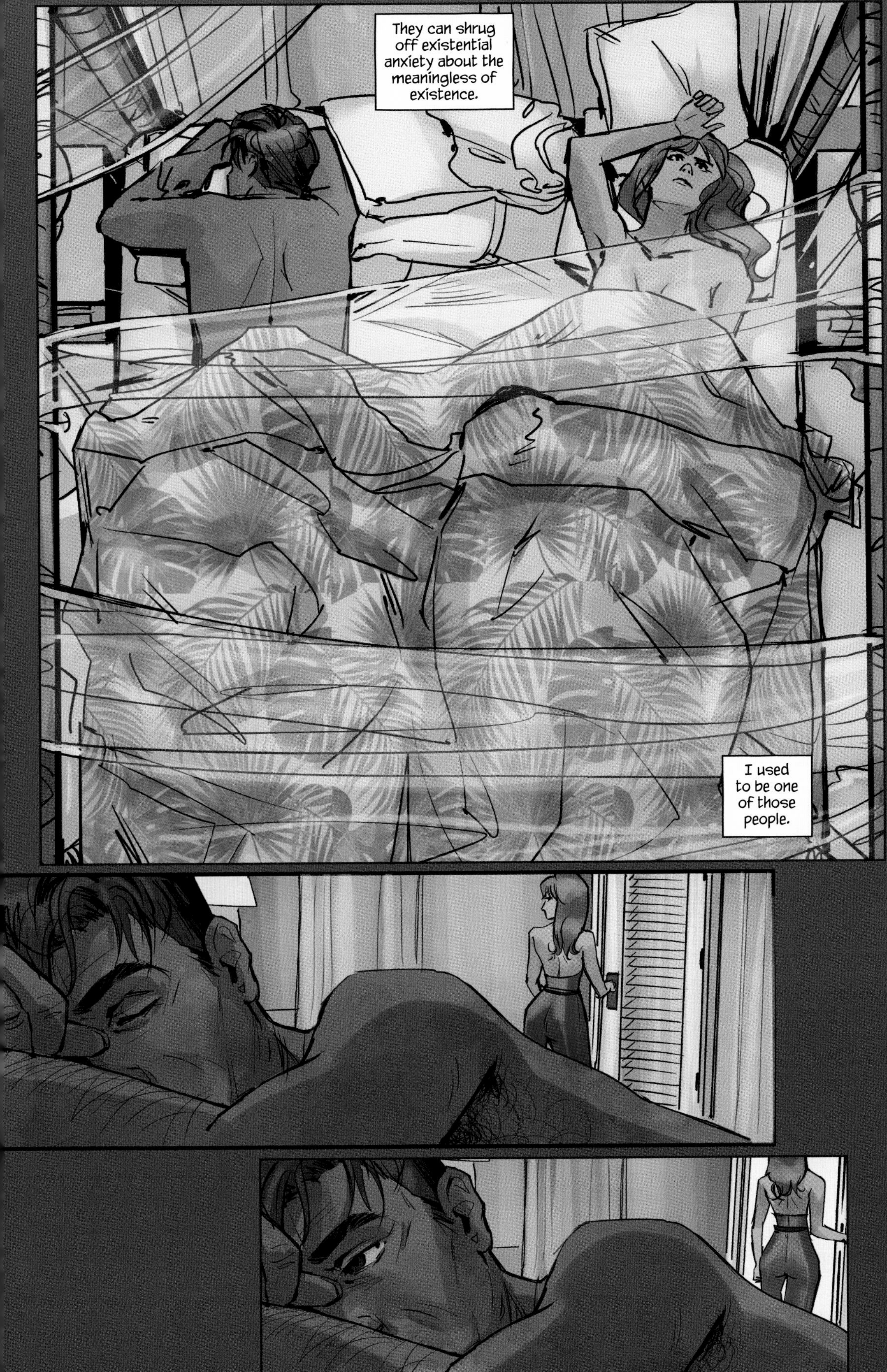
They can shrug off existential anxiety about the meaningless of existence.
I used to be one of those people.

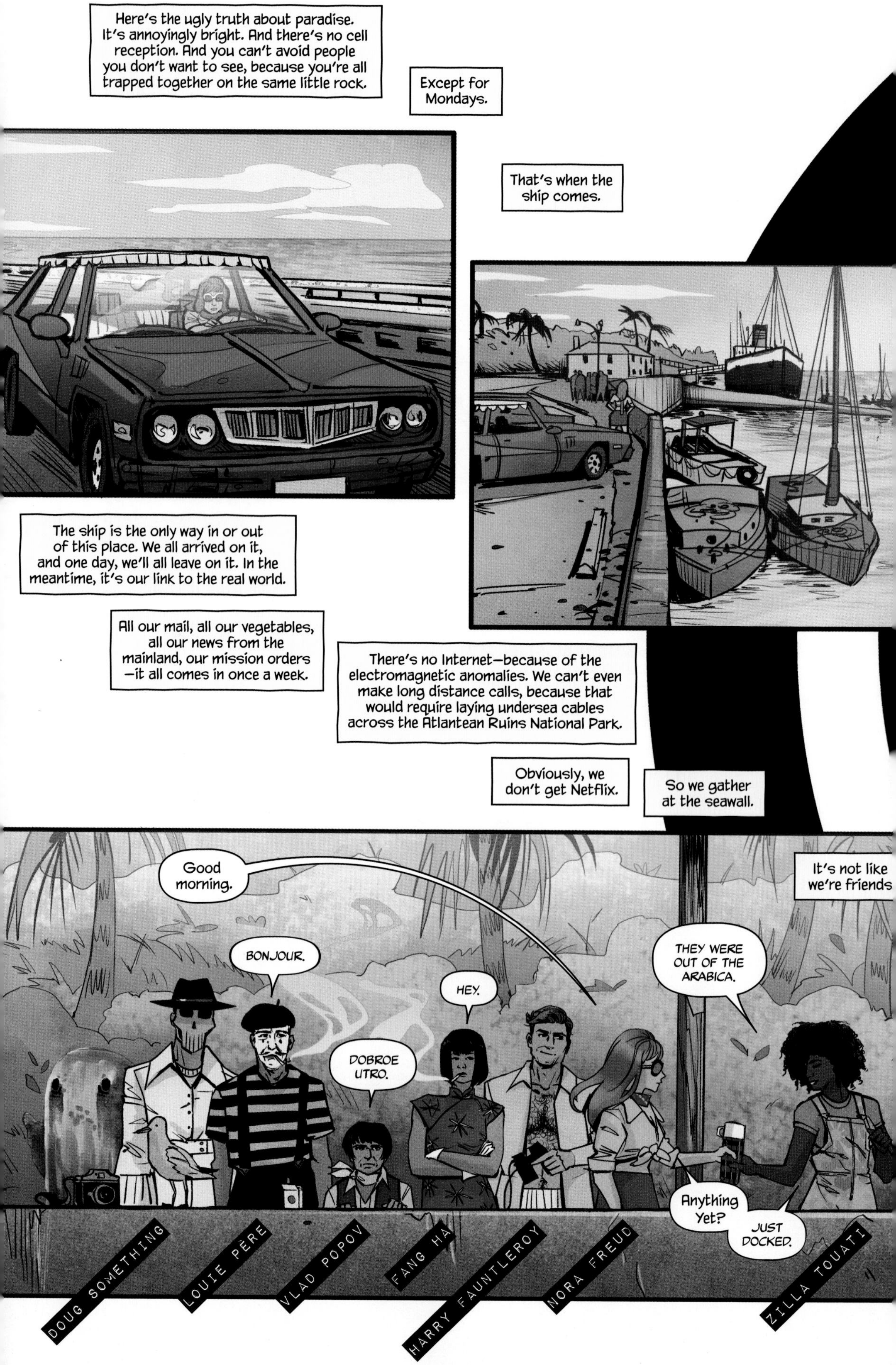
Here's the ugly truth about paradise. It's annoyingly bright. And there's no cell reception. And you can't avoid people you don't want to see, because you're all trapped together on the same little rock.
Except for Mondays.
That's when the ship comes.
The ship is the only way in or out of this place. We all arrived on it, and one day, we'll all leave on it. In the meantime, it's our link to the real world.
All our mail, all our vegetables, all our news from the mainland, our mission orders —it all comes in once a week.
There's no Internet—because of the electromagnetic anomalies. We can't even make long distance calls, because that would require laying undersea cables across the Atlantean Ruins National Park.
Obviously, we don't get Netflix.
So we gather at the seawall.
Good morning.
It's not like we're friends
BONJOUR.
HEY.
THEY WERE OUT OF THE ARABICA.
DOBROE UTRO.
Anything Yet?
JUST DOCKED.
DOUG SOMETHING
LOUIE PÈRE
VLAD POPOV
FANG HA
HARRY FAUNTLEROY
NORA FREUD
ZILLA TOUATI

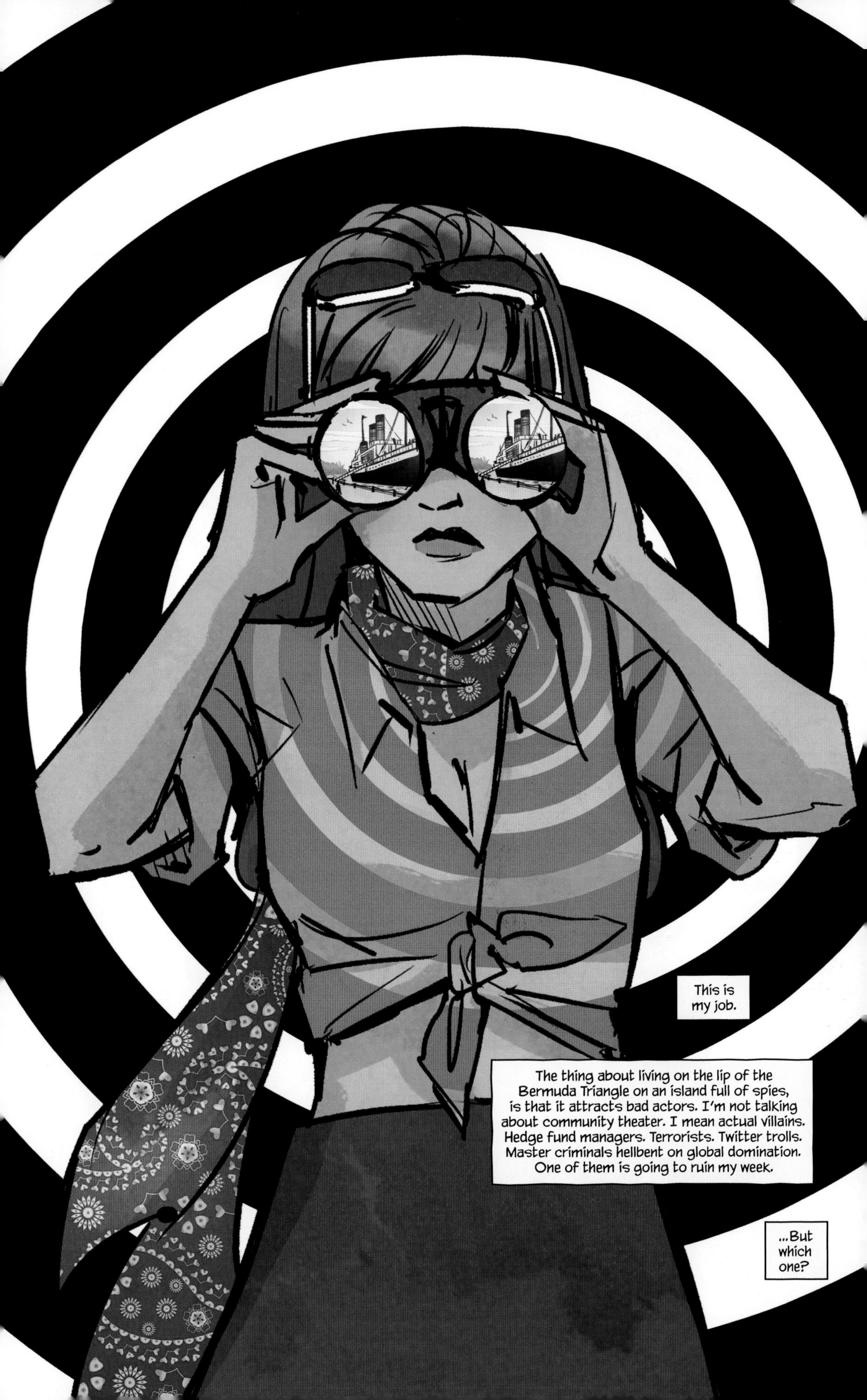
This is my job.
The thing about living on the lip of the Bermuda Triangle on an island full of spies, is that it attracts bad actors. I'm not talking about community theater. I mean actual villains. Hedge fund managers. Terrorists. Twitter trolls. Master criminals hellbent on global domination. One of them is going to ruin my week.
...But which one?

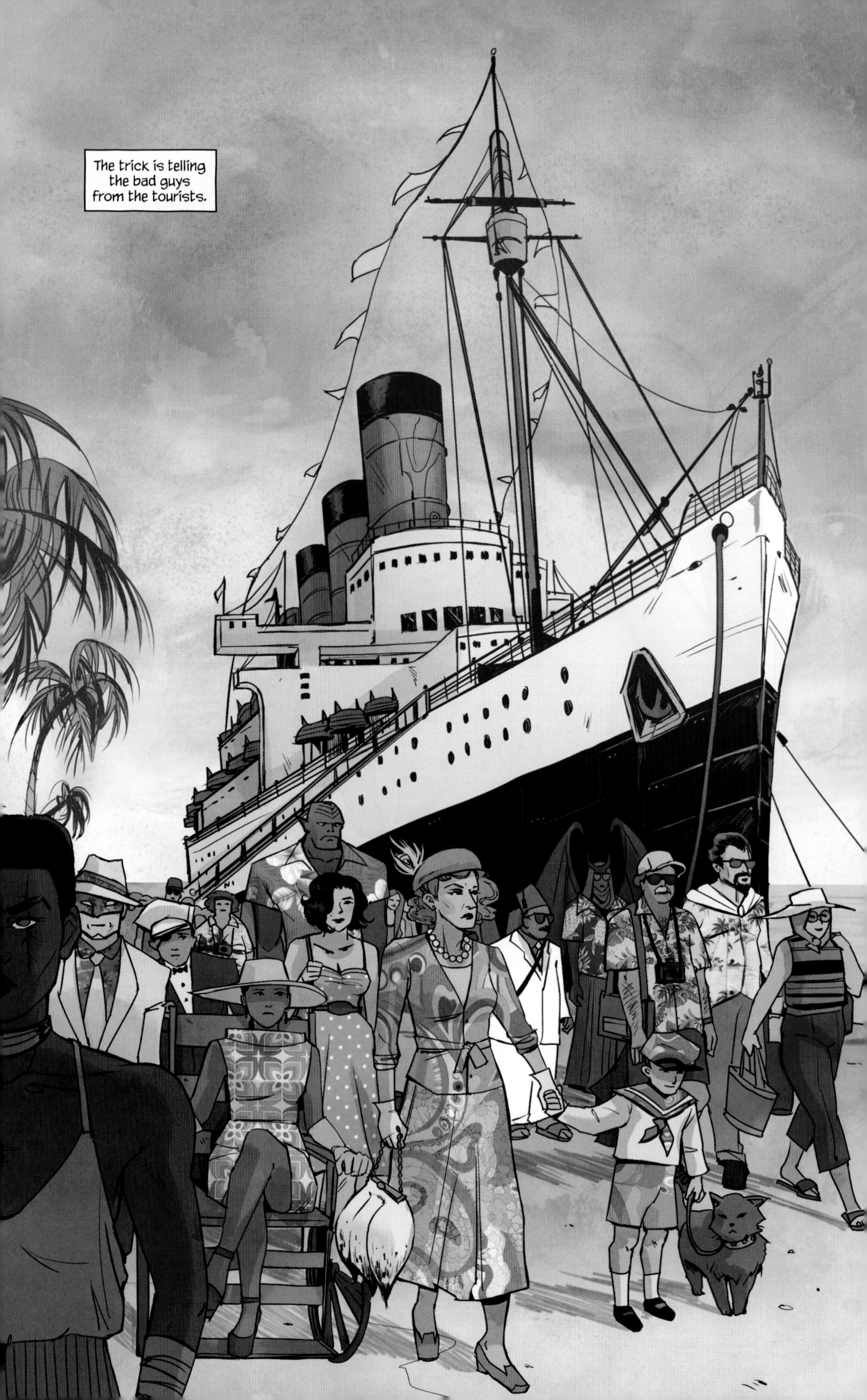
The trick is telling the bad guys from the tourists.

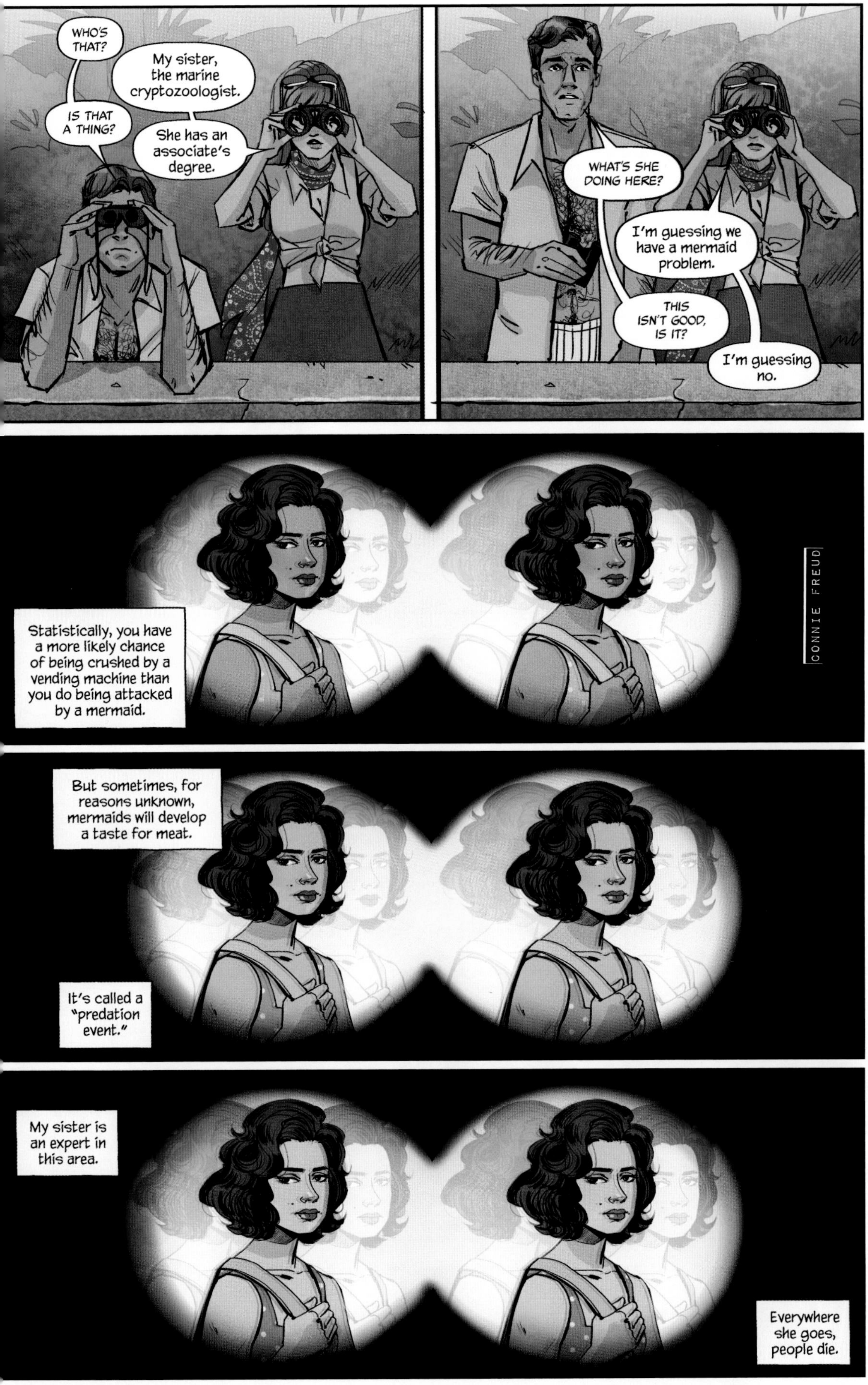
WHO'S THAT?
My sister, the marine cryptozoologist.
IS THAT A THING?
She has an associate's degree.
WHAT'S SHE DOING HERE?
I'm guessing we have a mermaid problem.
THIS ISN'T GOOD, IS IT?
I'm guessing no.
CONNIE FREUD
Statistically, you have a more likely chance of being crushed by a vending machine than you do being attacked by a mermaid.
But sometimes, for reasons unknown, mermaids will develop a taste for meat.
It's called a "predation event."
My sister is an expert in this area.
Everywhere she goes, people die.

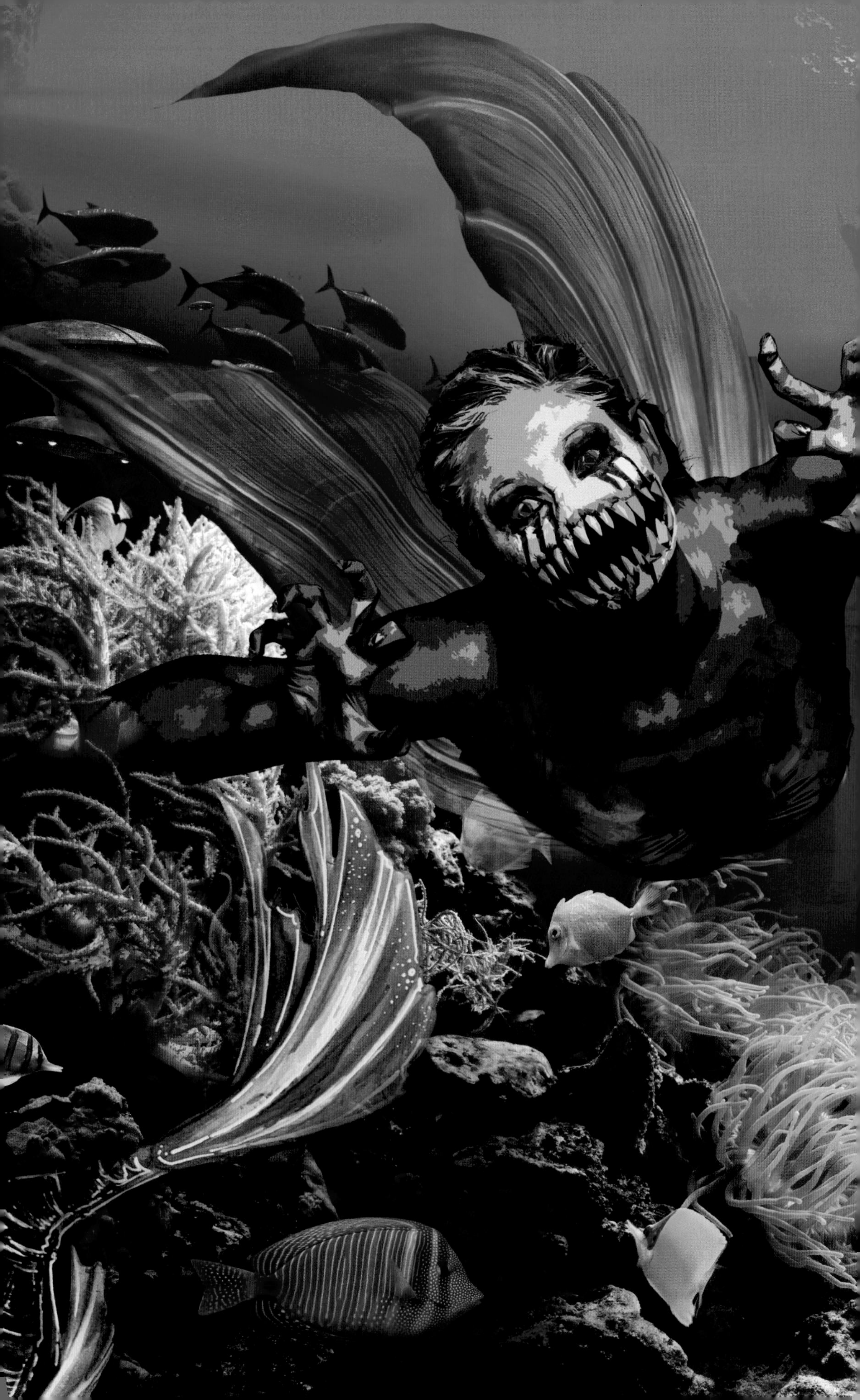

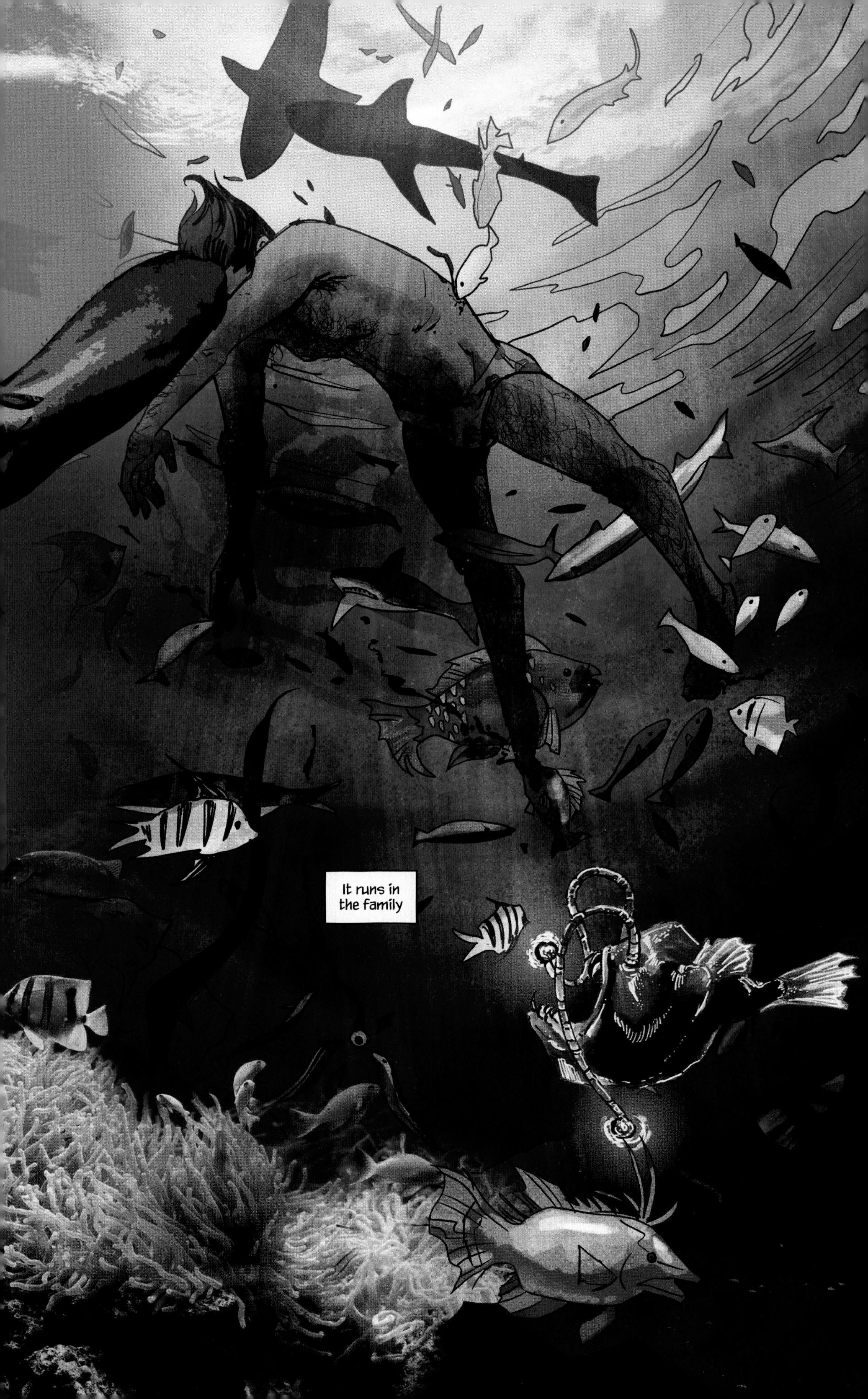
It runs in the family

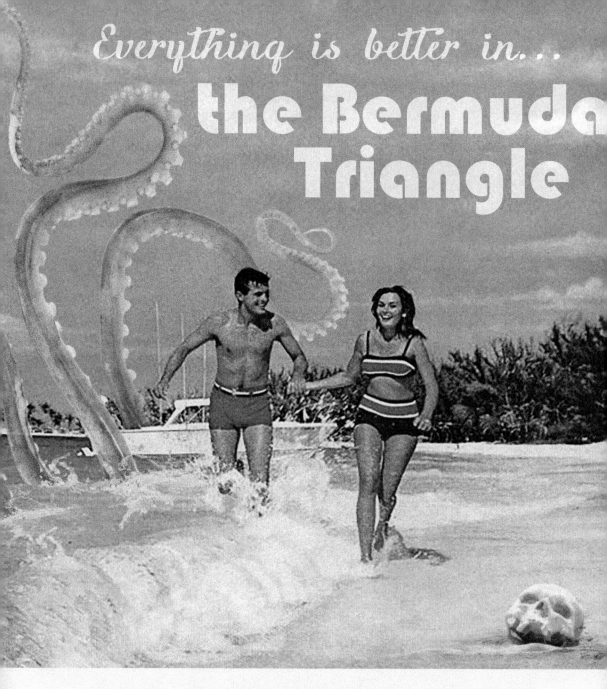

Everything is better in...

the Bermuda Triangle

It's like nowhere else.

The islands of the Bermuda Triangle await you. Pink beaches. Soft skies. Ghost pirate ships. Enjoy swimming with mermaids, the evening call to the Kraken, UFO spotting, and poolside temporal anomalies. The Bermuda Triangle offers something for the whole family.

You might not ever want to go home.

Your vacation will include:*

Exotic marine life	Whirlpool surfing	Ancient alien burial grounds	A sunset catamaran trip
Sunbathing	Ghost encounters	Traditional dance lessons	Kid-friendly sea serpent swims
Sunken City Tours	Kayaking	Boutique shopping	Beach combing for bones
Zip lines	Rogue waves	Scuba diving	Breakfast buffet

*All experiences not guaranteed. Some may result in death.

THE BERMUDA TRIANGLE

Want a unique job? Try cryptozoology! It pays very well.

ISLAND LINES
Cruise The Bermuda Triangle

Poolside Cocktail

~ Daily Special ~

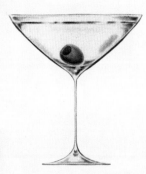

DAY 2

DRY MARTINI

1/5 French (dry) Vermouth
4/5 Gin
Stir well with ice
Strain into cocktail glass and add olive

ISLAND LINES
Cruise The Bermuda Triangle

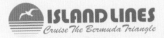

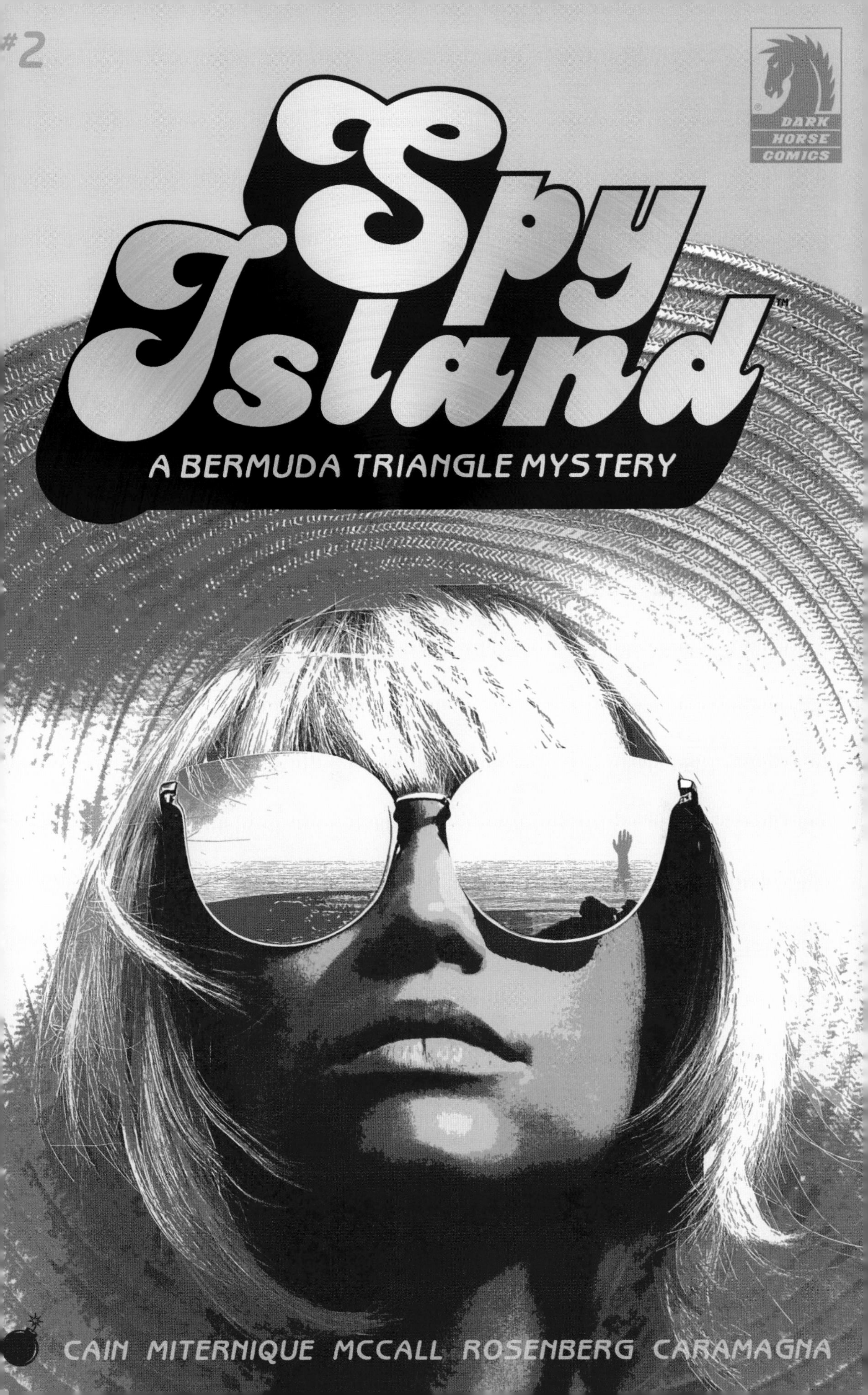
#2
DARK HORSE COMICS
Spy Island™
A BERMUDA TRIANGLE MYSTERY
CAIN MITERNIQUE MCCALL ROSENBERG CARAMAGNA

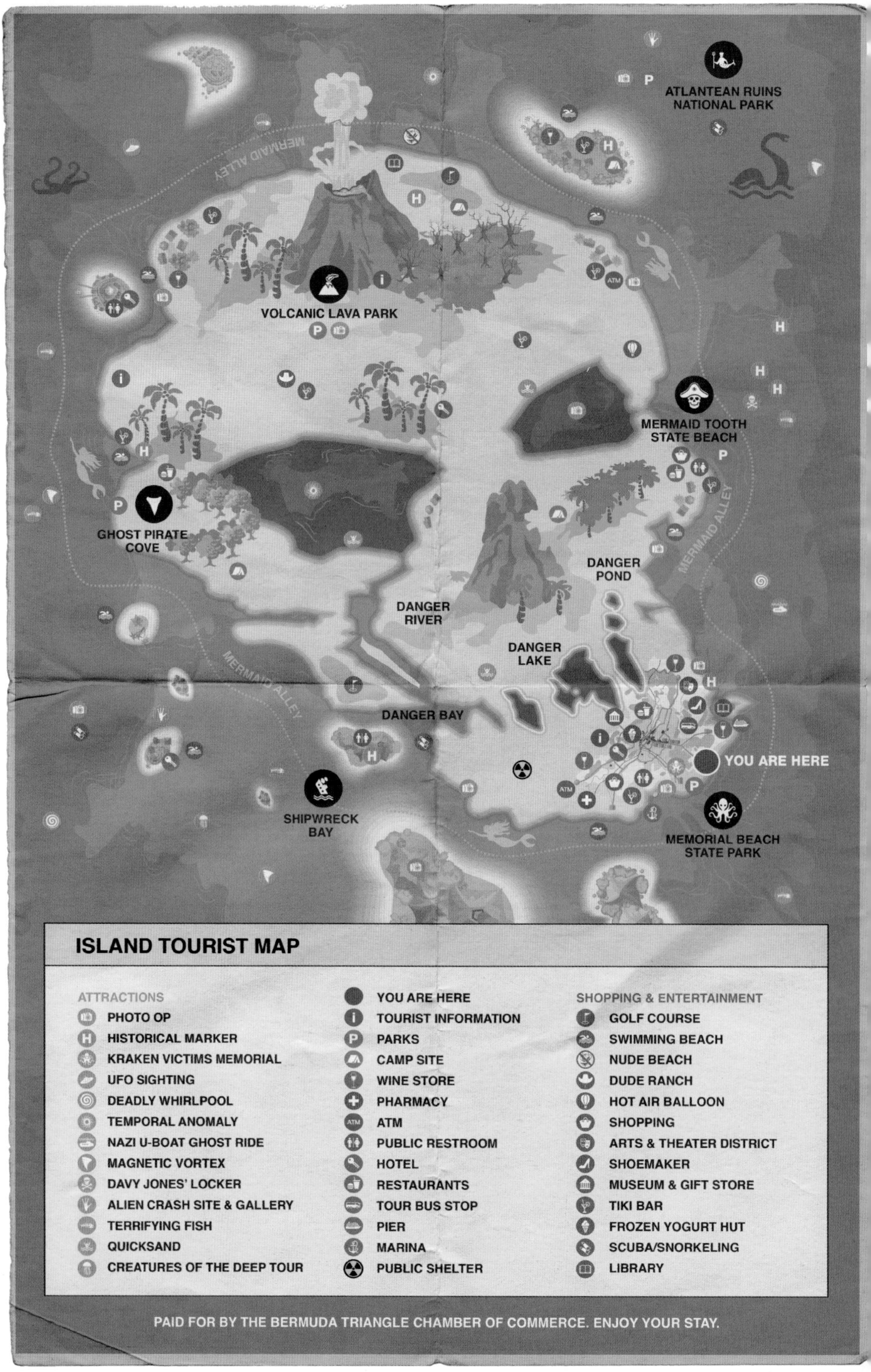
ATLANTEAN RUINS NATIONAL PARK
MERMAID ALLEY
VOLCANIC LAVA PARK
MERMAID TOOTH STATE BEACH
GHOST PIRATE COVE
MERMAID ALLEY
DANGER POND
DANGER RIVER
DANGER LAKE
MERMAID ALLEY
DANGER BAY
YOU ARE HERE
SHIPWRECK BAY
MEMORIAL BEACH STATE PARK
P
H
i
ATM

ISLAND TOURIST MAP

ATTRACTIONS		SHOPPING & ENTERTAINMENT
PHOTO OP	YOU ARE HERE	GOLF COURSE
HISTORICAL MARKER	TOURIST INFORMATION	SWIMMING BEACH
KRAKEN VICTIMS MEMORIAL	PARKS	NUDE BEACH
UFO SIGHTING	CAMP SITE	DUDE RANCH
DEADLY WHIRLPOOL	WINE STORE	HOT AIR BALLOON
TEMPORAL ANOMALY	PHARMACY	SHOPPING
NAZI U-BOAT GHOST RIDE	ATM	ARTS & THEATER DISTRICT
MAGNETIC VORTEX	PUBLIC RESTROOM	SHOEMAKER
DAVY JONES' LOCKER	HOTEL	MUSEUM & GIFT STORE
ALIEN CRASH SITE & GALLERY	RESTAURANTS	TIKI BAR
TERRIFYING FISH	TOUR BUS STOP	FROZEN YOGURT HUT
QUICKSAND	PIER	SCUBA/SNORKELING
CREATURES OF THE DEEP TOUR	MARINA	LIBRARY
	PUBLIC SHELTER	

PAID FOR BY THE BERMUDA TRIANGLE CHAMBER OF COMMERCE. ENJOY YOUR STAY.

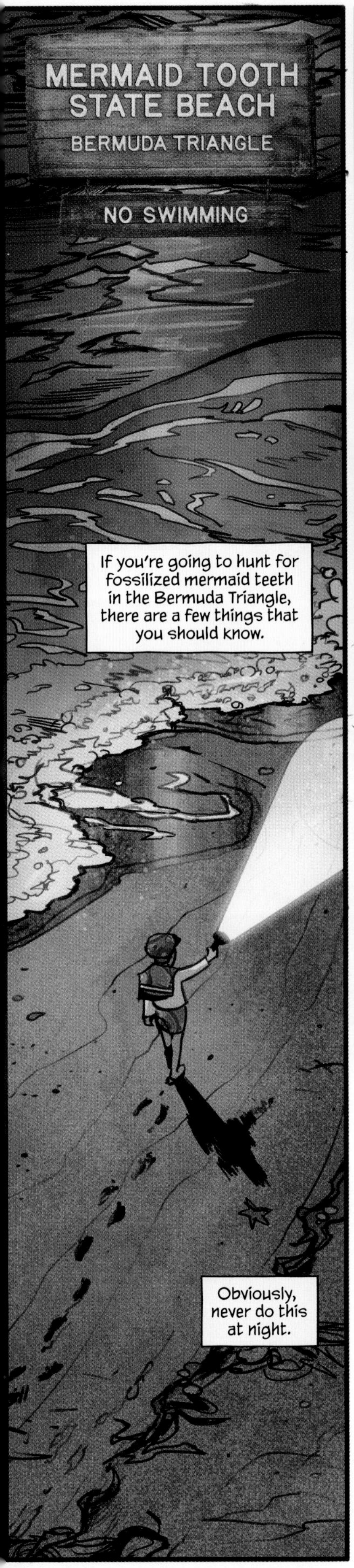
MERMAID TOOTH
STATE BEACH
BERMUDA TRIANGLE
NO SWIMMING
If you're going to hunt for fossilized mermaid teeth in the Bermuda Triangle, there are a few things that you should know.
Obviously, never do this at night.

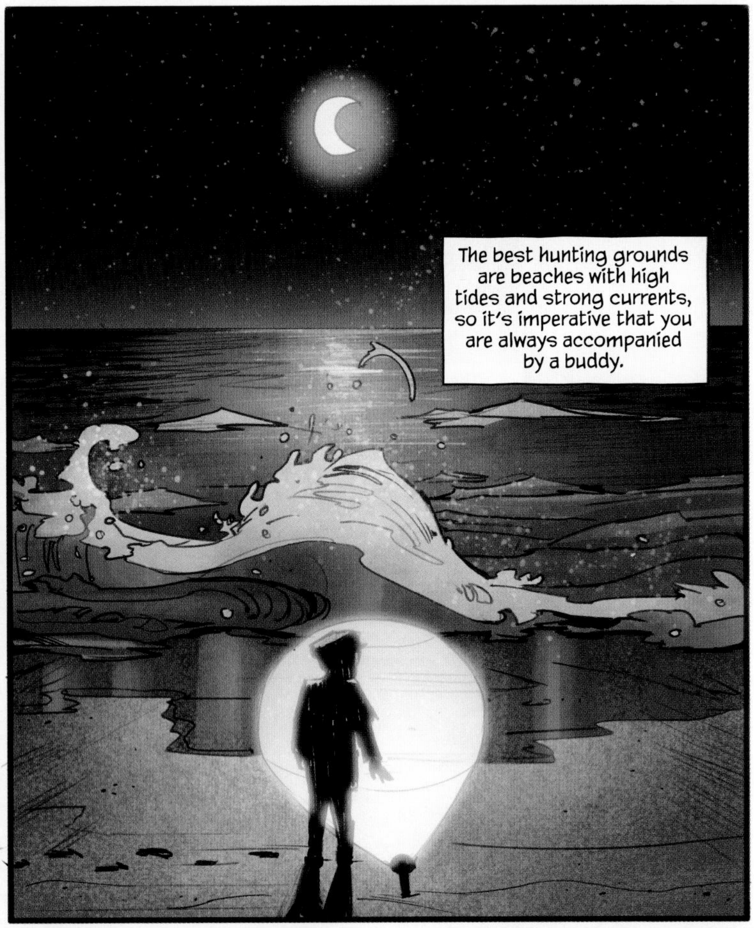
The best hunting grounds are beaches with high tides and strong currents, so it's imperative that you are always accompanied by a buddy.

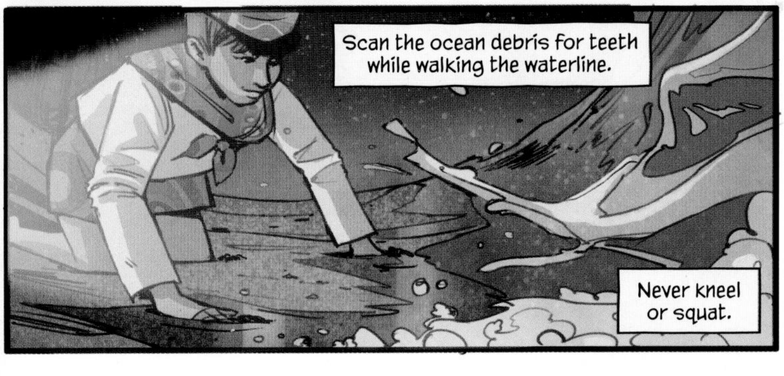
Scan the ocean debris for teeth while walking the waterline.
Never kneel or squat.

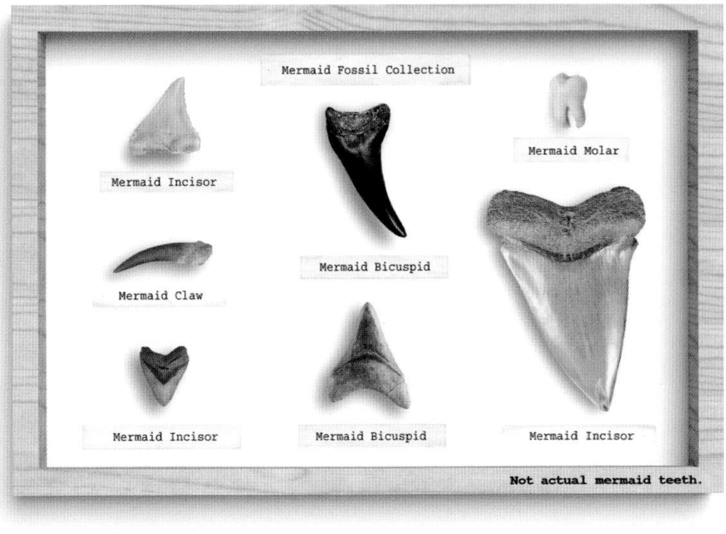
Mermaid Fossil Collection
Mermaid Incisor
Mermaid Bicuspid
Mermaid Molar
Mermaid Claw
Mermaid Incisor
Mermaid Bicuspid
Mermaid Incisor
Not actual mermaid teeth.

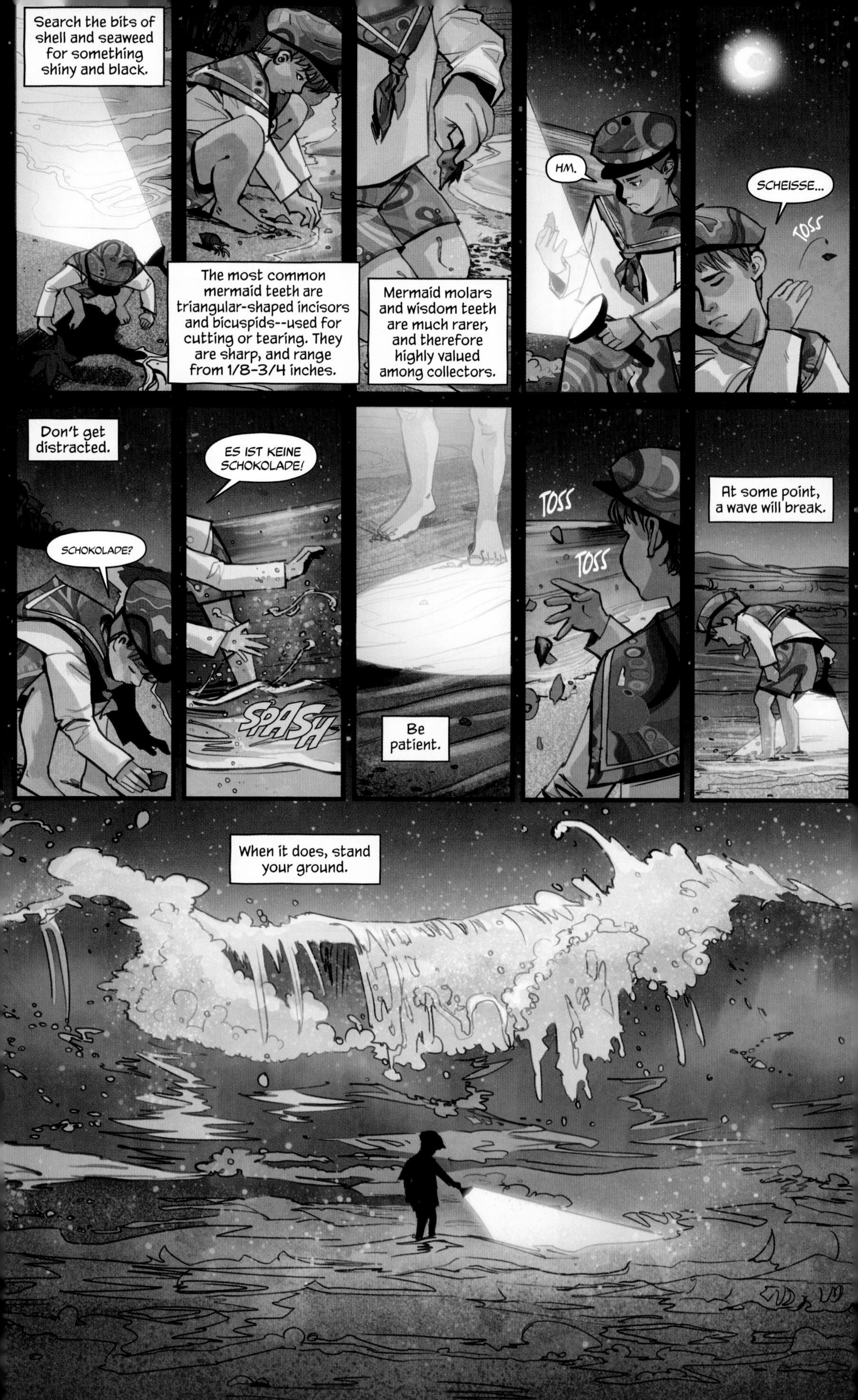
Search the bits of shell and seaweed for something shiny and black.
The most common mermaid teeth are triangular-shaped incisors and bicuspids--used for cutting or tearing. They are sharp, and range from 1/8-3/4 inches.
Mermaid molars and wisdom teeth are much rarer, and therefore highly valued among collectors.
HM.
SCHEISSE...
TOSS
Don't get distracted.
SCHOKOLADE?
ES IST KEINE SCHOKOLADE!
SPASH
Be patient.
TOSS
TOSS
At some point, a wave will break.
When it does, stand your ground.

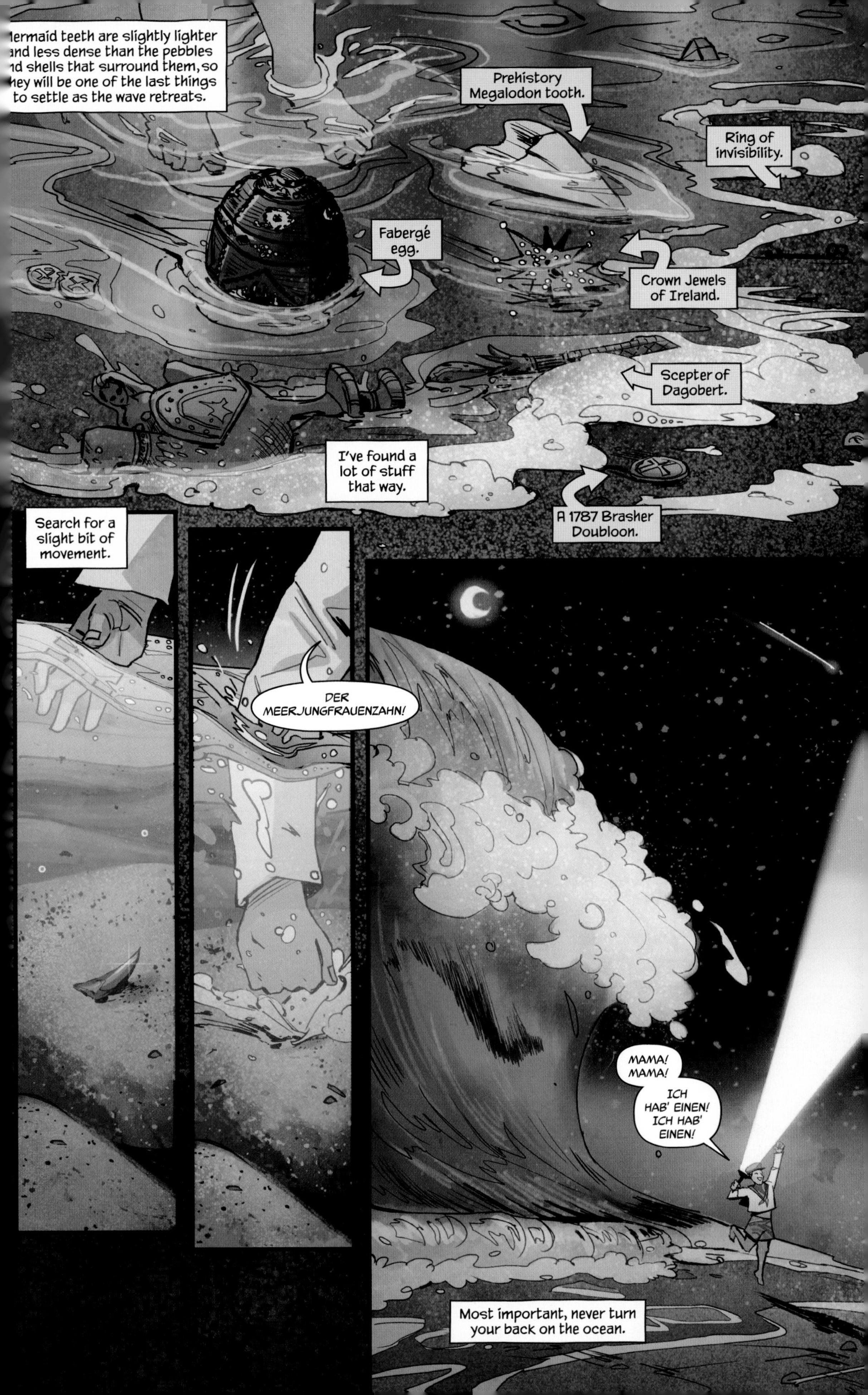

lermaid teeth are slightly lighter and less dense than the pebbles nd shells that surround them, so hey will be one of the last things to settle as the wave retreats.
Prehistory Megalodon tooth.
Ring of invisibility.
Fabergé egg.
Crown Jewels of Ireland.
Scepter of Dagobert.
I've found a lot of stuff that way.
A 1787 Brasher Doubloon.
Search for a slight bit of movement.
DER MEERJUNGFRAUENZAHN!
MAMA! MAMA!
ICH HAB' EINEN! ICH HAB' EINEN!
Most important, never turn your back on the ocean.

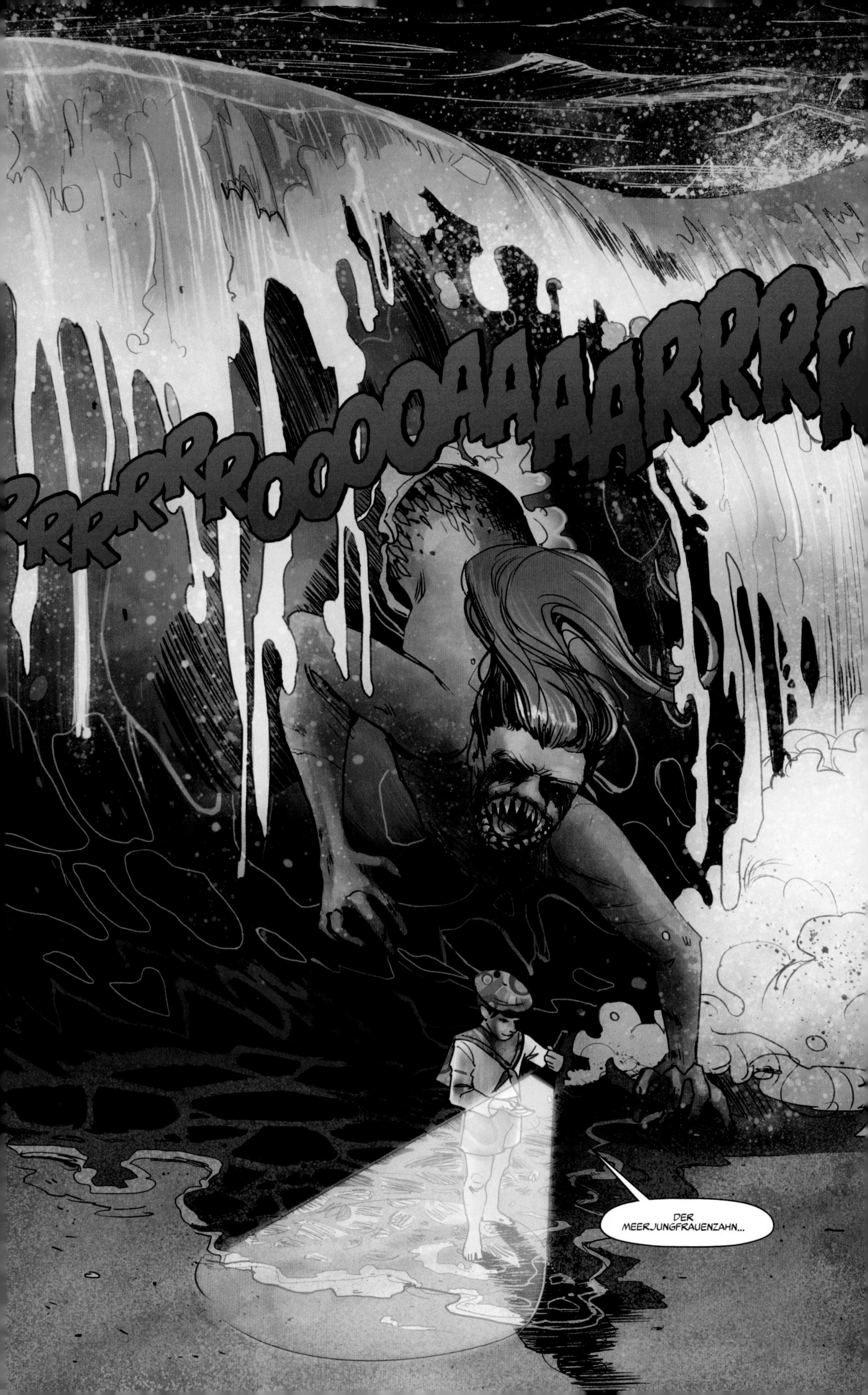
RRRRROOOOAAAARRRR
DER MEERJUNGFRAUENZAHN...

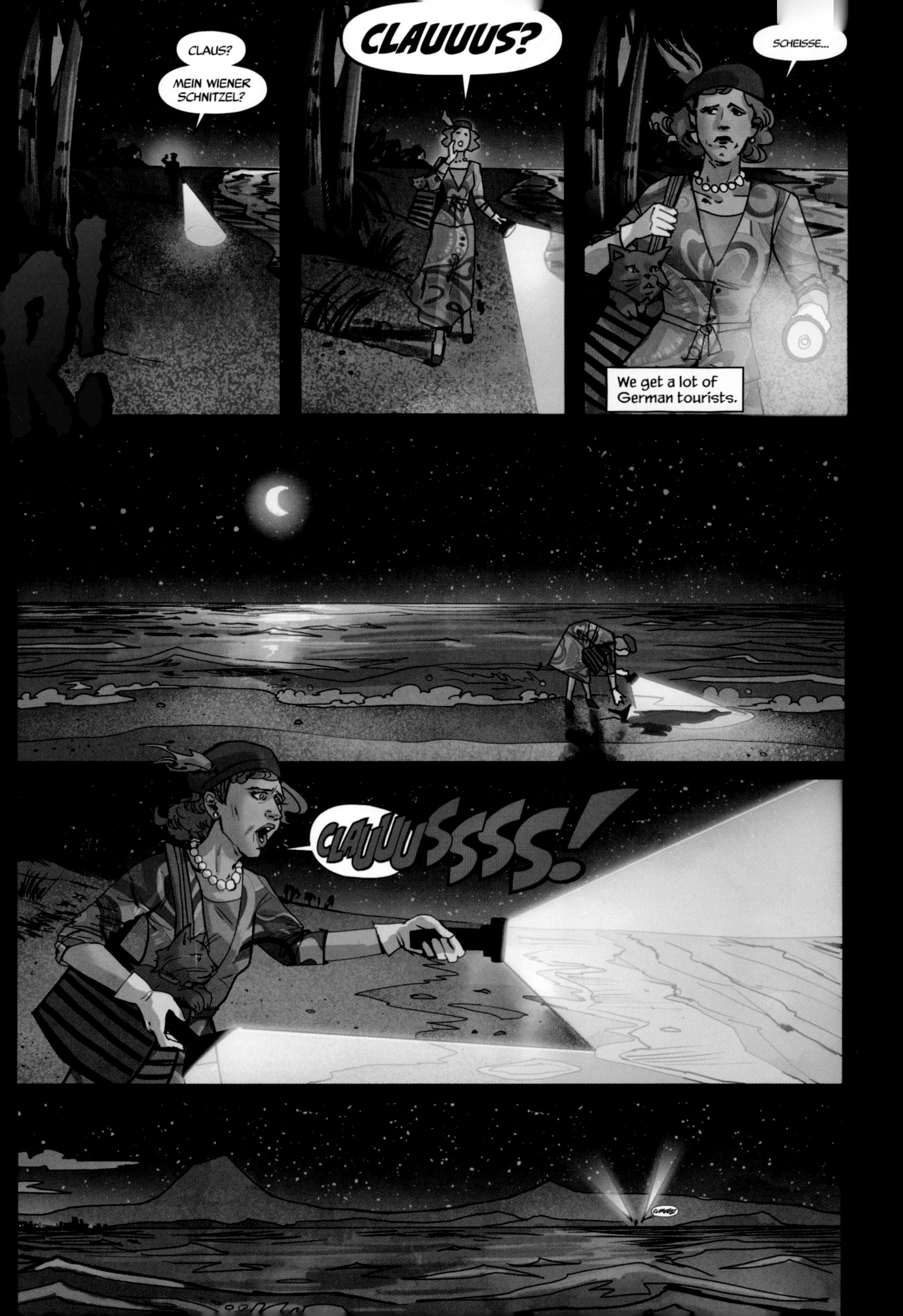
CLAUS?
MEIN WIENER SCHNITZEL?
CLAUUUS?
SCHEISSE...
We get a lot of German tourists.
CLAUUUSSSS!

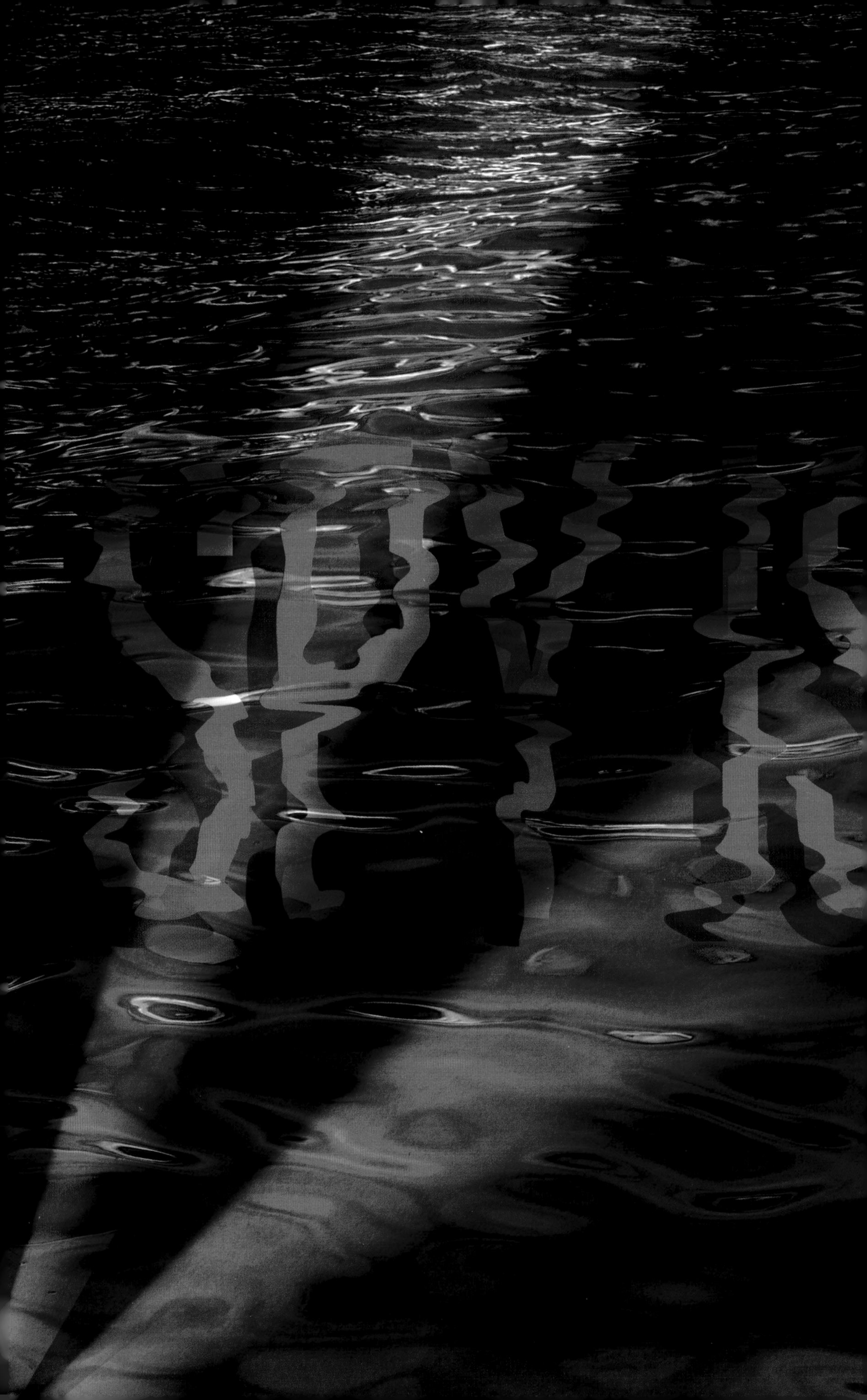

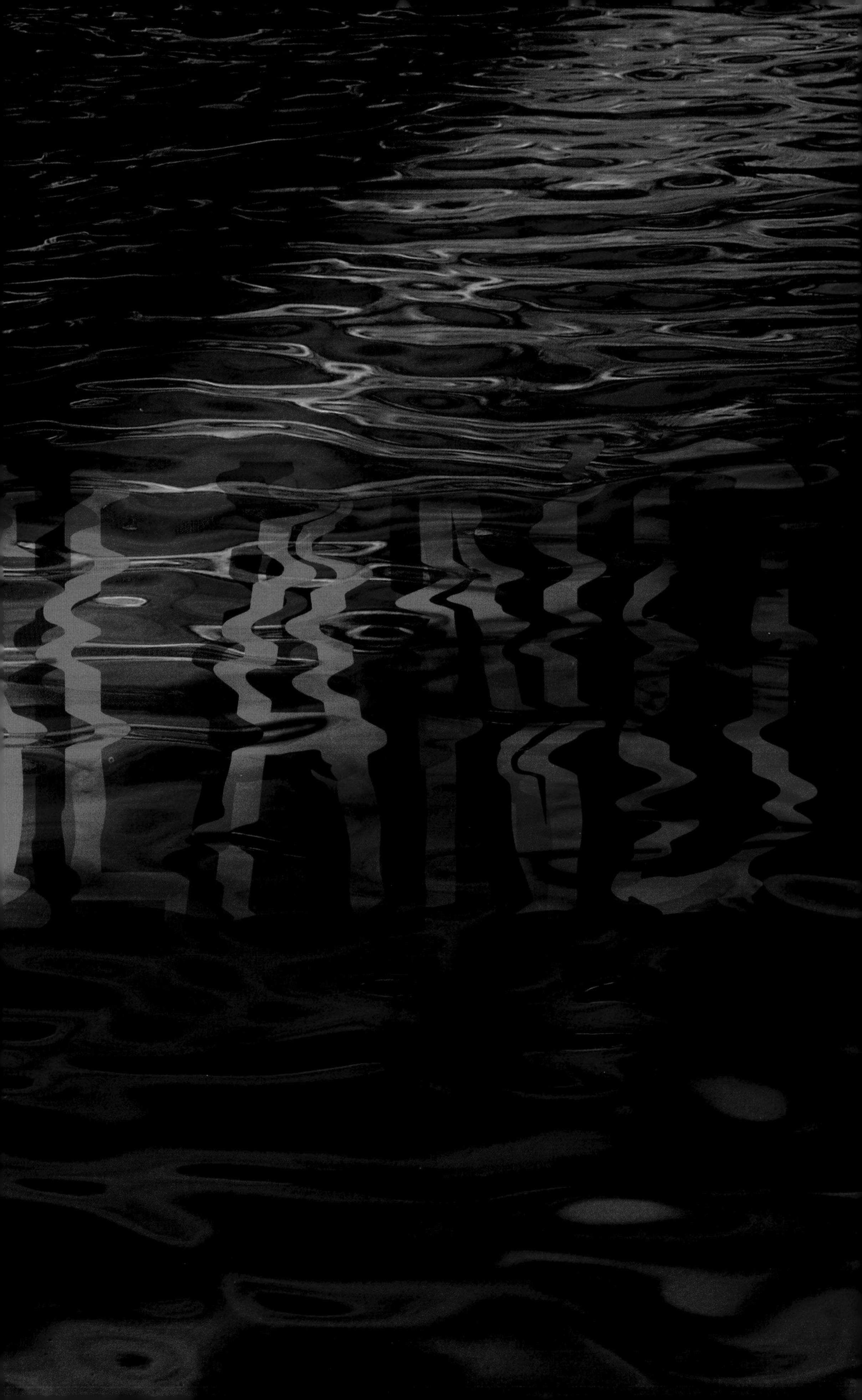

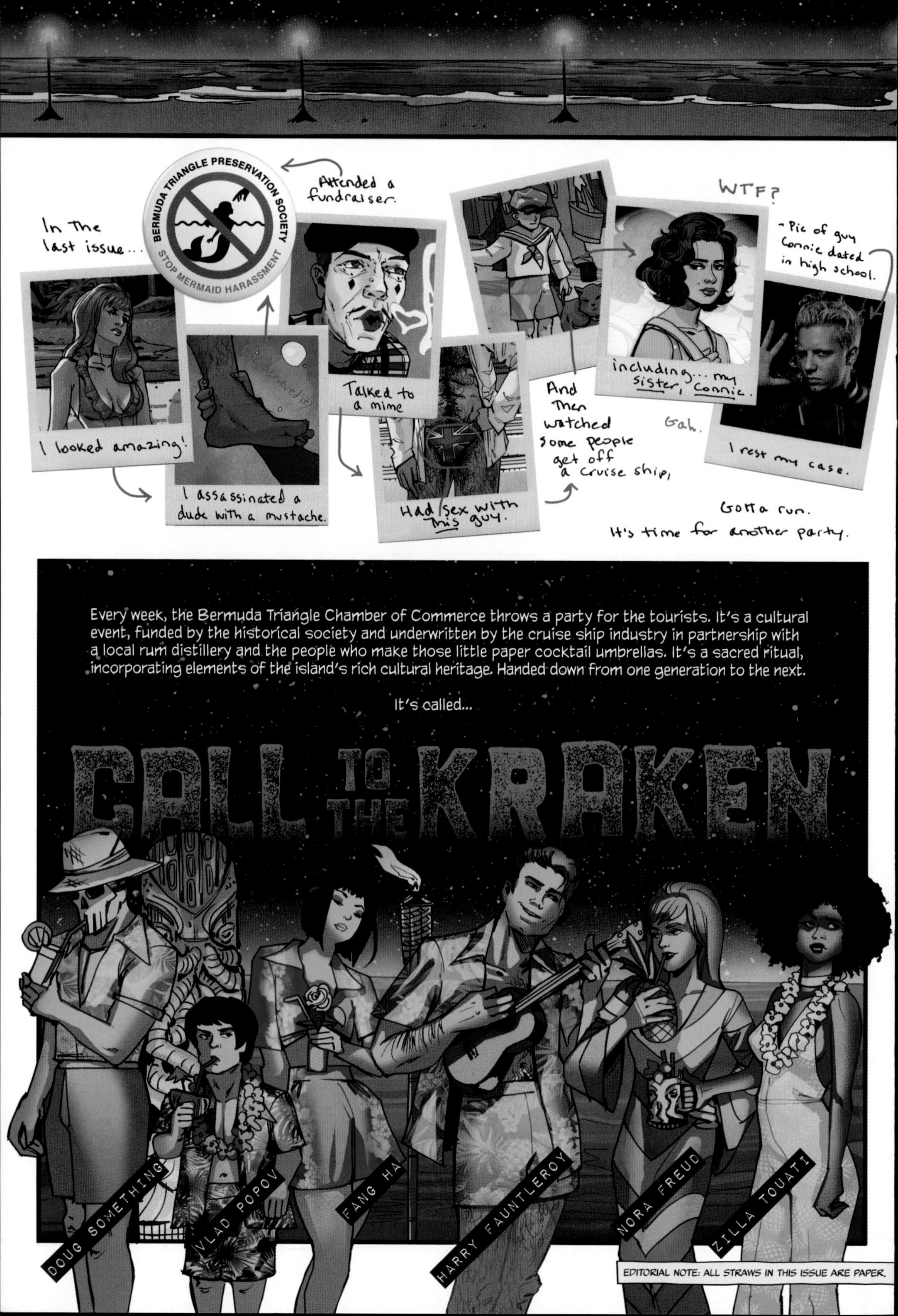
In the last issue...
BERMUDA TRIANGLE PRESERVATION SOCIETY
STOP MERMAID HARASSMENT
Attended a fundraiser.
I looked amazing!
I assassinated a dude with a mustache.
Talked to a mime
Had sex with this guy.
And Then watched some people get off a cruise ship,
including... my sister, Connie.
WTF?
Gah.
- Pic of guy Connie dated in high school.
I rest my case.
Gotta run.
It's time for another party.
Every week, the Bermuda Triangle Chamber of Commerce throws a party for the tourists. It's a cultural event, funded by the historical society and underwritten by the cruise ship industry in partnership with a local rum distillery and the people who make those little paper cocktail umbrellas. It's a sacred ritual, incorporating elements of the island's rich cultural heritage. Handed down from one generation to the next.
It's called...
CALL TO THE KRAKEN
DOUG SOMETHING
VLAD POPOV
FANG HA
HARRY FAUNTLEROY
NORA FREUD
ZILLA TOUATI
EDITORIAL NOTE: ALL STRAWS IN THIS ISSUE ARE PAPER.

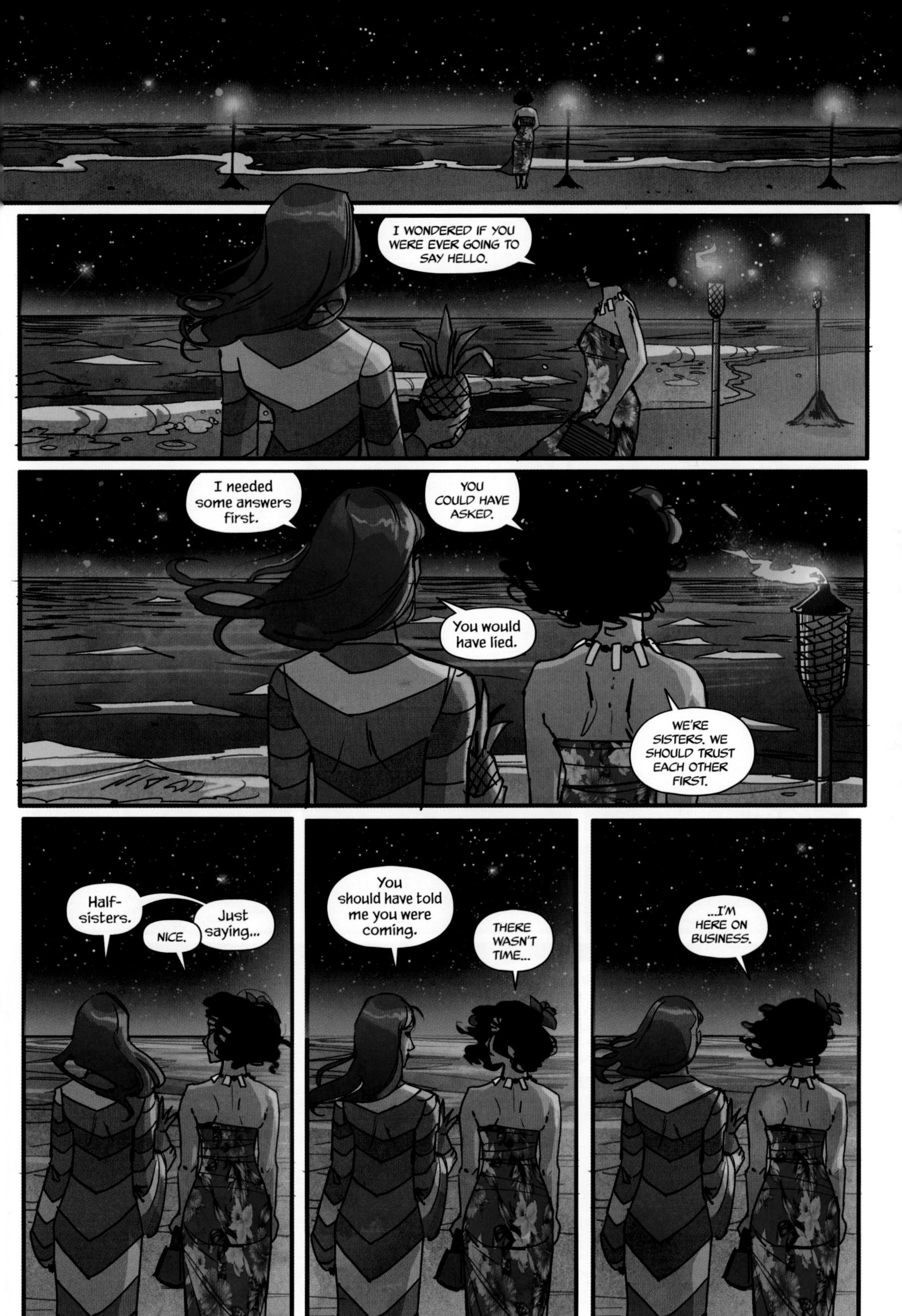
I WONDERED IF YOU WERE EVER GOING TO SAY HELLO.
I needed some answers first.
YOU COULD HAVE ASKED.
You would have lied.
WE'RE SISTERS. WE SHOULD TRUST EACH OTHER FIRST.
Half-sisters.
NICE.
Just saying...
You should have told me you were coming.
THERE WASN'T TIME...
...I'M HERE ON BUSINESS.

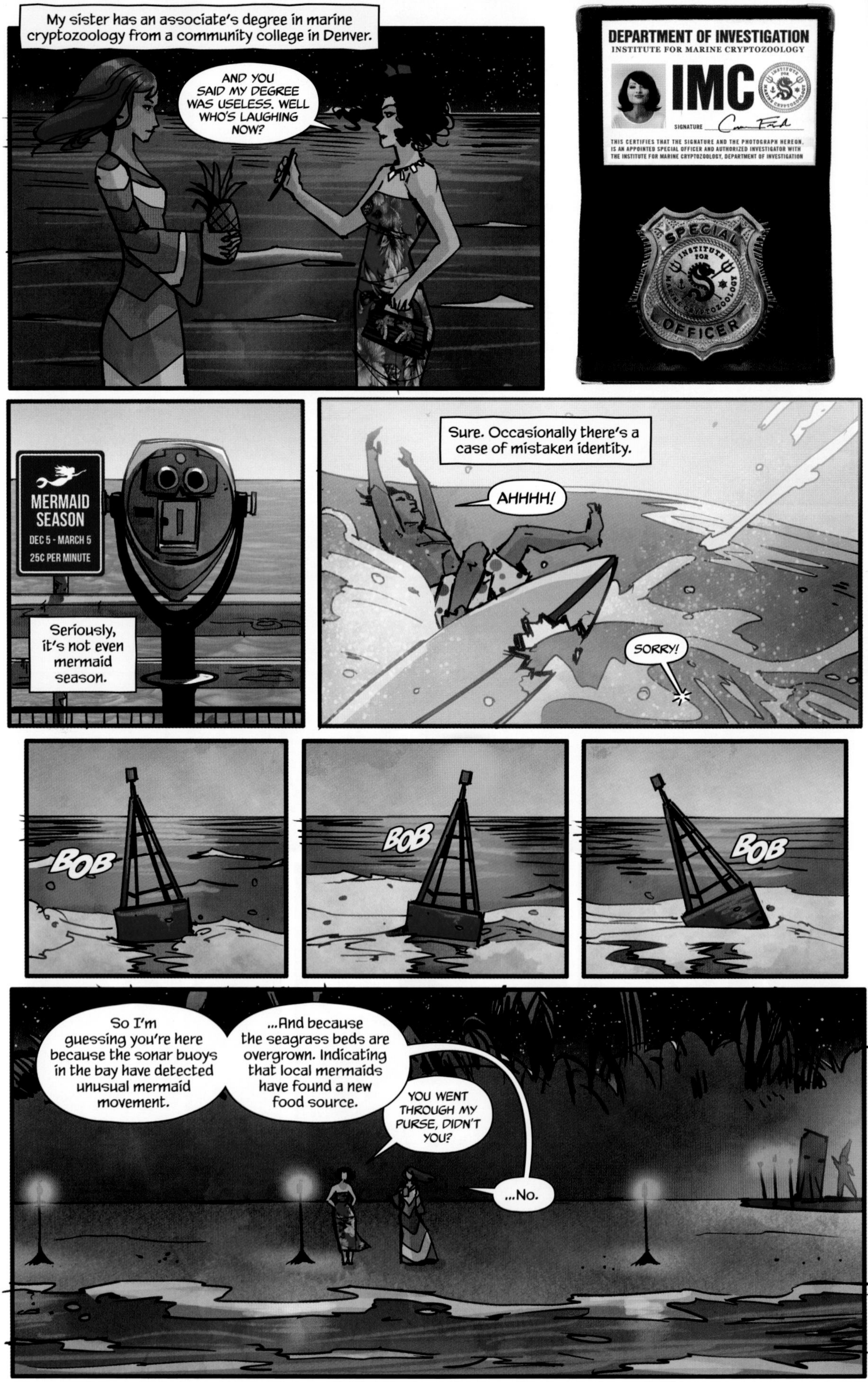

My sister has an associate's degree in marine cryptozoology from a community college in Denver.
AND YOU SAID MY DEGREE WAS USELESS. WELL WHO'S LAUGHING NOW?
DEPARTMENT OF INVESTIGATION
INSTITUTE FOR MARINE CRYPTOZOOLOGY
IMC
SIGNATURE
THIS CERTIFIES THAT THE SIGNATURE AND THE PHOTOGRAPH HEREON, IS AN APPOINTED SPECIAL OFFICER AND AUTHORIZED INVESTIGATOR WITH THE INSTITUTE FOR MARINE CRYPTOZOOLOGY, DEPARTMENT OF INVESTIGATION
SPECIAL
INSTITUTE FOR MARINE CRYPTOZOOLOGY
OFFICER
MERMAID SEASON
DEC 5 - MARCH 5
25¢ PER MINUTE
Seriously, it's not even mermaid season.
Sure. Occasionally there's a case of mistaken identity.
AHHHH!
SORRY!
BOB
BOB
BOB
So I'm guessing you're here because the sonar buoys in the bay have detected unusual mermaid movement.
...And because the seagrass beds are overgrown. Indicating that local mermaids have found a new food source.
YOU WENT THROUGH MY PURSE, DIDN'T YOU?
...No.

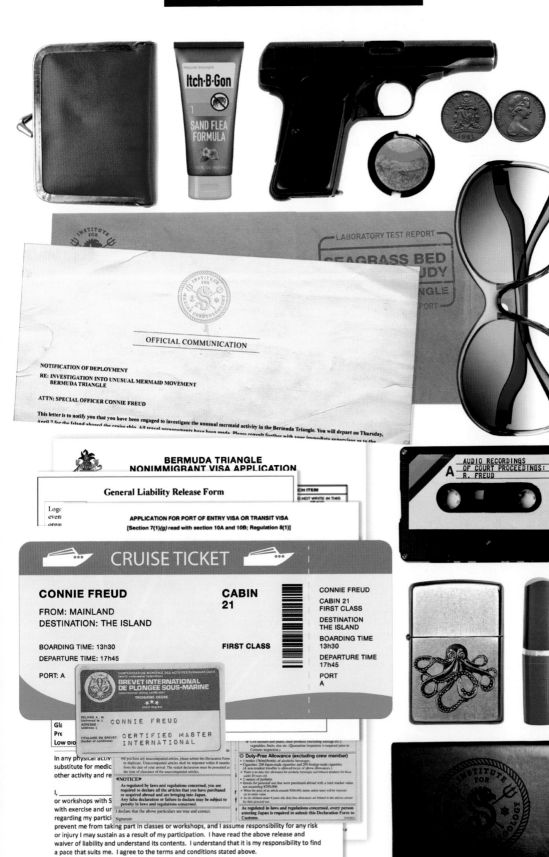

Regular Strength

Itch·B·Gon

SAND FLEA FORMULA

LABORATORY TEST REPORT

SEAGRASS BED STUDY

TRIANGLE

REPORT

OFFICIAL COMMUNICATION

NOTIFICATION OF DEPLOYMENT

RE: INVESTIGATION INTO UNUSUAL MERMAID MOVEMENT
   BERMUDA TRIANGLE

ATTN: SPECIAL OFFICER CONNIE FREUD

This letter is to notify you that you have been engaged to investigate the unusual mermaid activity in the Bermuda Triangle. You will depart on Thursday, April 7 for the Island aboard the cruise ship. All travel arrangements have been made. Please consult further with your immediate supervisor as to the

**BERMUDA TRIANGLE
NONIMMIGRANT VISA APPLICATION**

General Liability Release Form

APPLICATION FOR PORT OF ENTRY VISA OR TRANSIT VISA
[Section 7(1)(g) read with section 10A and 10B; Regulation 8(1)]

AUDIO RECORDINGS
OF COURT PROCEEDINGS:
R. FREUD

A

CRUISE TICKET

CONNIE FREUD

FROM: MAINLAND
DESTINATION: THE ISLAND

BOARDING TIME: 13h30
DEPARTURE TIME: 17h45

PORT: A

**CABIN
21**

FIRST CLASS

CONNIE FREUD

CABIN 21
FIRST CLASS

DESTINATION
THE ISLAND

BOARDING TIME
13h30

DEPARTURE TIME
17h45

PORT
A

CONFEDERATION MONDIALE DES ACTIVITES SUBAQUATIQUES
(world underwater federation)
**BREVET INTERNATIONAL
DE PLONGEE SOUS-MARINE**
International diving certificate
TROISIEME DEGRE
★★★
(third degree)

DELIVRE A : M.
(delivered to :)
ADRESSE :
(address :)   CONNIE FREUD

TITULAIRE DU BREVET   CERTIFIED MASTER
(holder of certificate)   INTERNATIONAL

INSTITUTE FOR ...OLOGY

In any physical activ...
substitute for medic...
other activity and re...

I, _____
or workshops with S...
with exercise and ur...
regarding my partici...
prevent me from taking part in classes or workshops, and I assume responsibility for any risk
or injury I may sustain as a result of my participation. I have read the above release and
waiver of liability and understand its contents. I understand that it is my responsibility to find
a pace that suits me. I agree to the terms and conditions stated above.

Date _____

Signature_____

«NOTICE»
As regulated by laws and regulations concerned, you are
required to declare all the articles that you have purchased
or acquired abroad and are bringing into Japan.
Any false declaration or failure to declare may be subject to
penalty in laws and regulations concerned.

I declare that the above particulars are true and correct.

Signature

○ **Duty-Free Allowance (excluding crew member)**

As regulated in laws and regulations concerned, every person
entering Japan is required to submit this Declaration Form to
Customs.

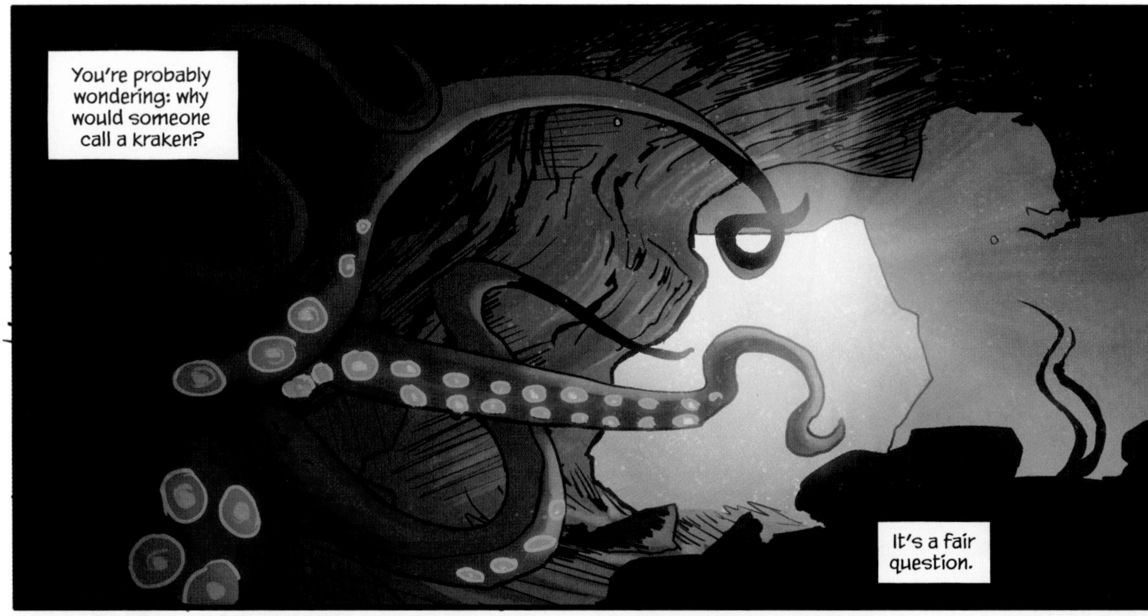
You're probably wondering: why would someone call a kraken?
It's a fair question.

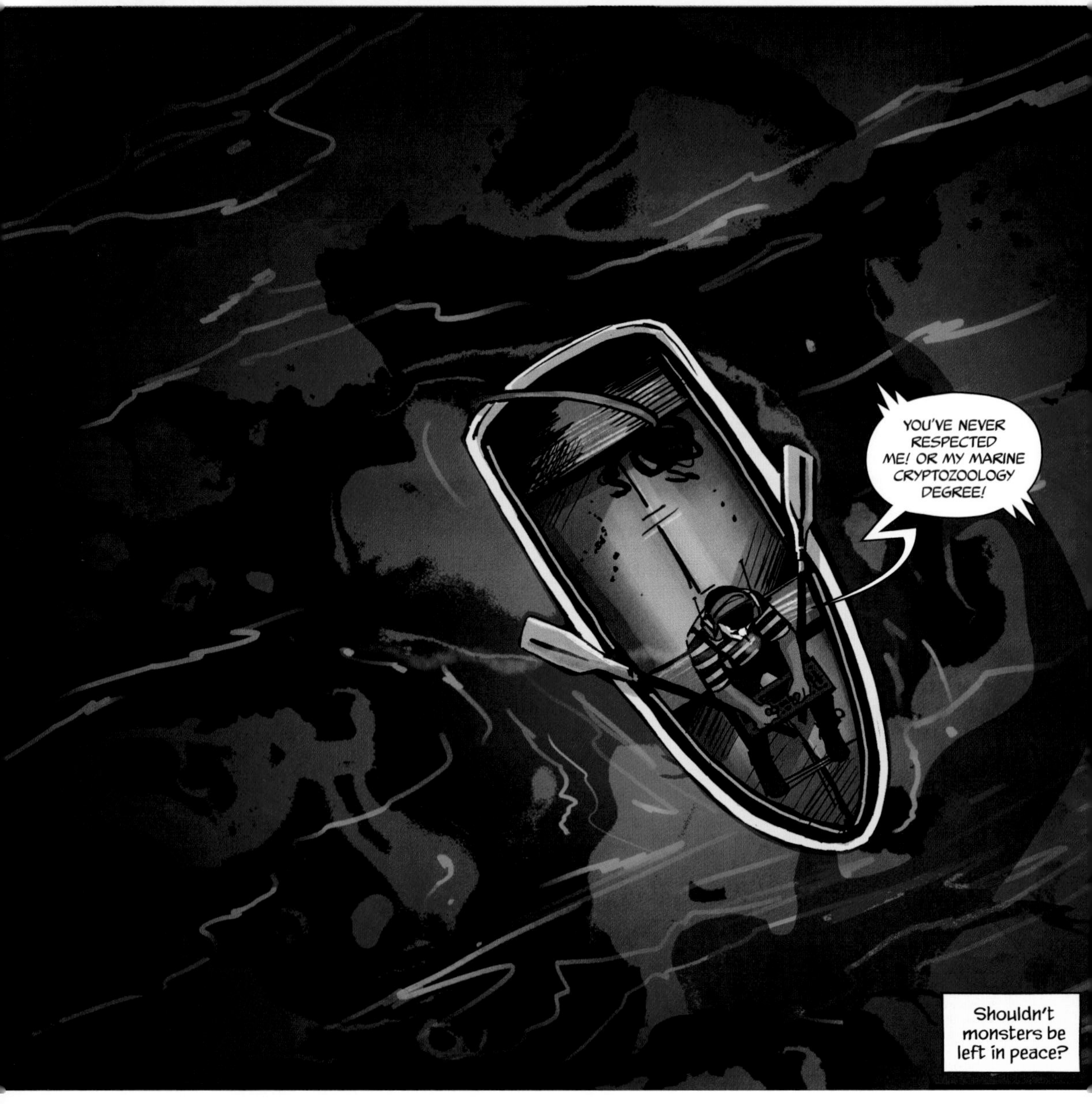
YOU'VE NEVER RESPECTED ME! OR MY MARINE CRYPTOZOOLOGY DEGREE!
Shouldn't monsters be left in peace?

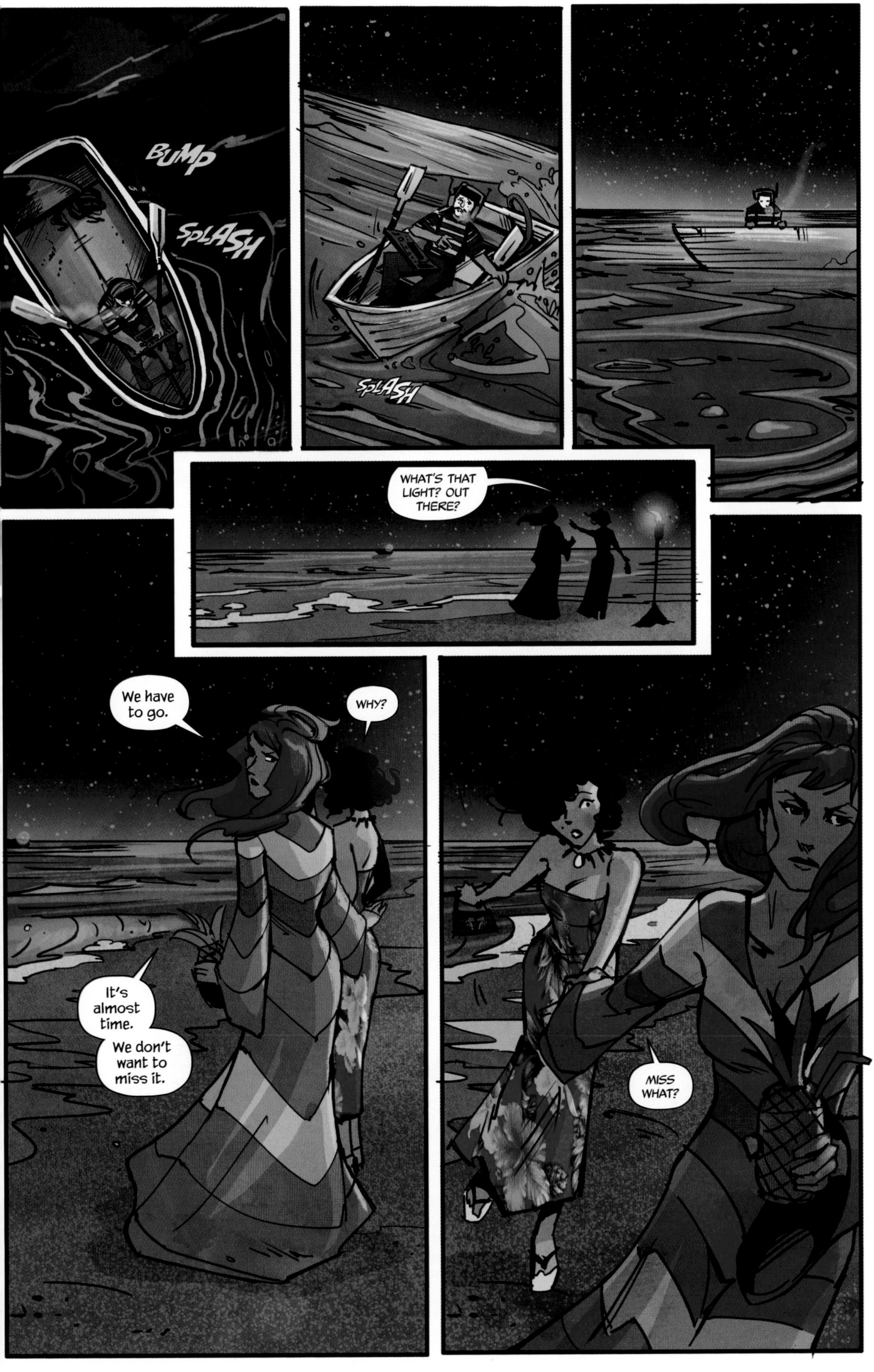
BUMP
SPLASH
SPLASH
WHAT'S THAT LIGHT? OUT THERE?
We have to go.
WHY?
It's almost time.
We don't want to miss it.
MISS WHAT?

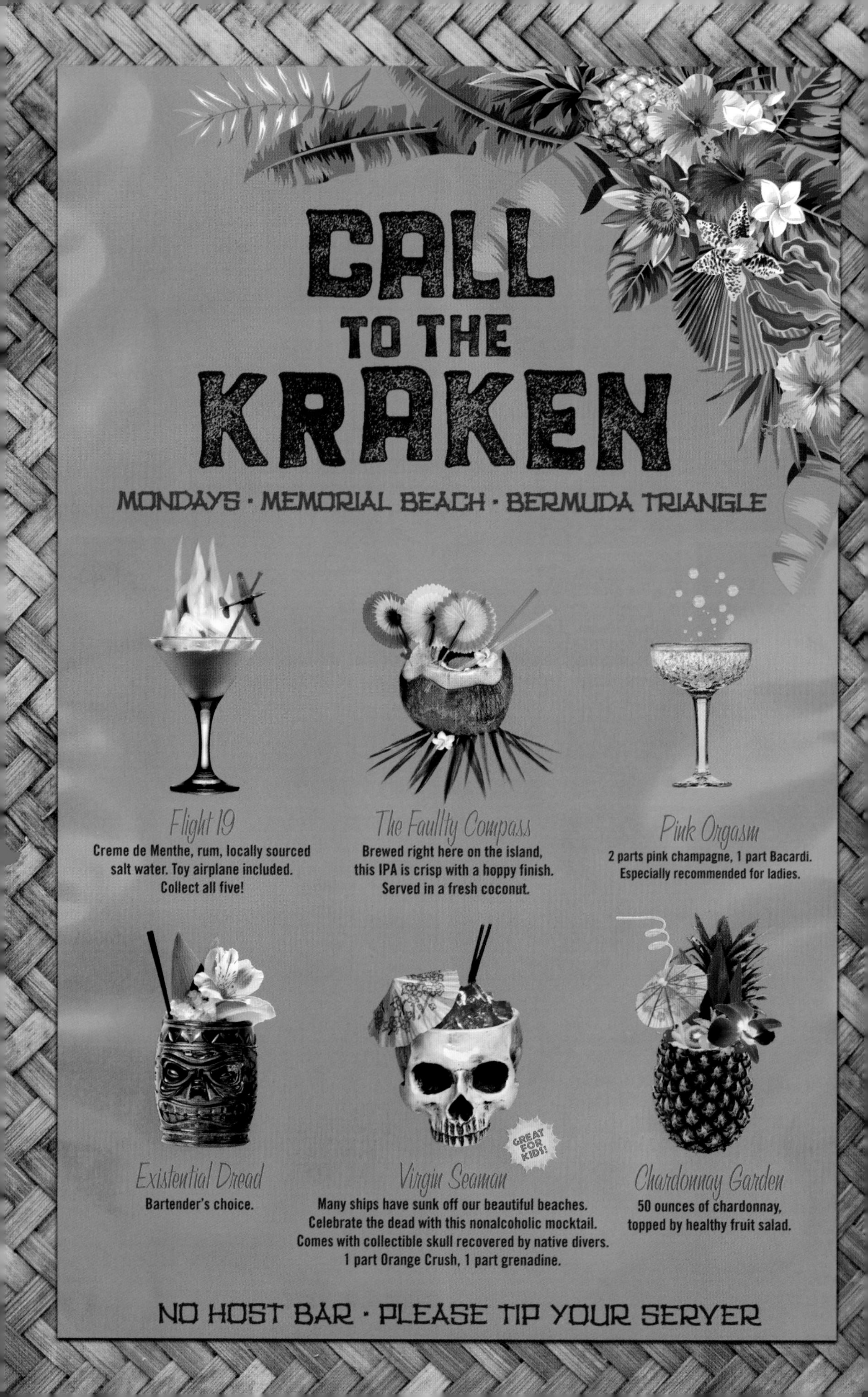
CALL
TO THE
KRAKEN
MONDAYS · MEMORIAL BEACH · BERMUDA TRIANGLE
Flight 19
Creme de Menthe, rum, locally sourced salt water. Toy airplane included. Collect all five!
The Faullty Compass
Brewed right here on the island, this IPA is crisp with a hoppy finish. Served in a fresh coconut.
Pink Orgasm
2 parts pink champagne, 1 part Bacardi. Especially recommended for ladies.
Existential Dread
Bartender's choice.
GREAT FOR KIDS!
Virgin Seaman
Many ships have sunk off our beautiful beaches. Celebrate the dead with this nonalcoholic mocktail. Comes with collectible skull recovered by native divers. 1 part Orange Crush, 1 part grenadine.
Chardonnay Garden
50 ounces of chardonnay, topped by healthy fruit salad.
NO HOST BAR · PLEASE TIP YOUR SERVER

TODAY'S SPECIAL

Mermaid Chum Punch

Market Price

Tomato juice, vodka, Worcestershire sauce,
Bermuda onion, and other spices, served with bait fish and a splash of lemon.

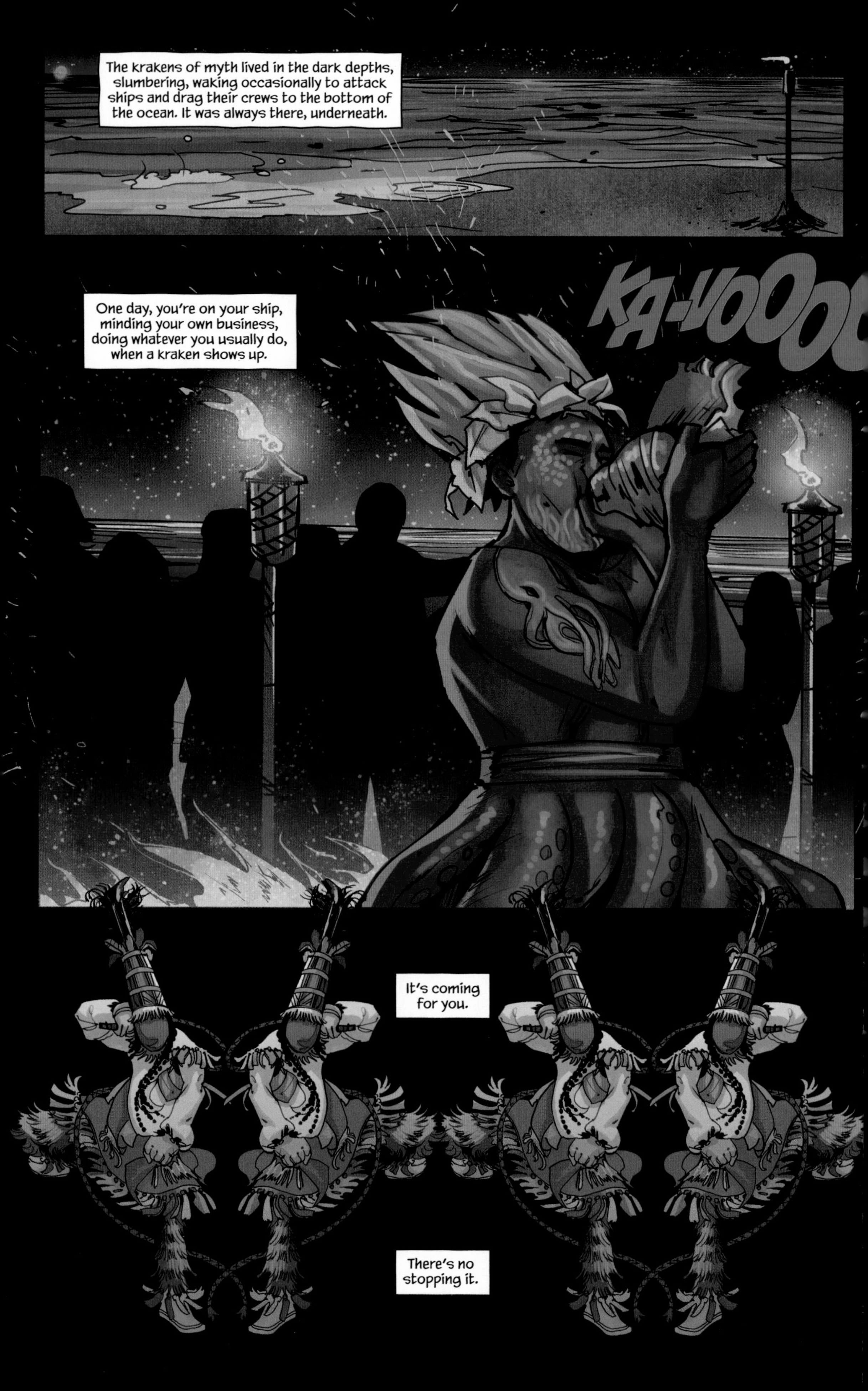
The krakens of myth lived in the dark depths, slumbering, waking occasionally to attack ships and drag their crews to the bottom of the ocean. It was always there, underneath.
One day, you're on your ship, minding your own business, doing whatever you usually do, when a kraken shows up.
KA-VOOOO
It's coming for you.
There's no stopping it.

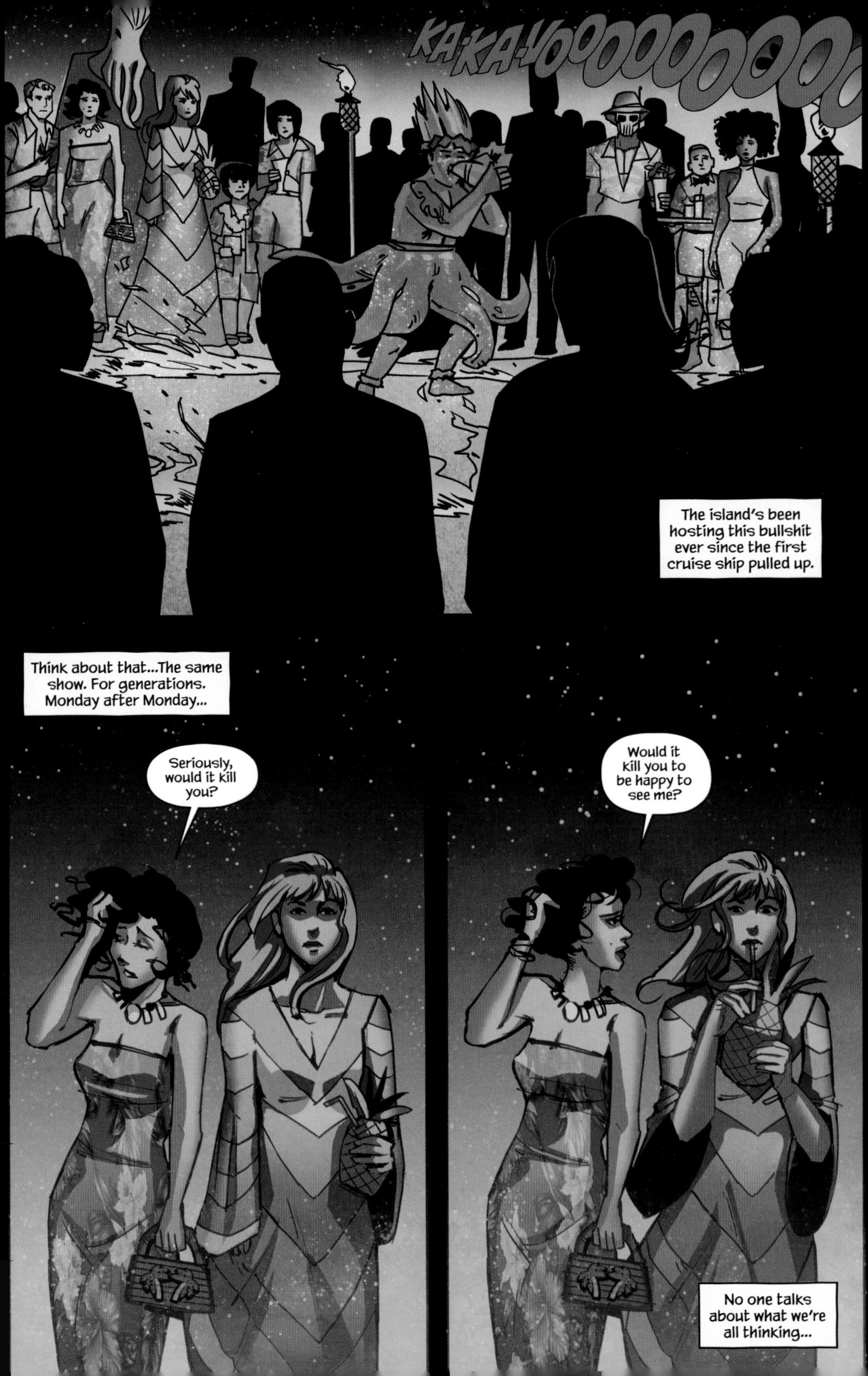
KA-KA-VOOOOOOOOO
The island's been hosting this bullshit ever since the first cruise ship pulled up.
Think about that...The same show. For generations. Monday after Monday...
Seriously, would it kill you?
Would it kill you to be happy to see me?
No one talks about what we're all thinking...

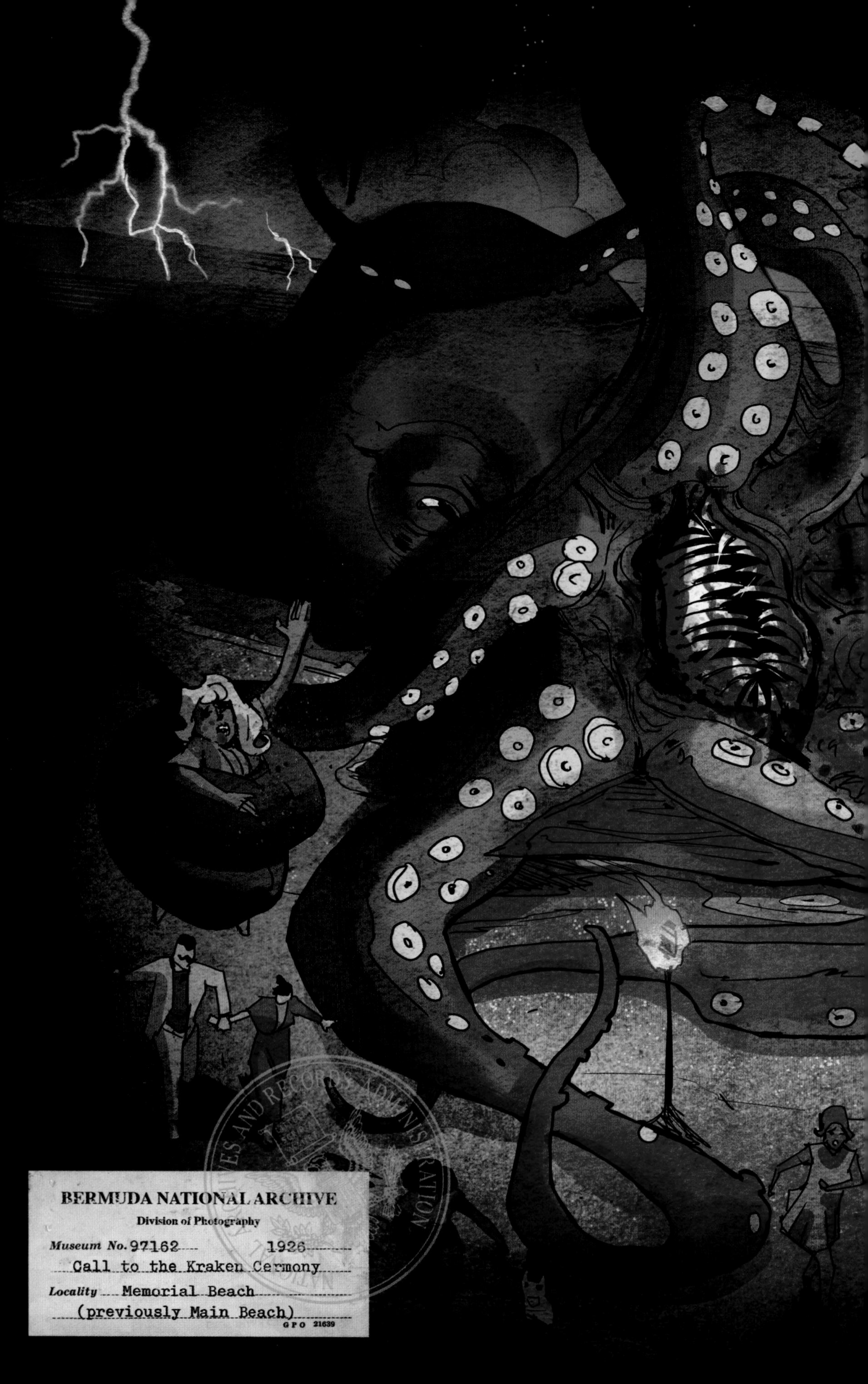
BERMUDA NATIONAL ARCHIVE
Division of Photography
Museum No. 97162 1926
Call to the Kraken Cermony
Locality Memorial Beach
(previously Main Beach)
GPO 21639

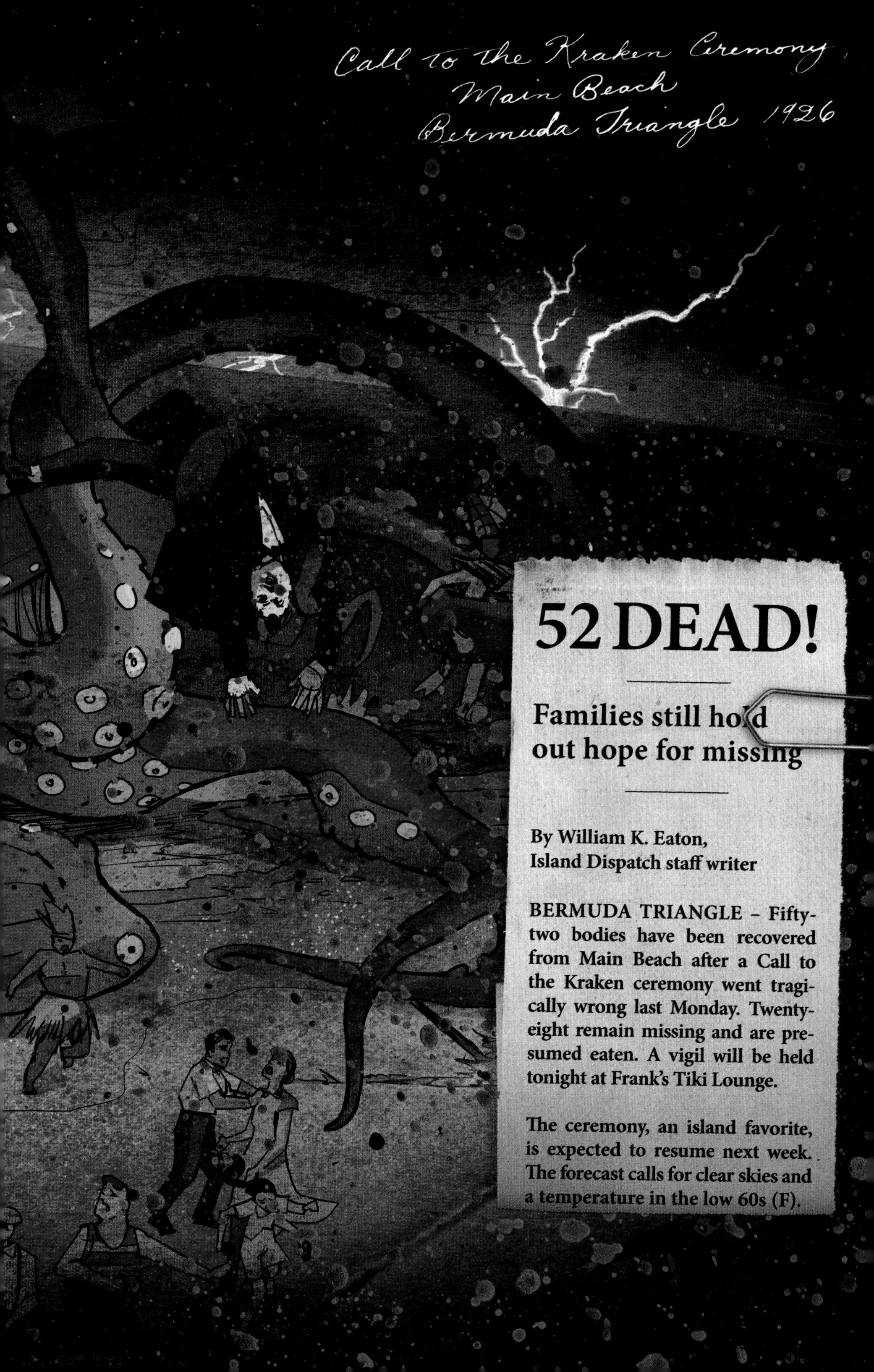
Call to the Kraken Ceremony,
Main Beach
Bermuda Triangle 1926

52 DEAD!

Families still hold out hope for missing

By William K. Eaton,
Island Dispatch staff writer

BERMUDA TRIANGLE – Fifty-two bodies have been recovered from Main Beach after a Call to the Kraken ceremony went tragically wrong last Monday. Twenty-eight remain missing and are presumed eaten. A vigil will be held tonight at Frank's Tiki Lounge.

The ceremony, an island favorite, is expected to resume next week. The forecast calls for clear skies and a temperature in the low 60s (F).

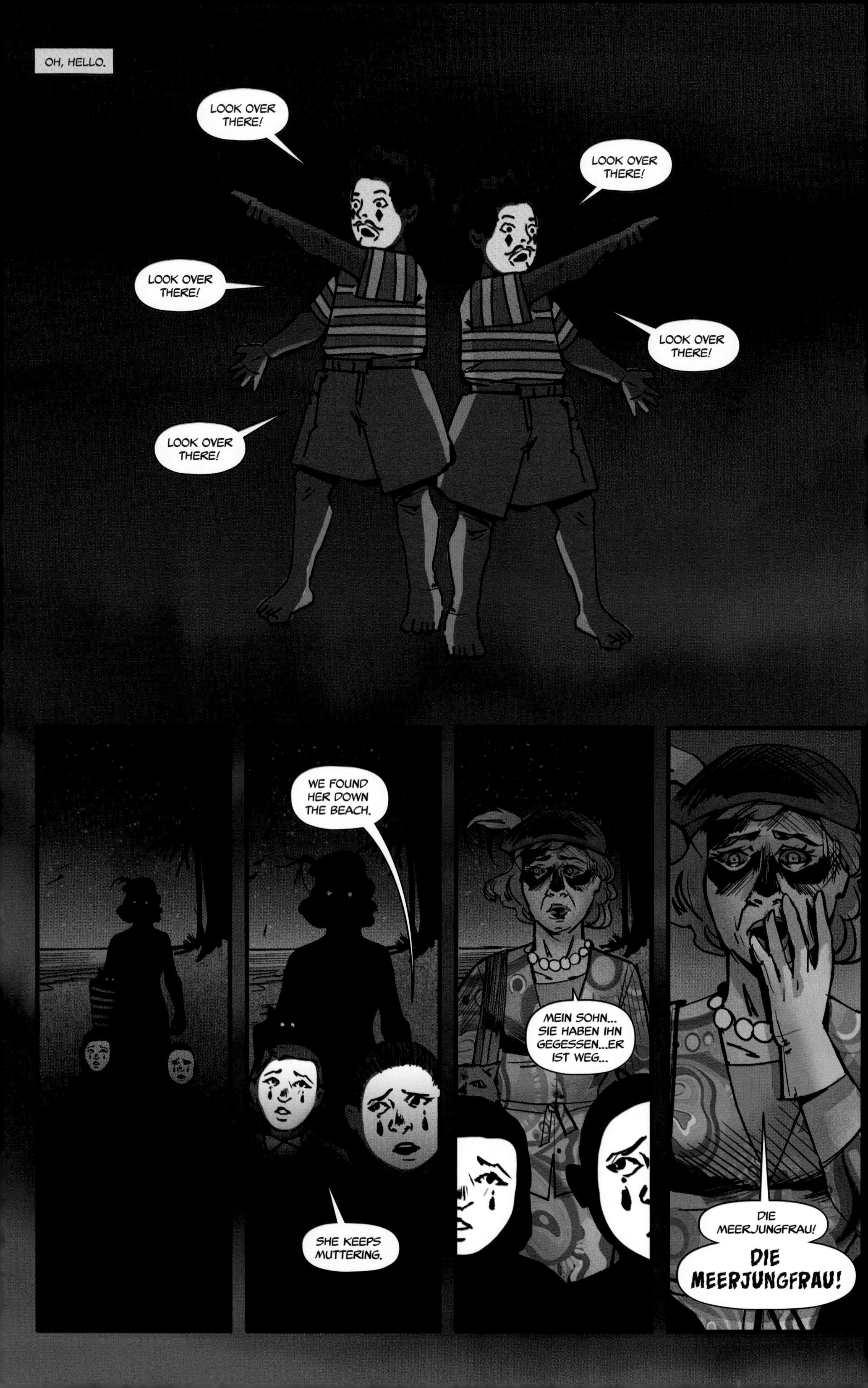
OH, HELLO.
LOOK OVER THERE!
LOOK OVER THERE!
LOOK OVER THERE!
LOOK OVER THERE!
LOOK OVER THERE!
WE FOUND HER DOWN THE BEACH.
SHE KEEPS MUTTERING.
MEIN SOHN... SIE HABEN IHN GEGESSEN...ER IST WEG...
DIE MEERJUNGFRAU!
DIE MEERJUNGFRAU!

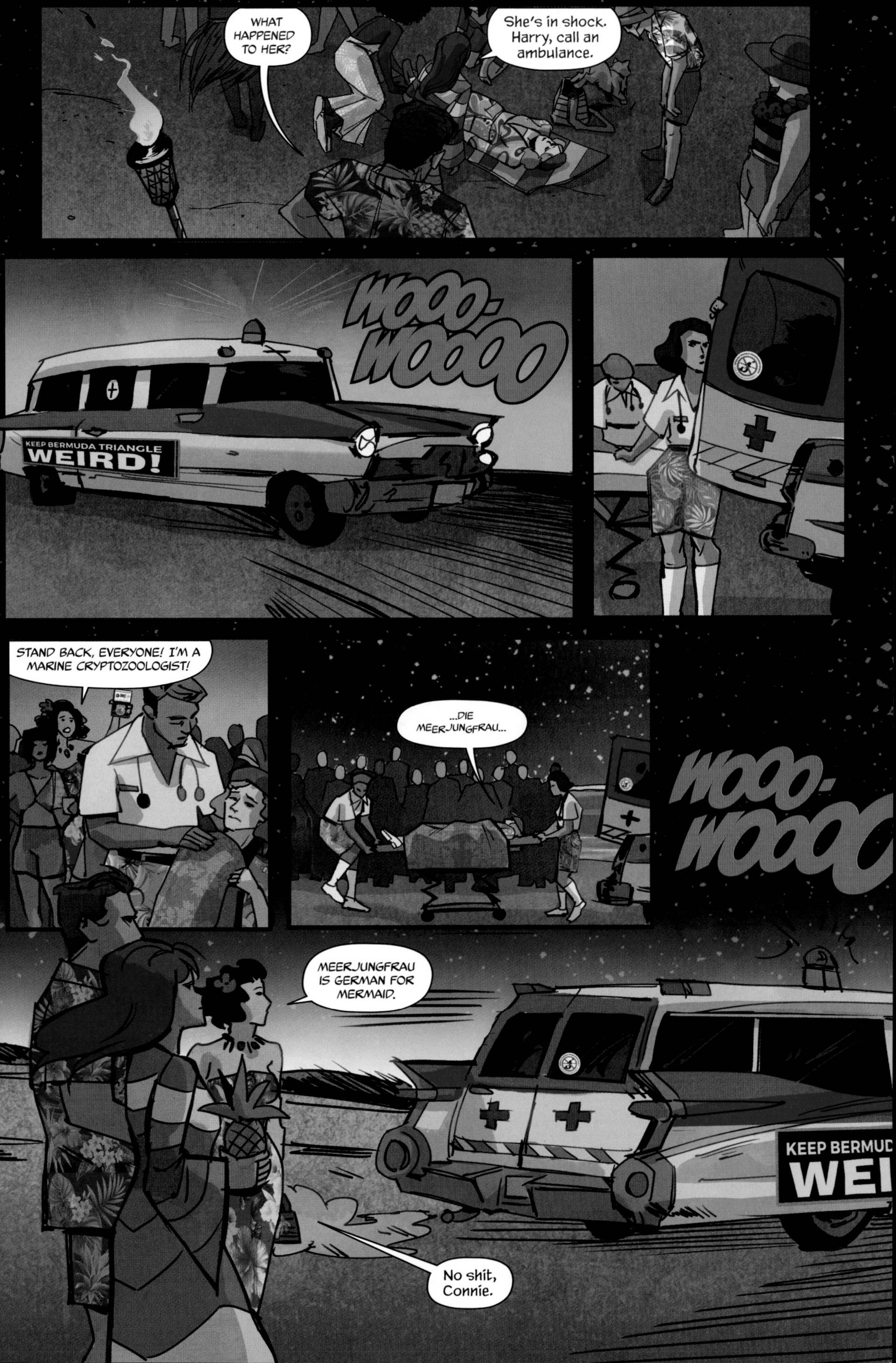
WHAT HAPPENED TO HER?
She's in shock. Harry, call an ambulance.
WOOO-WOOOOO
KEEP BERMUDA TRIANGLE
WEIRD!
STAND BACK, EVERYONE! I'M A MARINE CRYPTOZOOLOGIST!
...DIE MEERJUNGFRAU...
WOOO-WOOOO
MEERJUNGFRAU IS GERMAN FOR MERMAID.
KEEP BERMUD
WEI
No shit, Connie.

DANGEROUS

MERMAIDS and other animals are WILD

They cause many injuries to visitors

TO PROTECT YOU, OUR REGULATIONS PRO-
HIBIT FEEDING OR MOLESTING THEM

Watch them from a safe distance

PULL OFF THE ROAD AND STAY IN YOUR CAR

NATIONAL PARK SERVICE
DEPARTMENT OF THE INTERIOR

Reprint 1954   16—63682-4   GOVERNMENT PRINTING OFFICE

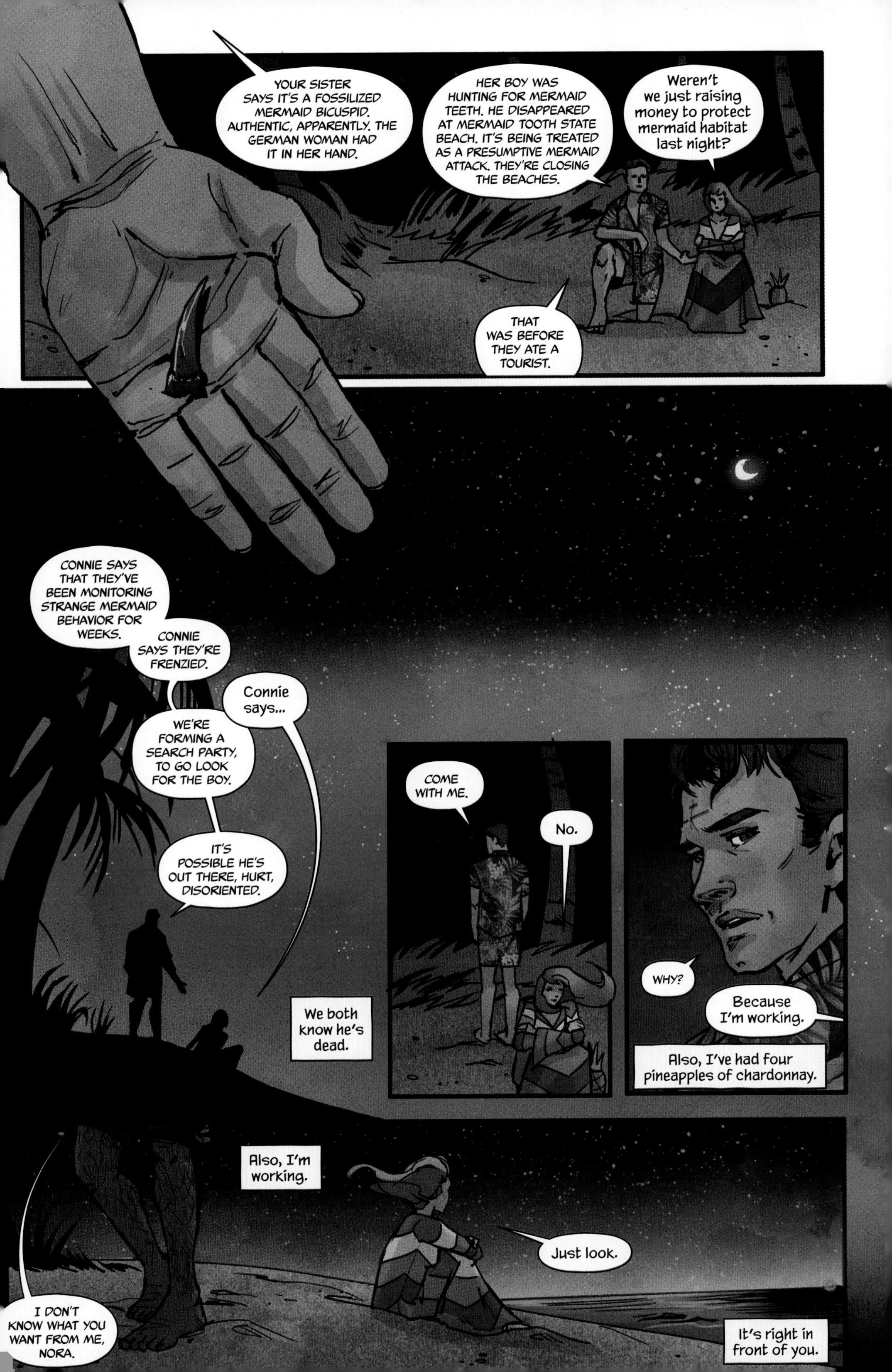
YOUR SISTER SAYS IT'S A FOSSILIZED MERMAID BICUSPID. AUTHENTIC, APPARENTLY. THE GERMAN WOMAN HAD IT IN HER HAND.
HER BOY WAS HUNTING FOR MERMAID TEETH. HE DISAPPEARED AT MERMAID TOOTH STATE BEACH. IT'S BEING TREATED AS A PRESUMPTIVE MERMAID ATTACK. THEY'RE CLOSING THE BEACHES.
Weren't we just raising money to protect mermaid habitat last night?
THAT WAS BEFORE THEY ATE A TOURIST.
CONNIE SAYS THAT THEY'VE BEEN MONITORING STRANGE MERMAID BEHAVIOR FOR WEEKS.
CONNIE SAYS THEY'RE FRENZIED.
Connie says...
WE'RE FORMING A SEARCH PARTY, TO GO LOOK FOR THE BOY.
IT'S POSSIBLE HE'S OUT THERE, HURT, DISORIENTED.
We both know he's dead.
COME WITH ME.
No.
WHY?
Because I'm working.
Also, I've had four pineapples of chardonnay.
Also, I'm working.
Just look.
I DON'T KNOW WHAT YOU WANT FROM ME, NORA.
It's right in front of you.

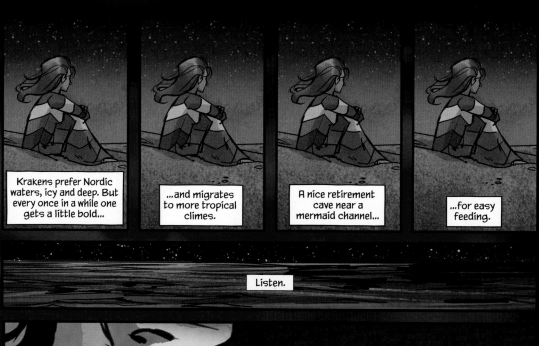

Krakens prefer Nordic waters, icy and deep. But every once in a while one gets a little bold...

...and migrates to more tropical climes.

A nice retirement cave near a mermaid channel...

...for easy feeding.

Listen.

FLCK

The definition of a wave is something that repeats over time.

LAP

LAP

LAP

LAP

LAP

KRAKEN
MEMORIAL

ALWAYS REMEMBER

GEOF DOWD
JOSHUA SENIOR
ALICIA RANDALL
KATE LEE
PHIL MARTIN
FAITH ALSOP
BENJAMIN MACKENZIE
WILLIAM KING
ANGELA GIBSON
ALEXANDER LYMAN
CARL TAYLOR
EDDIE PERI
FAITH WRIGHT
WARREN ROBERTSON
MELANIE GLOVER
BLAKE PARR
LISA DAVIDSON
CHLOE PETERS
GABRIELLE LEE
STEPHANIE GRAHAM
ANNA GLOVER
GABRIELLE JACKSON
MAX BAKER
ALISON GIBSON

VICTOR MURRAY
PER
BLAKE
CHARLOTTE UNDERWOOD
JUSTIN HOWARD
LUCAS AVERY
MICHELLE DAVIDSON
JOAN LEWIS
LOWEN KISS
FAITH CORNISH
AUDREY ELLERFORD
VICTOR HARDACRE
GABRIELLE RAMPLING
OLIVIA LAMBERT
WENDY McPHERSON
PIPPA BAILEY
SAM PAIGE
JOSEPH CLAPTON
JOE CRAMPTON
MEGAN MacLEOD
PETER KELLY
CASSANDRA ROBERTSON
CAROLINE BEAUS
LILIA BUTLER

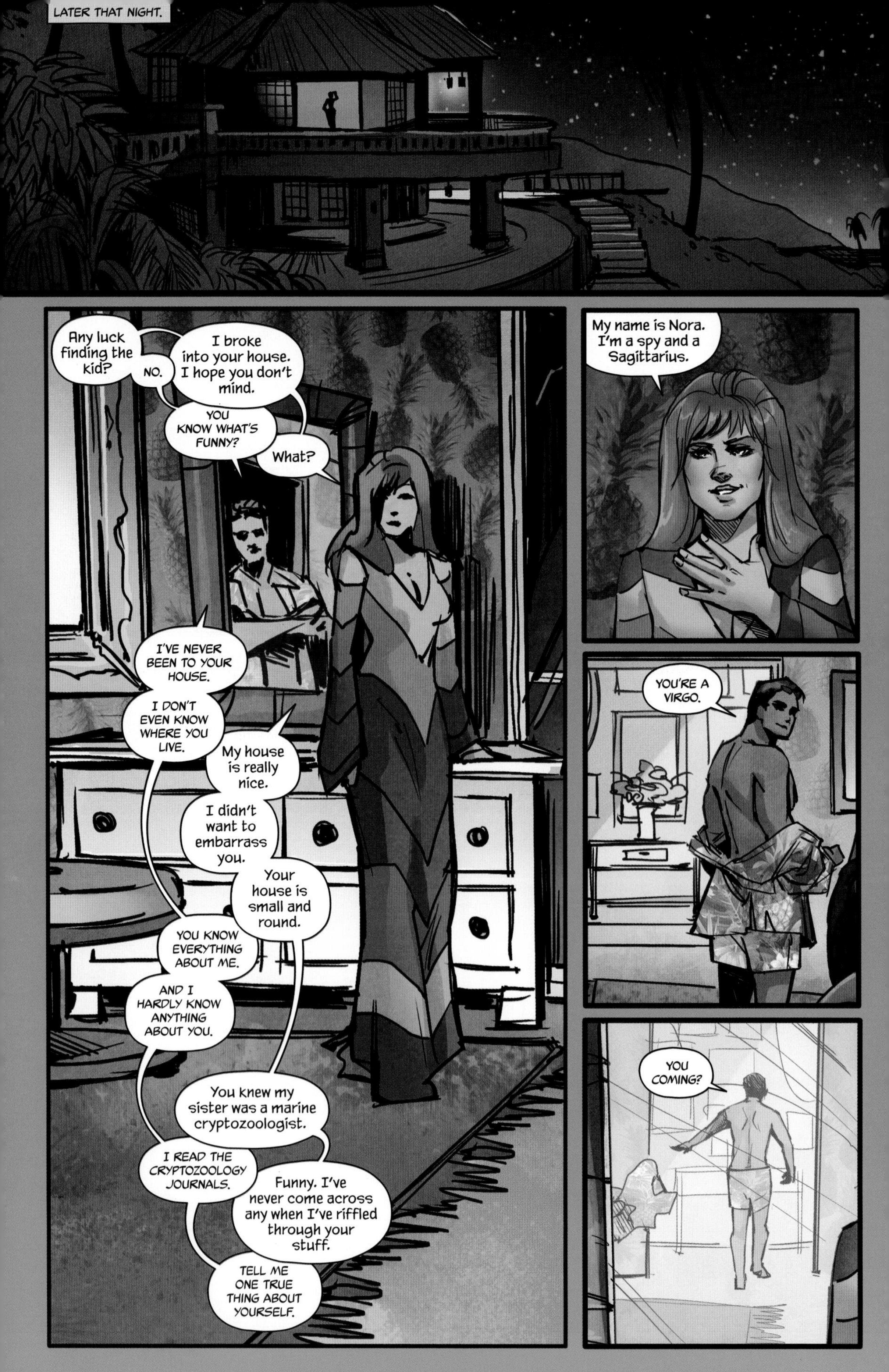
LATER THAT NIGHT.
Any luck finding the kid?
NO.
I broke into your house. I hope you don't mind.
YOU KNOW WHAT'S FUNNY?
What?
I'VE NEVER BEEN TO YOUR HOUSE.
I DON'T EVEN KNOW WHERE YOU LIVE.
My house is really nice.
I didn't want to embarrass you.
Your house is small and round.
YOU KNOW EVERYTHING ABOUT ME.
AND I HARDLY KNOW ANYTHING ABOUT YOU.
You knew my sister was a marine cryptozoologist.
I READ THE CRYPTOZOOLOGY JOURNALS.
Funny. I've never come across any when I've riffled through your stuff.
TELL ME ONE TRUE THING ABOUT YOURSELF.
My name is Nora. I'm a spy and a Sagittarius.
YOU'RE A VIRGO.
YOU COMING?

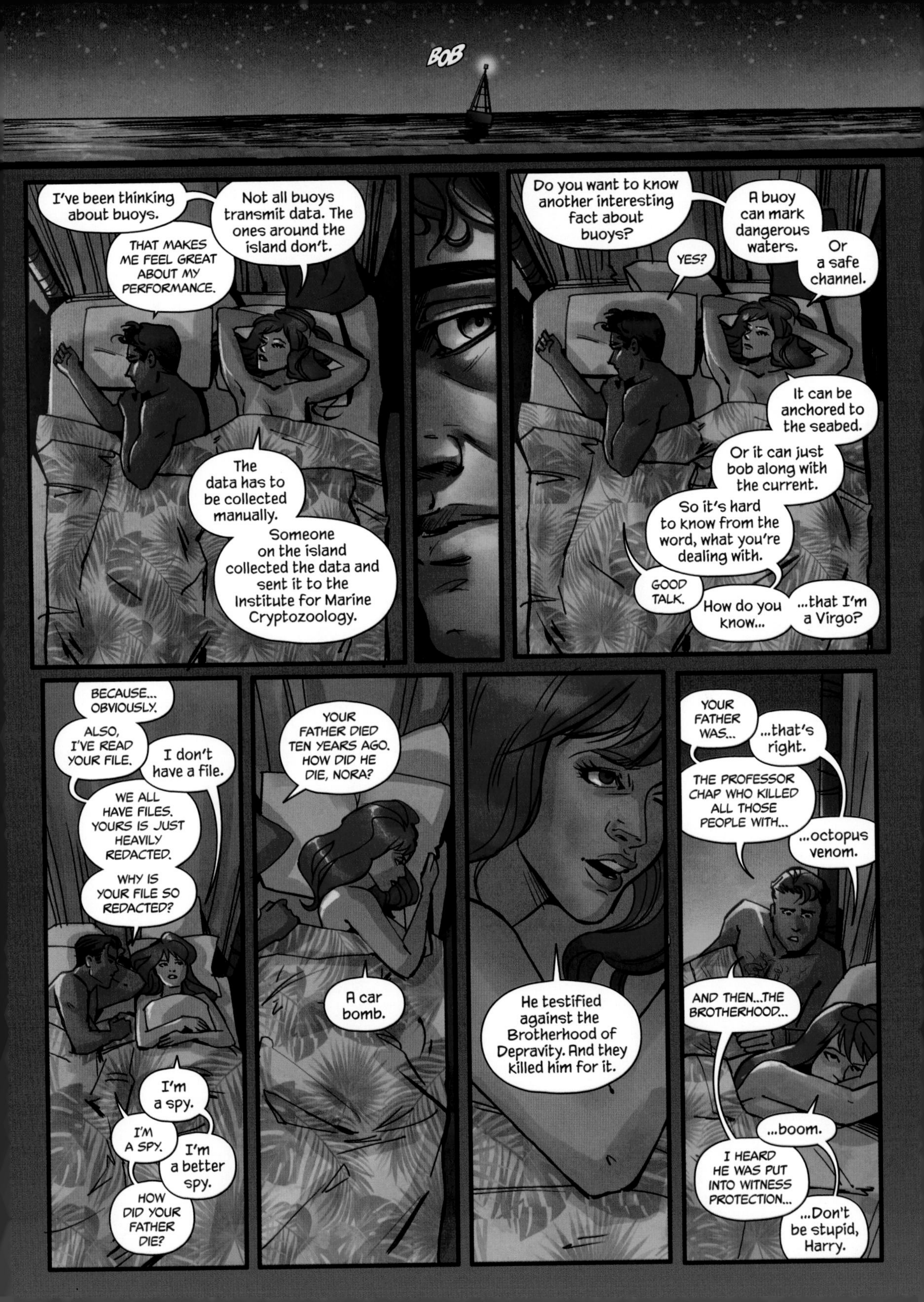
BOB
I've been thinking about buoys.
Not all buoys transmit data. The ones around the island don't.
THAT MAKES ME FEEL GREAT ABOUT MY PERFORMANCE.
The data has to be collected manually.
Someone on the island collected the data and sent it to the Institute for Marine Cryptozoology.
Do you want to know another interesting fact about buoys?
YES?
A buoy can mark dangerous waters.
Or a safe channel.
It can be anchored to the seabed.
Or it can just bob along with the current.
So it's hard to know from the word, what you're dealing with.
GOOD TALK.
How do you know...
...that I'm a Virgo?
BECAUSE... OBVIOUSLY.
ALSO, I'VE READ YOUR FILE.
I don't have a file.
WE ALL HAVE FILES. YOURS IS JUST HEAVILY REDACTED.
WHY IS YOUR FILE SO REDACTED?
I'm a spy.
I'M A SPY.
I'm a better spy.
HOW DID YOUR FATHER DIE?
YOUR FATHER DIED TEN YEARS AGO. HOW DID HE DIE, NORA?
A car bomb.
He testified against the Brotherhood of Depravity. And they killed him for it.
YOUR FATHER WAS...
...that's right.
THE PROFESSOR CHAP WHO KILLED ALL THOSE PEOPLE WITH...
...octopus venom.
AND THEN...THE BROTHERHOOD...
...boom.
I HEARD HE WAS PUT INTO WITNESS PROTECTION...
...Don't be stupid, Harry.

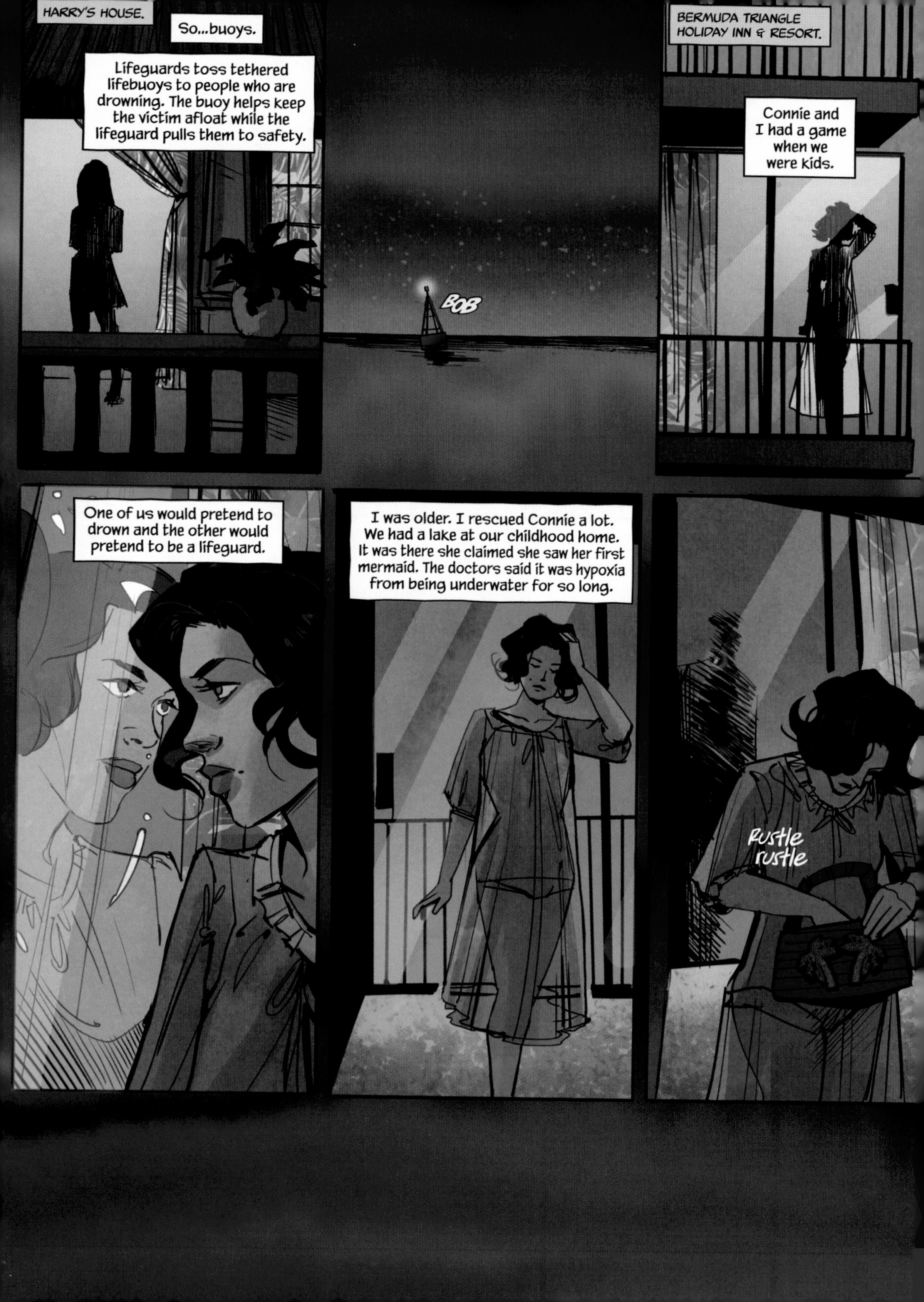

HARRY'S HOUSE.
So...buoys.
Lifeguards toss tethered lifebuoys to people who are drowning. The buoy helps keep the victim afloat while the lifeguard pulls them to safety.
BOB
BERMUDA TRIANGLE HOLIDAY INN & RESORT.
Connie and I had a game when we were kids.
One of us would pretend to drown and the other would pretend to be a lifeguard.
I was older. I rescued Connie a lot. We had a lake at our childhood home. It was there she claimed she saw her first mermaid. The doctors said it was hypoxia from being underwater for so long.
Rustle rustle

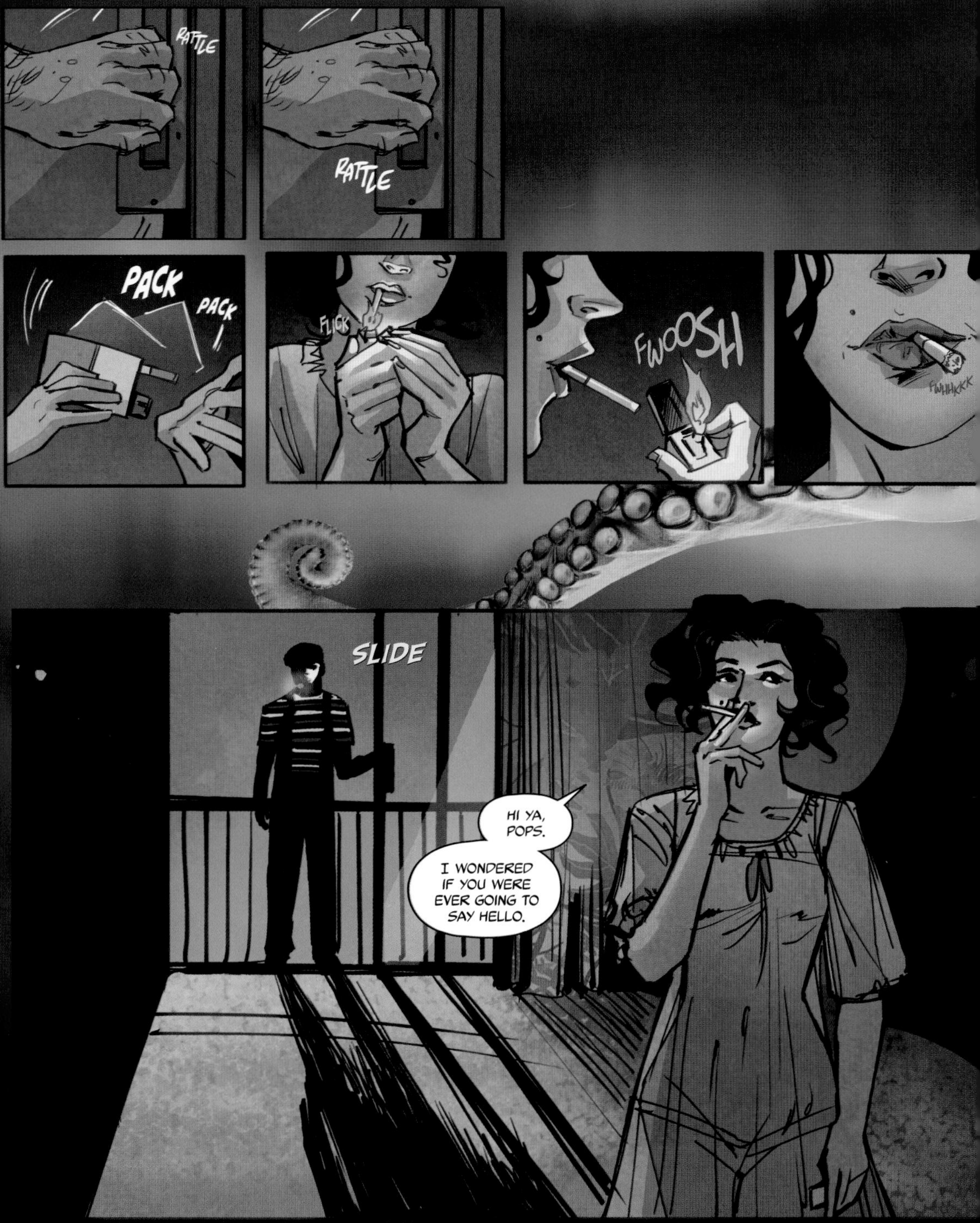
RATTLE
RATTLE
PACK
PACK
FLICK
FWOOSH
FWHHKKK
SLIDE
HI YA, POPS.
I WONDERED IF YOU WERE EVER GOING TO SAY HELLO.

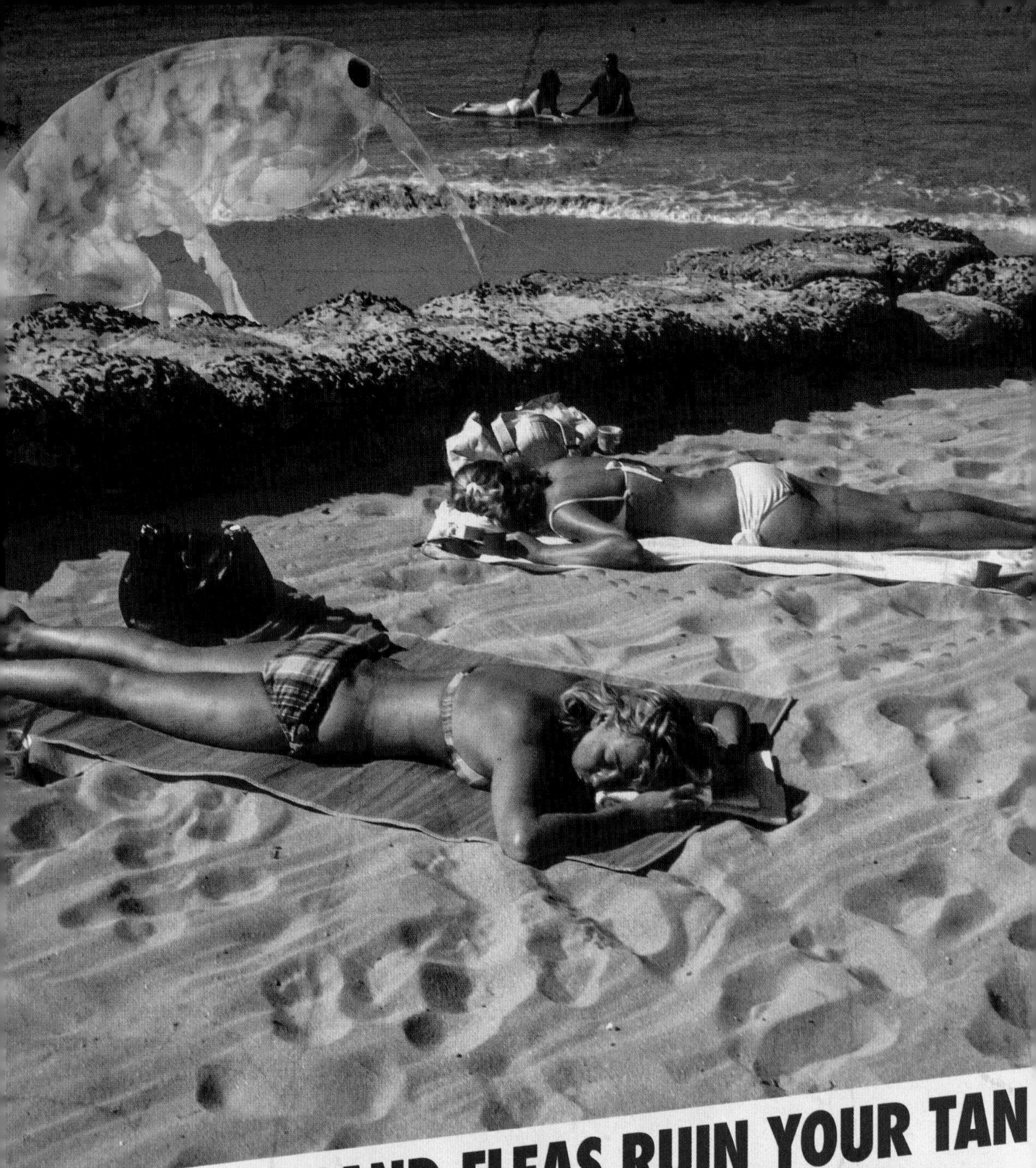

DON'T LET SAND FLEAS RUIN YOUR TAN

Sand flea bites and welts can be unsightly. Protect your tan with our anti-itch products, so you can keep sunbathing. You'll barely feel the parasites that have burrowed under your skin to reproduce! (Sand flea infestations are self-limiting; most will die naturally within three weeks.) New Pina Colada scent!

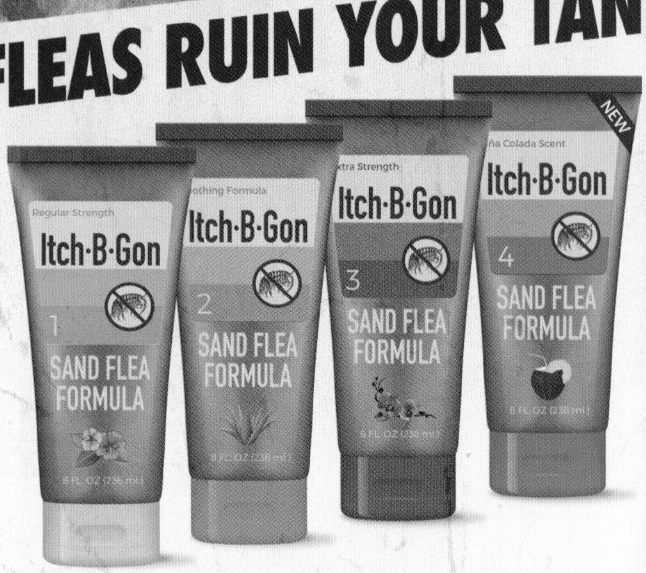
NEW
Regular Strength
Itch·B·Gon
1
SAND FLEA FORMULA
Itch·B·Gon
2
SAND FLEA FORMULA
Itch·B·Gon
3
SAND FLEA FORMULA
Itch·B·Gon
4
SAND FLEA FORMULA

THE BERMUDA TRIANGLE

Bring a friend with you. And hunt during the daytime. Never kneel or squat.

ISLAND LINES
Cruise The Bermuda Triangle

Poolside Cocktail
~ Daily Special ~

DAY 3

MERMAID ATTACK

Pour 1 oz grenadine in glass
Add 1 oz each Rum and Blue Curaçao
Stir with ½ oz sour mix
Add cherry, slice of orange and mint

ISLAND LINES
Cruise The Bermuda Triangle

#3

DARK HORSE COMICS

SPY ISLAND™

A Bermuda Triangle Mystery

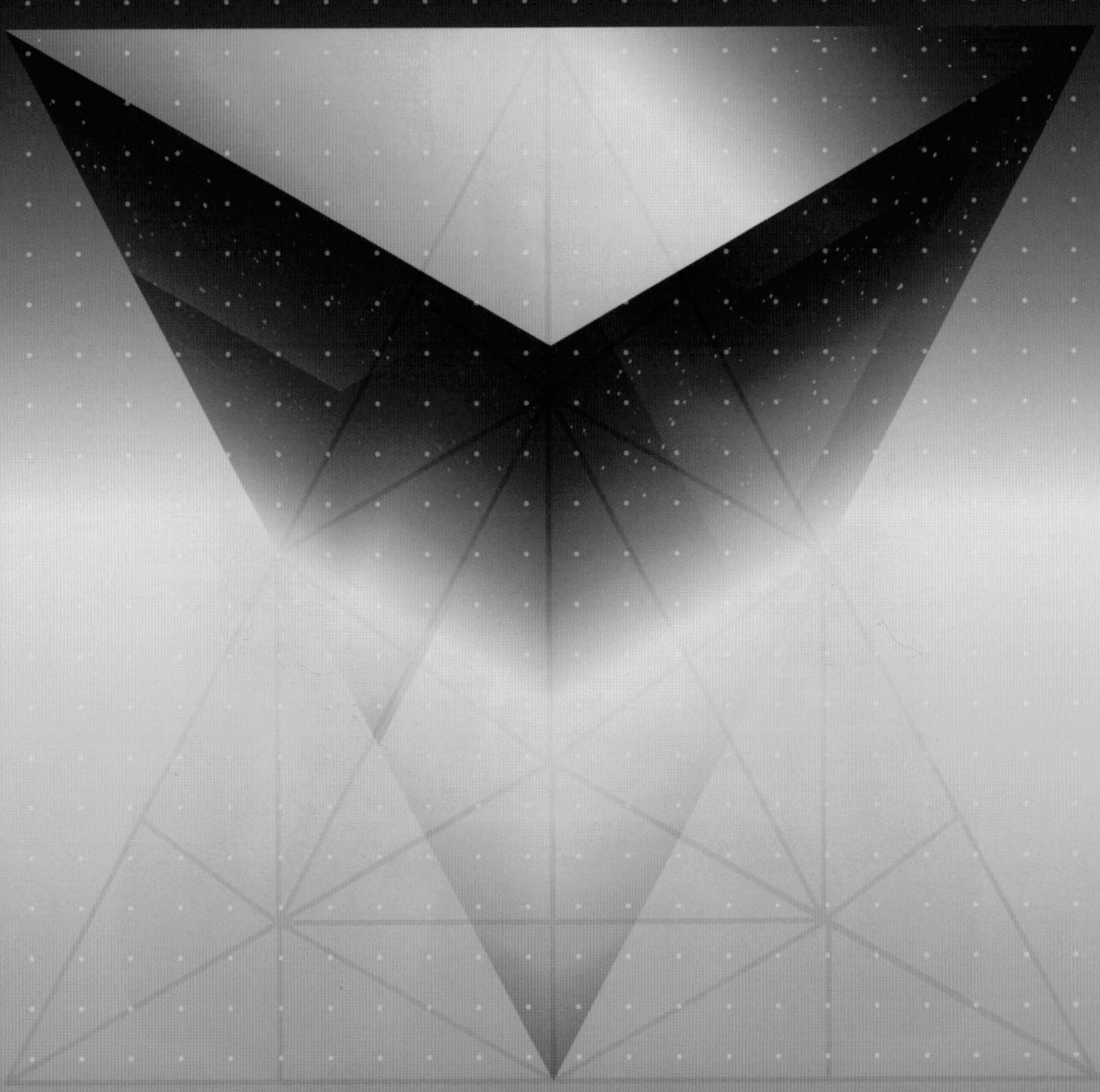

Cain Miternique McCall Rosenberg Caramagna

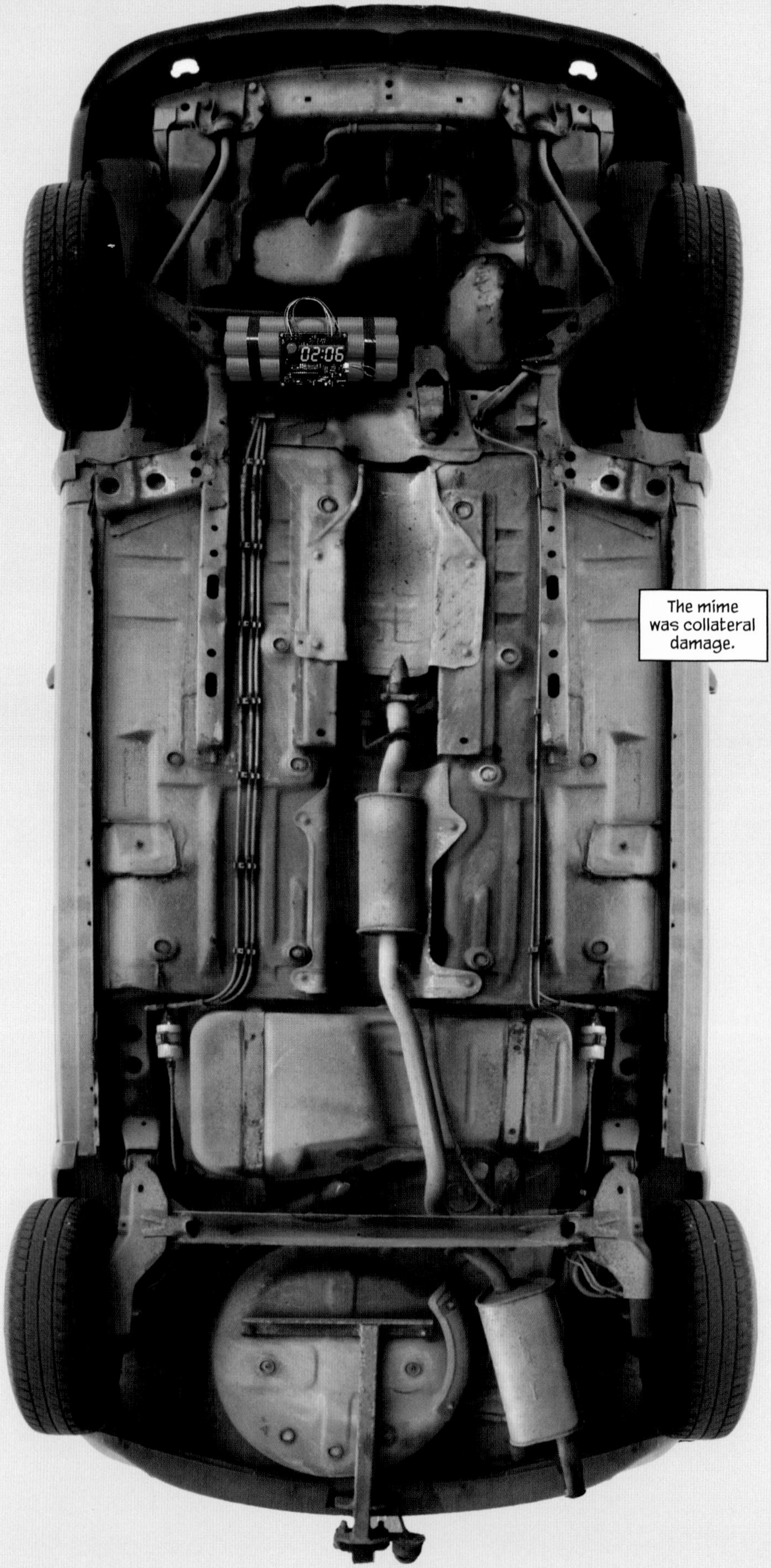
02:06
The mime was collateral damage.

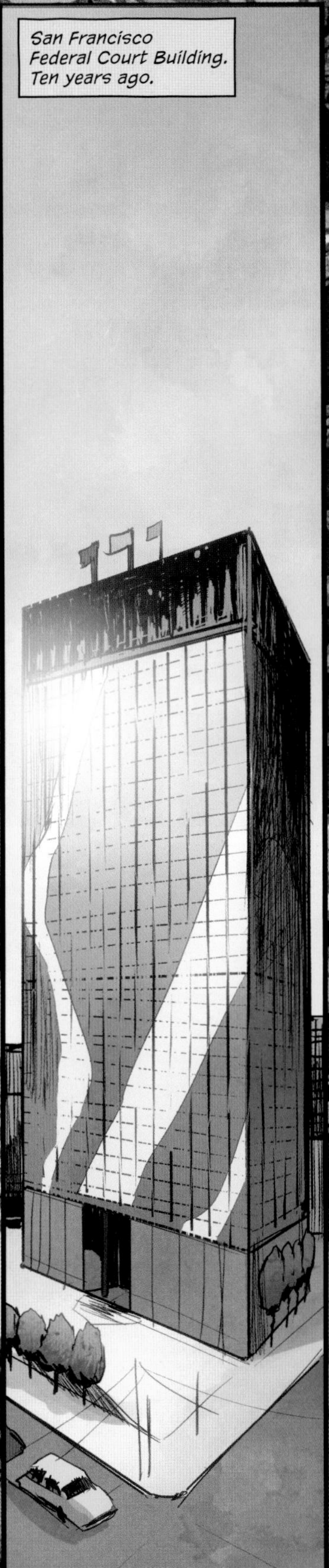
San Francisco
Federal Court Building.
Ten years ago.

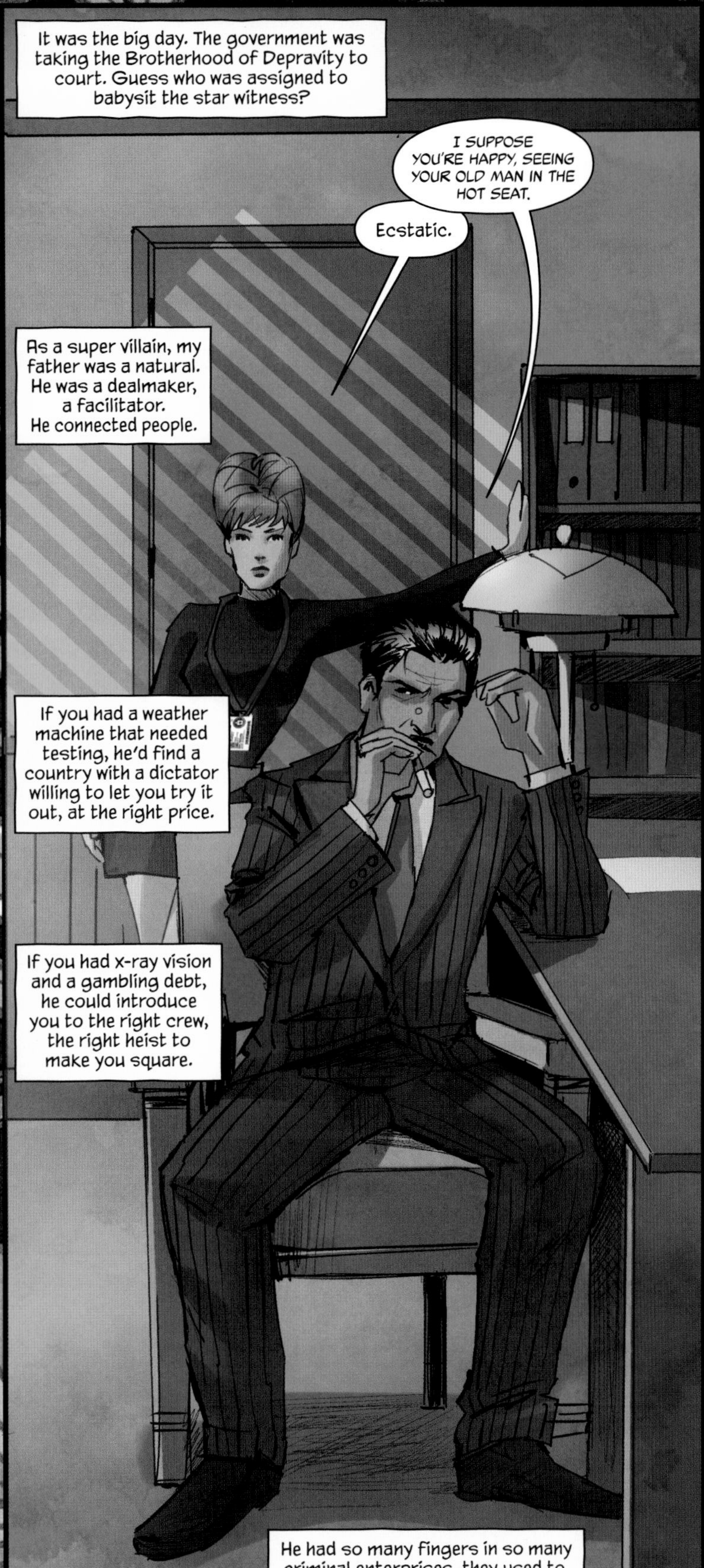
It was the big day. The government was taking the Brotherhood of Depravity to court. Guess who was assigned to babysit the star witness?
I SUPPOSE YOU'RE HAPPY, SEEING YOUR OLD MAN IN THE HOT SEAT.
Ecstatic.
As a super villain, my father was a natural. He was a dealmaker, a facilitator. He connected people.
If you had a weather machine that needed testing, he'd find a country with a dictator willing to let you try it out, at the right price.
If you had x-ray vision and a gambling debt, he could introduce you to the right crew, the right heist to make you square.
He had so many fingers in so many criminal enterprises, they used to say it was like he had tentacles. That's how he got his nickname...

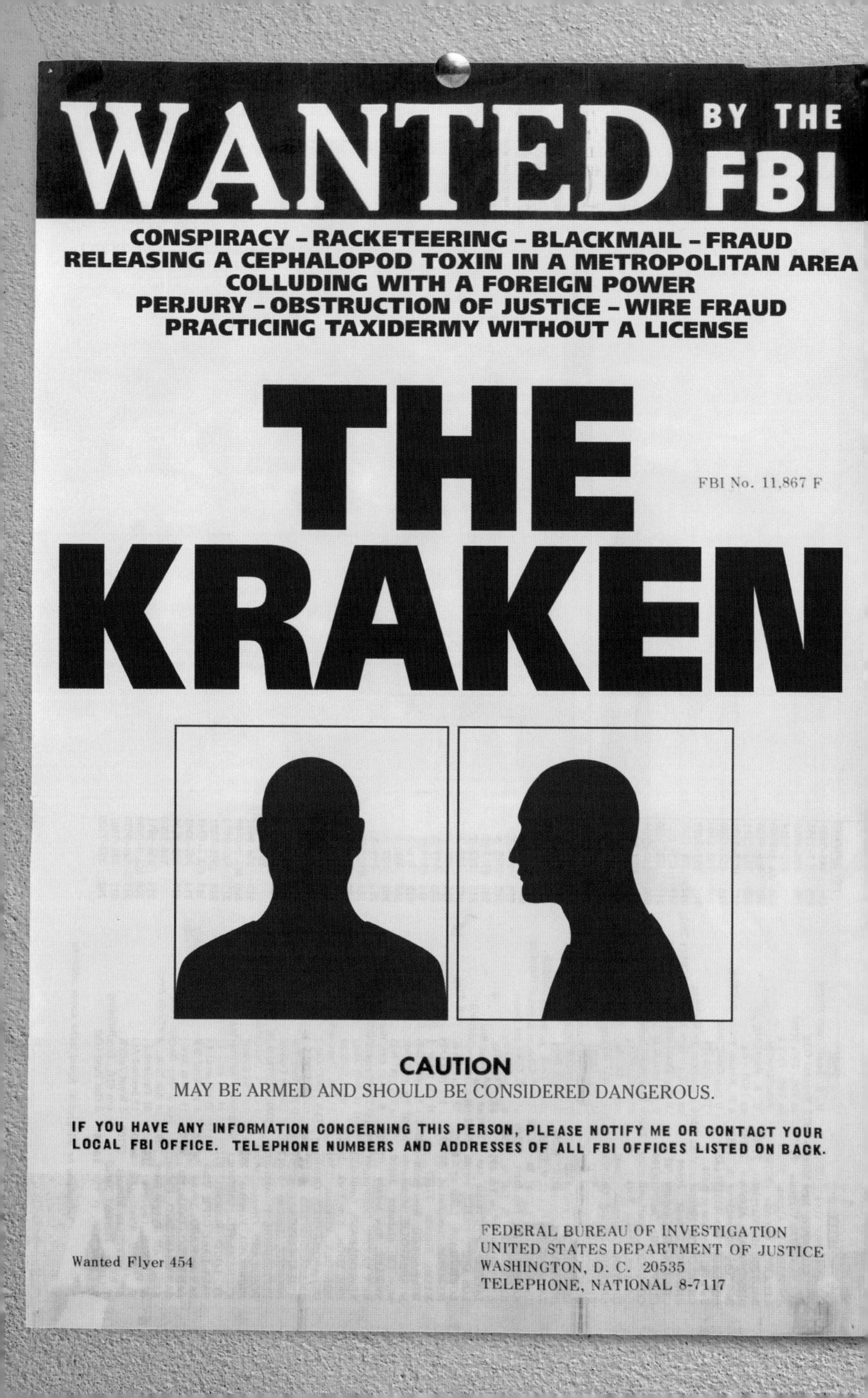

WANTED

BY THE FBI

CONSPIRACY – RACKETEERING – BLACKMAIL – FRAUD
RELEASING A CEPHALOPOD TOXIN IN A METROPOLITAN AREA
COLLUDING WITH A FOREIGN POWER
PERJURY – OBSTRUCTION OF JUSTICE – WIRE FRAUD
PRACTICING TAXIDERMY WITHOUT A LICENSE

THE KRAKEN

FBI No. 11,867 F

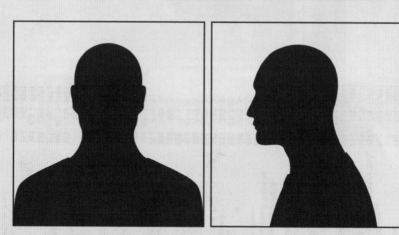

CAUTION
MAY BE ARMED AND SHOULD BE CONSIDERED DANGEROUS.

IF YOU HAVE ANY INFORMATION CONCERNING THIS PERSON, PLEASE NOTIFY ME OR CONTACT YOUR LOCAL FBI OFFICE. TELEPHONE NUMBERS AND ADDRESSES OF ALL FBI OFFICES LISTED ON BACK.

Wanted Flyer 454

FEDERAL BUREAU OF INVESTIGATION
UNITED STATES DEPARTMENT OF JUSTICE
WASHINGTON, D. C. 20535
TELEPHONE, NATIONAL 8-7117

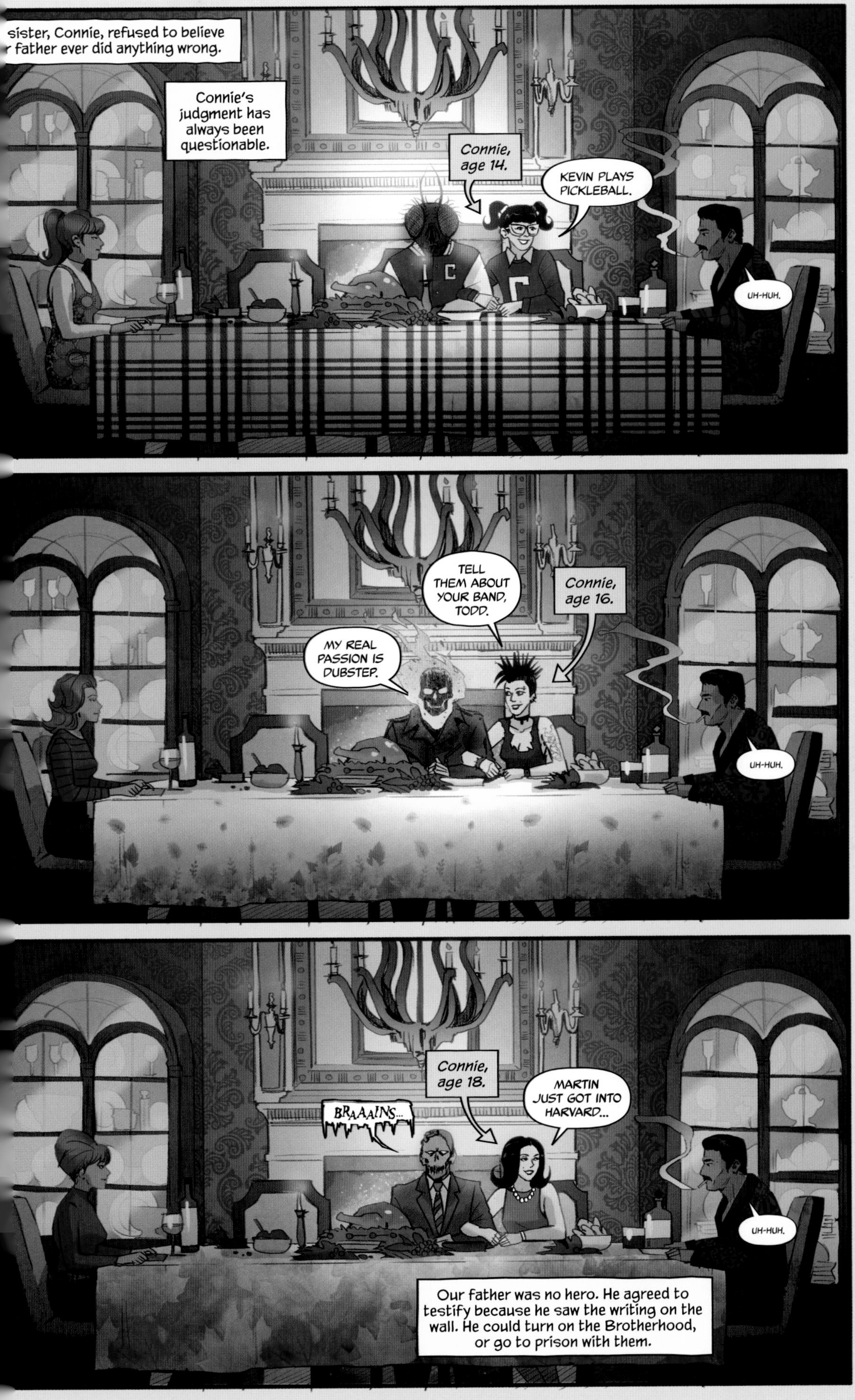

sister, Connie, refused to believe
r father ever did anything wrong.
Connie's judgment has always been questionable.
Connie, age 14.
KEVIN PLAYS PICKLEBALL.
UH-HUH.
TELL THEM ABOUT YOUR BAND, TODD.
Connie, age 16.
MY REAL PASSION IS DUBSTEP.
UH-HUH.
Connie, age 18.
MARTIN JUST GOT INTO HARVARD...
BRAAAINS...
UH-HUH.
Our father was no hero. He agreed to testify because he saw the writing on the wall. He could turn on the Brotherhood, or go to prison with them.

UNITED STATES V.
THE BROTHERHOOD OF DEPRAVITY

When the government prosecuted the Brotherhood of Depravity for violating the RICO Act, cameras were not allowed inside the federal courtroom. Only these courtroom sketches survive as a visual record of the proceedings. Originals are archived in Pam's office in the basement of the Phillip Burton Federal Building.

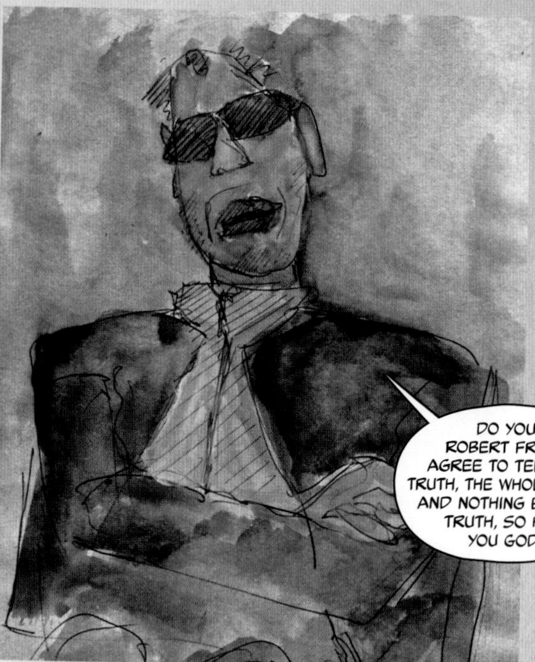

DO YOU, ROBERT FREUD, AGREE TO TELL THE TRUTH, THE WHOLE TRUTH, AND NOTHING BUT THE TRUTH, SO HELP YOU GOD?

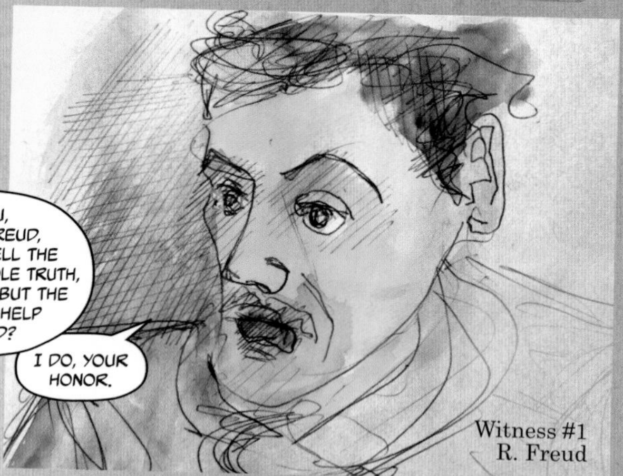

I DO, YOUR HONOR.
Witness #1
R. Freud

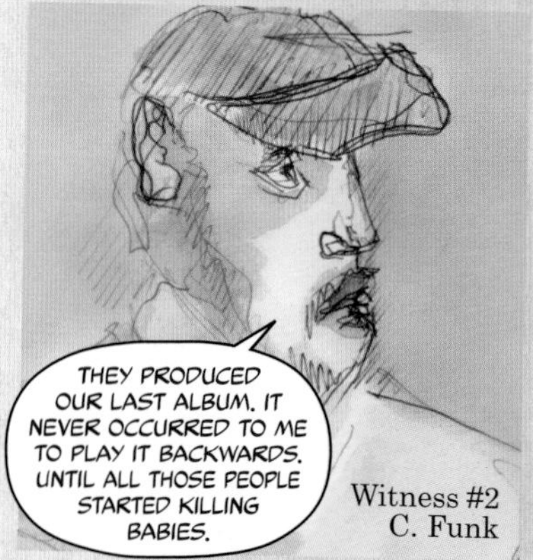

THEY PRODUCED OUR LAST ALBUM. IT NEVER OCCURRED TO ME TO PLAY IT BACKWARDS. UNTIL ALL THOSE PEOPLE STARTED KILLING BABIES.
Witness #2
C. Funk

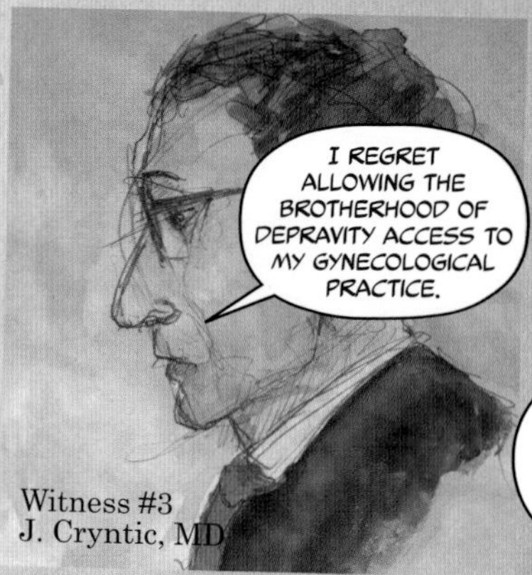

I REGRET ALLOWING THE BROTHERHOOD OF DEPRAVITY ACCESS TO MY GYNECOLOGICAL PRACTICE.
Witness #3
J. Cryntic, MD

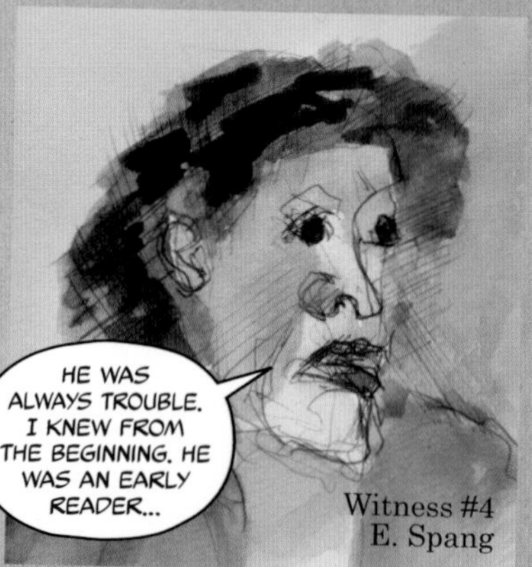

HE WAS ALWAYS TROUBLE. I KNEW FROM THE BEGINNING. HE WAS AN EARLY READER...
Witness #4
E. Spang

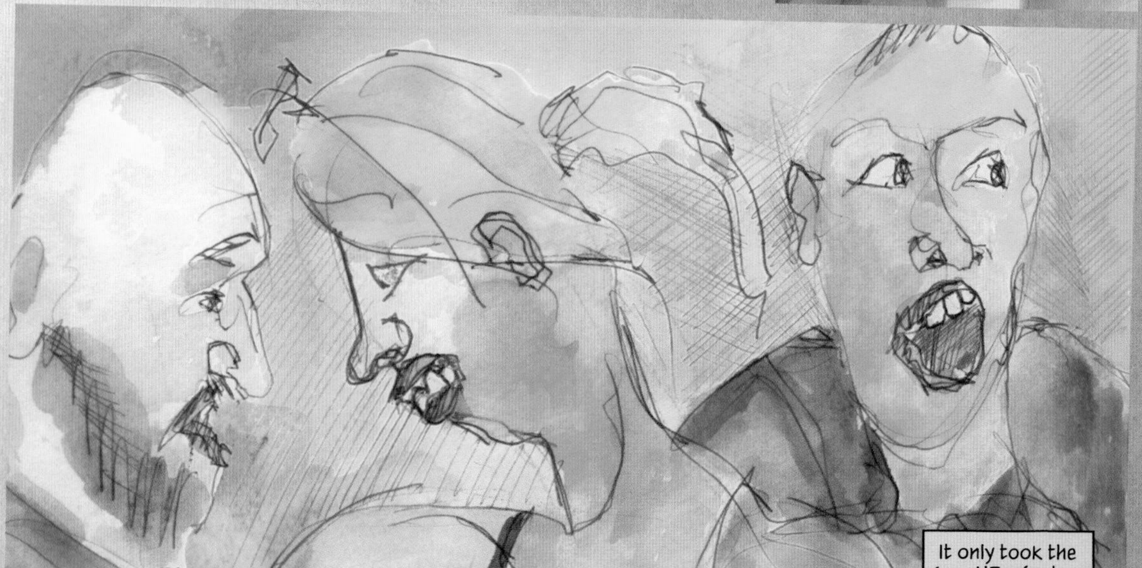

It only took the jury 45 minutes to deliberate.

pon this Affidavit, Complainant

or about the above date and at the above place did violate

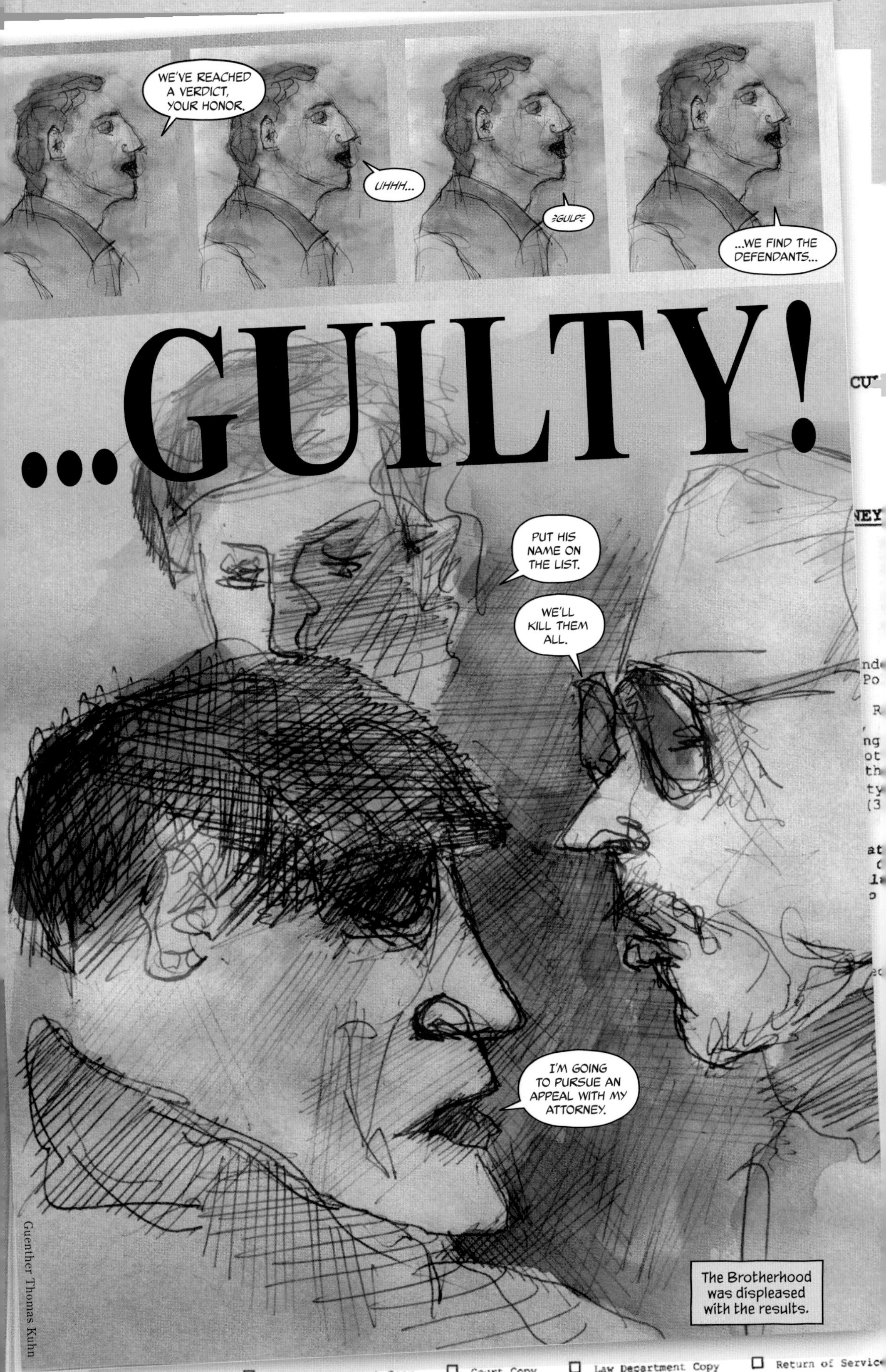

WE'VE REACHED A VERDICT, YOUR HONOR.
UHHH...
GULP
...WE FIND THE DEFENDANTS...
...GUILTY!
PUT HIS NAME ON THE LIST.
WE'LL KILL THEM ALL.
I'M GOING TO PURSUE AN APPEAL WITH MY ATTORNEY.
The Brotherhood was displeased with the results.
Guenther Thomas Kuhn

☐ Defendant's Copy ☐ Police Department Copy ☐ Court Copy ☐ Law Department Copy ☐ Return of Service

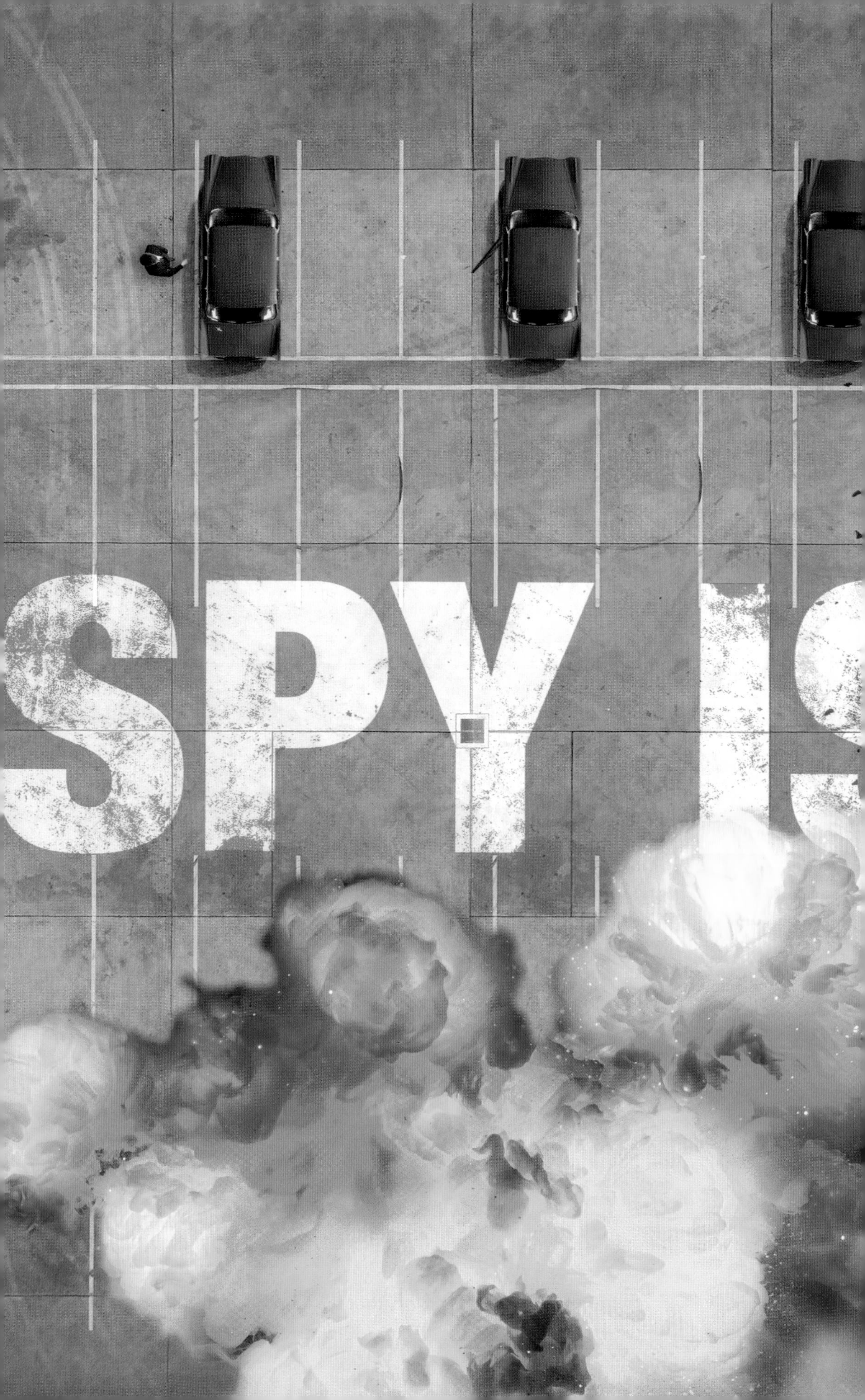
SPY IS

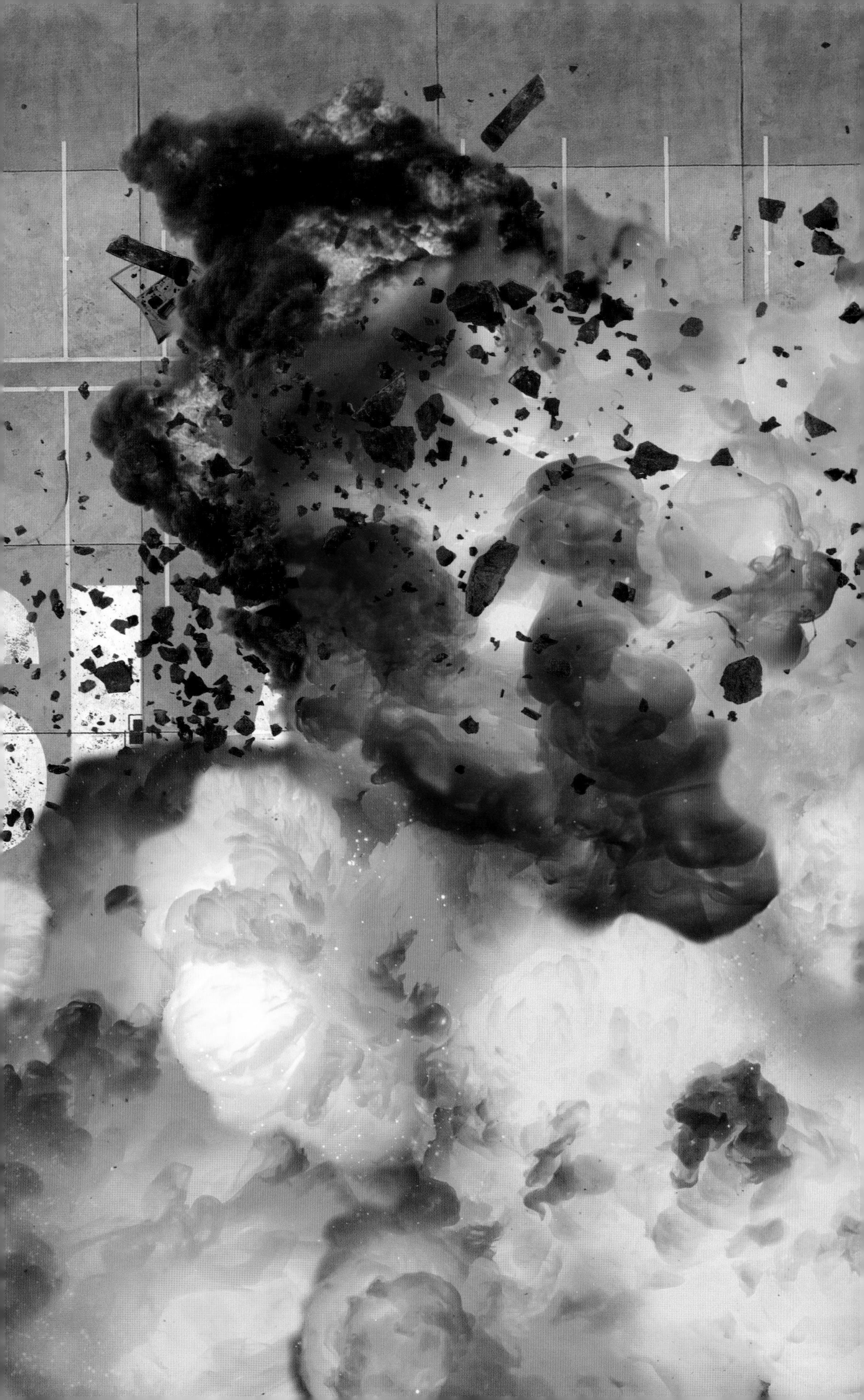

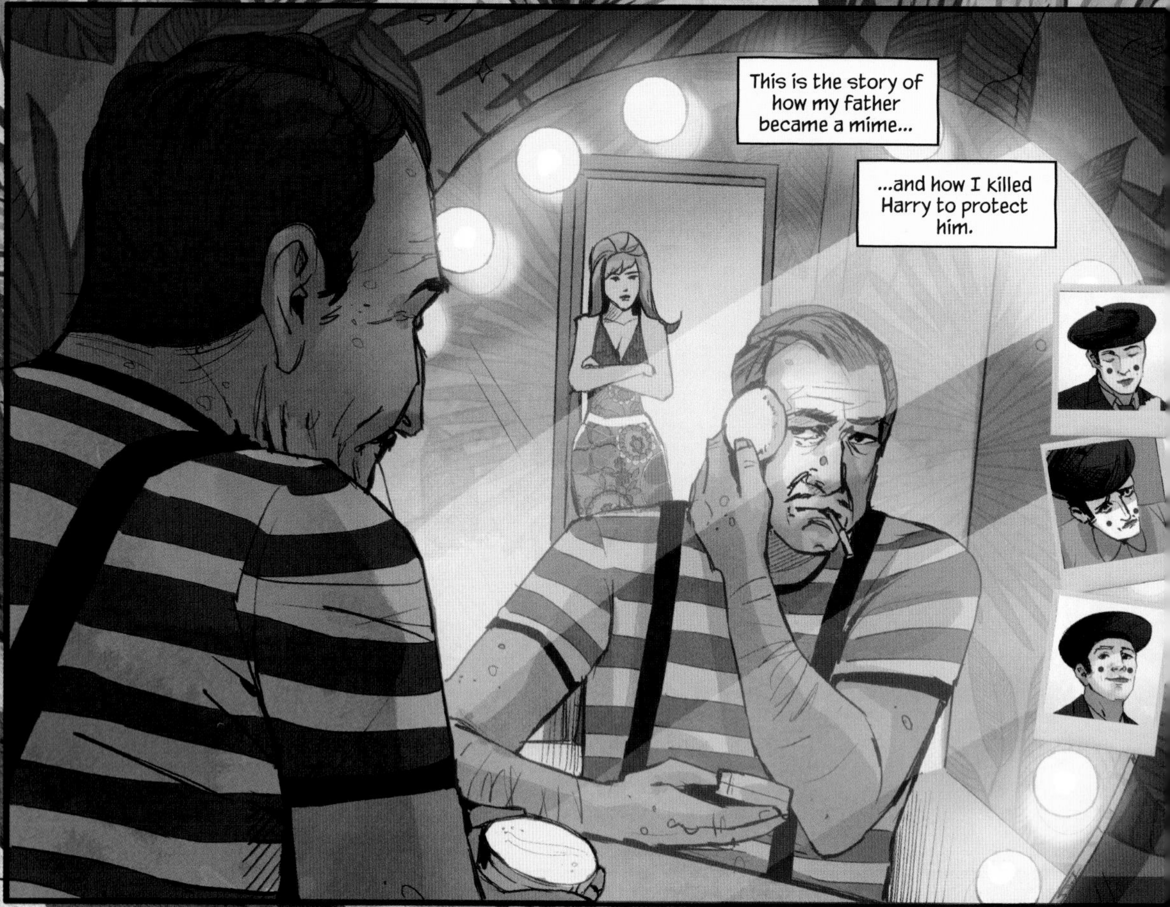
This is the story of how my father became a mime...
...and how I killed Harry to protect him.

FIELD AGENT'S GUIDE TO THE
WITNESS PROTECTION PROGRAM

STEP ONE:
Fake Subject's Death.

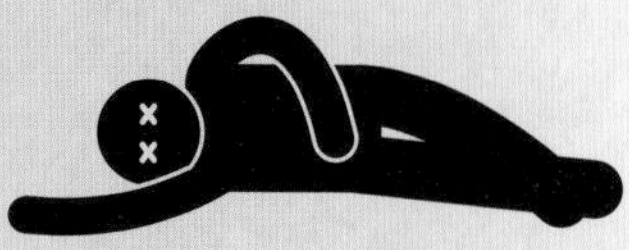

STEP TWO:
Provide Subject with False Identity.

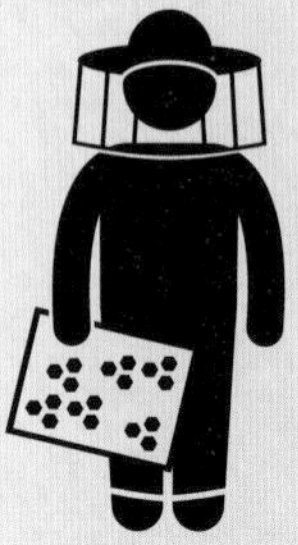

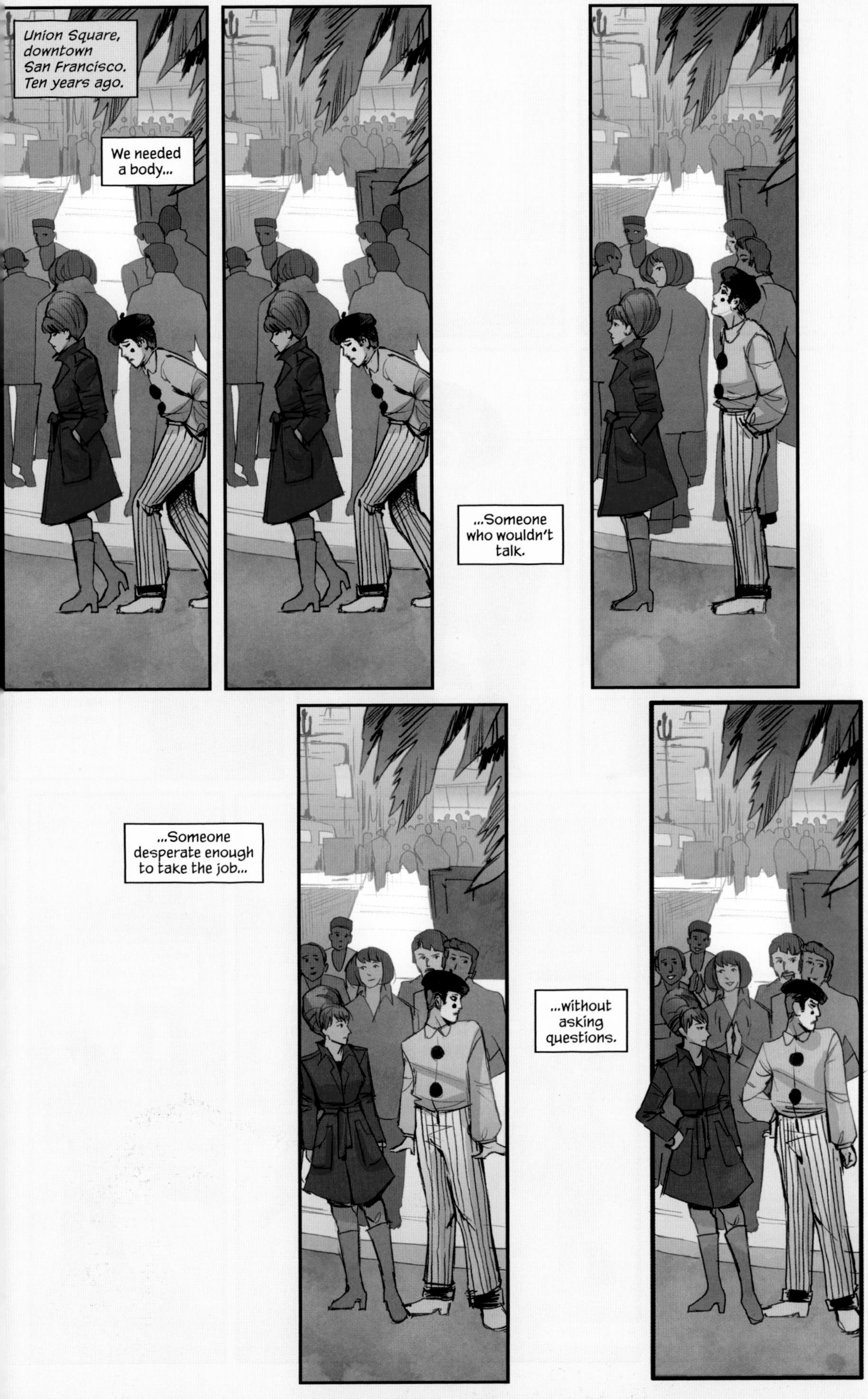
Union Square, downtown San Francisco. Ten years ago.
We needed a body...
...Someone who wouldn't talk.
...Someone desperate enough to take the job...
...without asking questions.

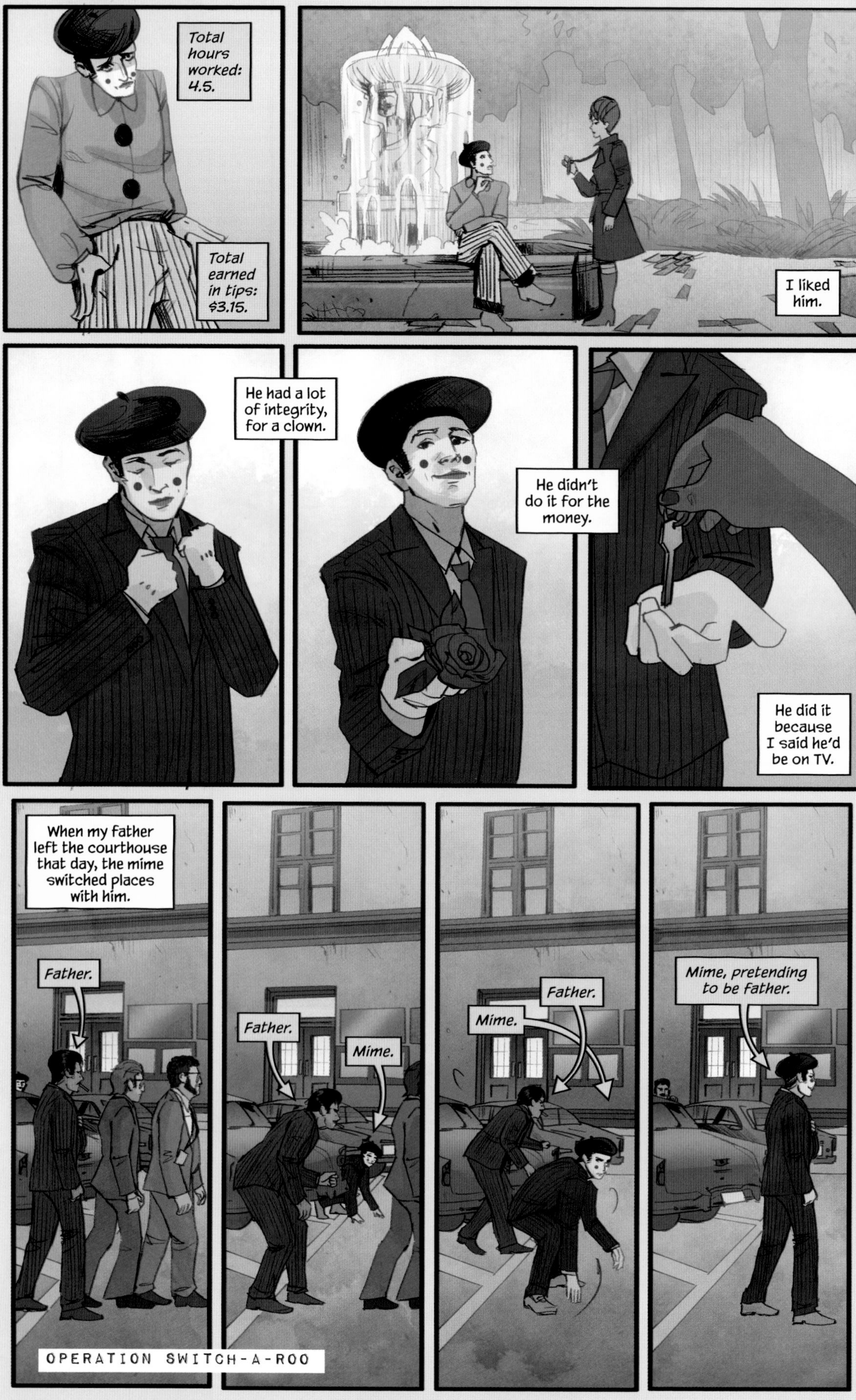
Total hours worked: 4.5.
Total earned in tips: $3.15.
I liked him.
He had a lot of integrity, for a clown.
He didn't do it for the money.
He did it because I said he'd be on TV.
When my father left the courthouse that day, the mime switched places with him.
Father.
OPERATION SWITCH-A-ROO
Father.
Mime.
Mime.
Father.
Mime, pretending to be Father.

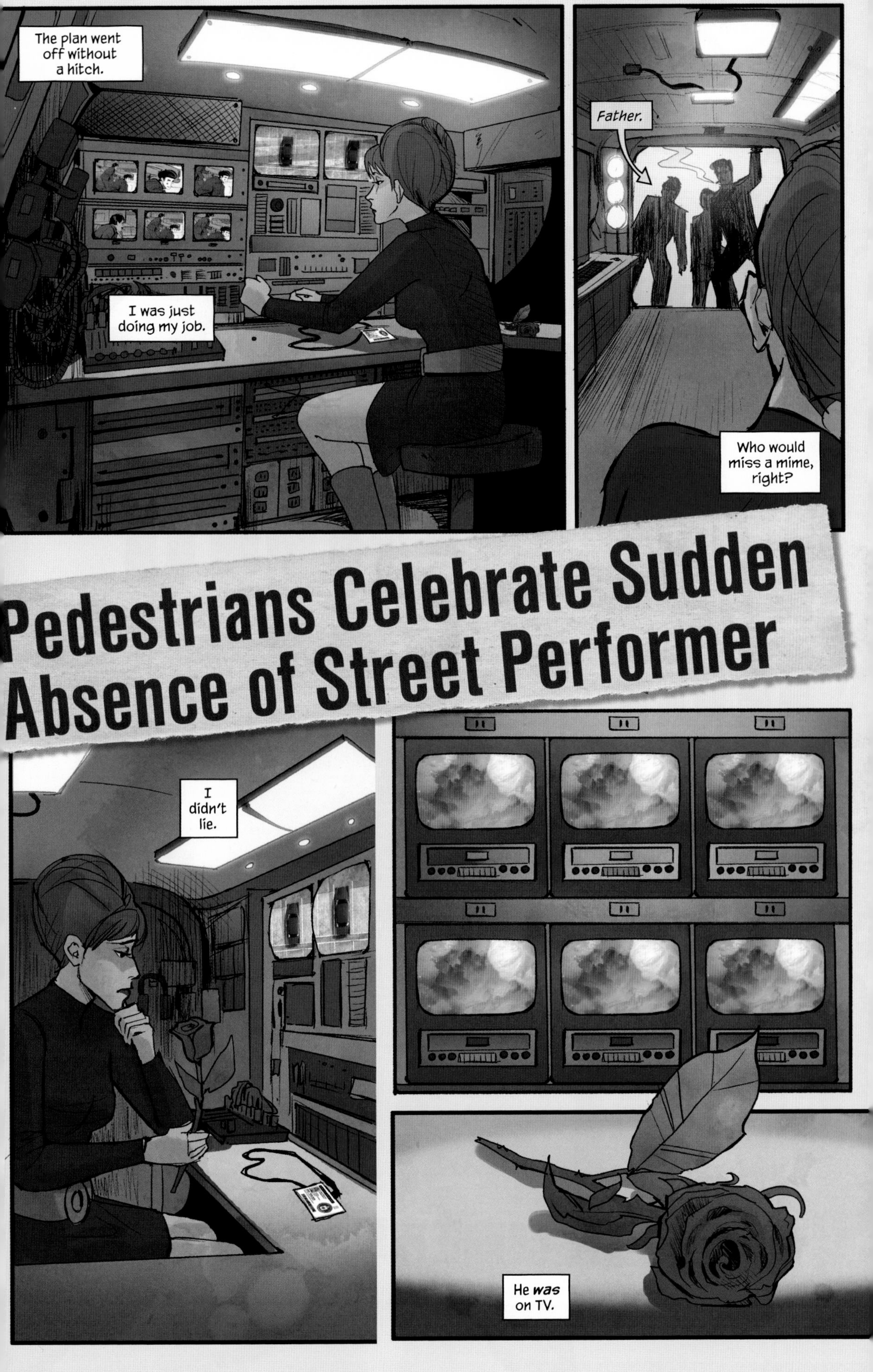

The plan went off without a hitch.
I was just doing my job.
Father.
Who would miss a mime, right?
Pedestrians Celebrate Sudden Absence of Street Performer
I didn't lie.
He *was* on TV.

FINAL ★★

Vol. 49, No. 296   Copr. 1961 News Syndicate Co. Inc.

DAILY NEWS

Tuesday, June 4

WEATHER: Sunny and warm.

8¢
10¢ OUTSIDE L.I. AND SUBURBS

LOCAL TEEN'S DAD BLOWS UP!

BOYFRIEND A SUSPECT

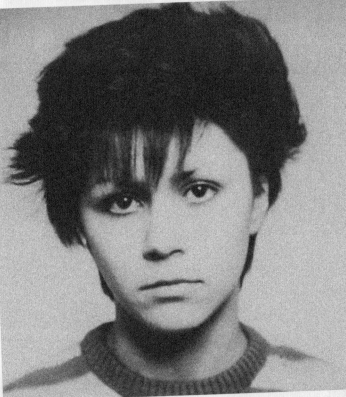

CONNIE FREUD: 'MY LIFE IS RUINED'

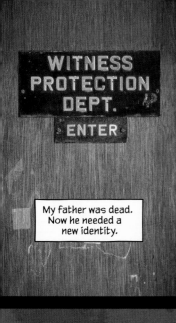

WITNESS PROTECTION DEPT.
ENTER

My father was dead. Now he needed a new identity.

Hm...

#3 SAILOR

#12 PRIEST

#17 KNIGHT

#24 COWBOY

No matter what we tried, he was still too recognizable.

MAYBE IF I TAKE IN THE SASH...?

I have an idea.

#31 MIME

Perfect.

It's not like I volunteered to go to the Bermuda Triangle to keep an eye on my super villain ex-con father. It was a promotion. A lot of extra responsibilities. A raise. I was sent to keep the world safe from vortexes and sea monsters. This island is dangerous. That's why they sent him here.

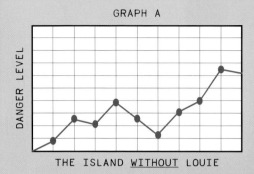

GRAPH A

DANGER LEVEL

THE ISLAND <u>WITHOUT</u> LOUIE

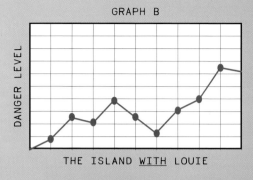

GRAPH B

DANGER LEVEL

THE ISLAND <u>WITH</u> LOUIE

They ran the numbers.

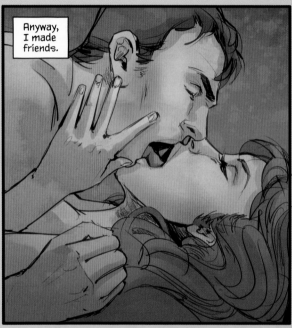

Anyway, I made friends.

GRROOR!

I love your bangs.

THANKS.

anxiety and neurosis

Seriously?

Louie found it harder to adjust.

Are you following me?

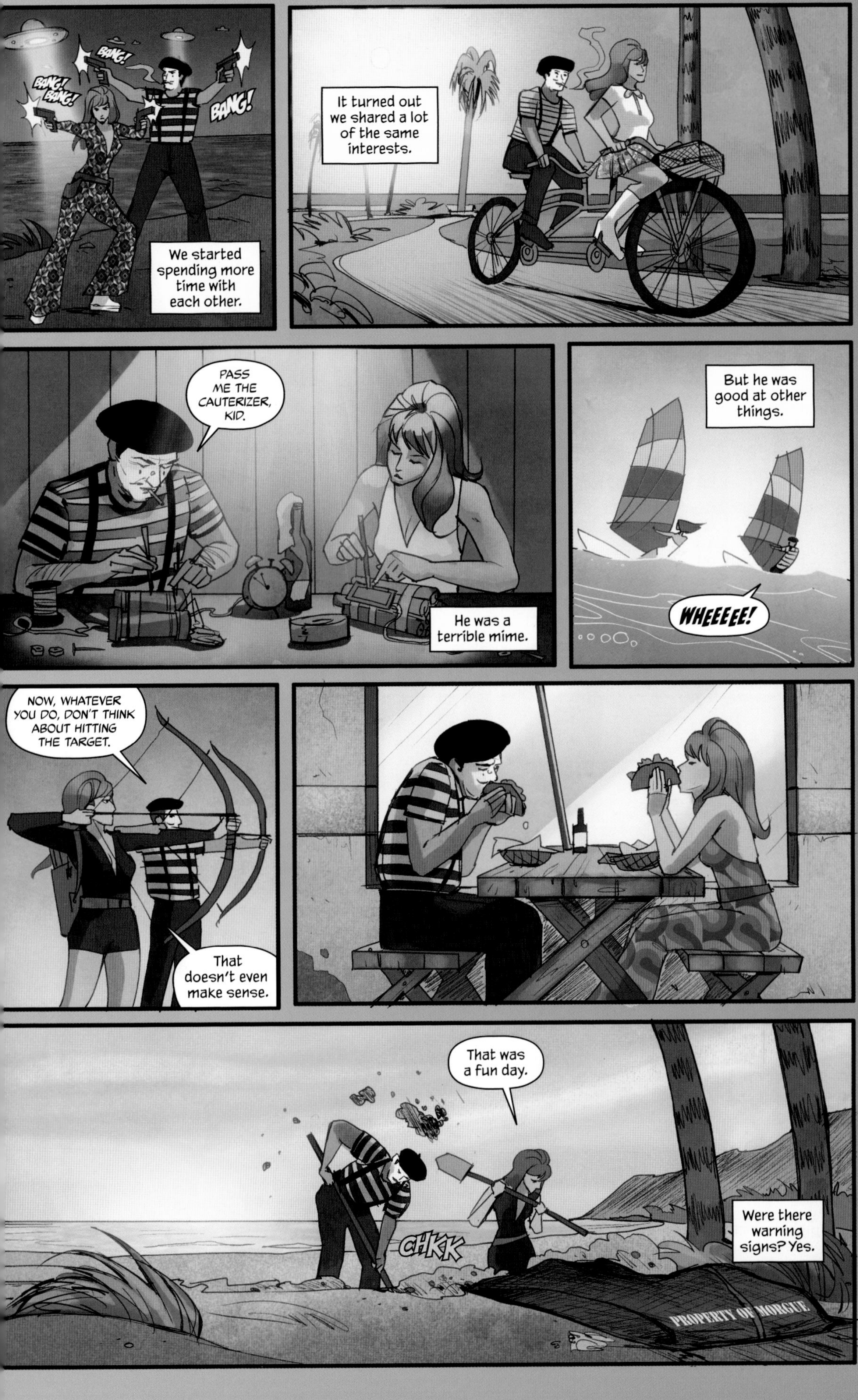
BANG!
BANG!
BANG!
BANG!
We started spending more time with each other.
It turned out we shared a lot of the same interests.
PASS ME THE CAUTERIZER, KID.
He was a terrible mime.
But he was good at other things.
WHEEEEE!
NOW, WHATEVER YOU DO, DON'T THINK ABOUT HITTING THE TARGET.
That doesn't even make sense.
That was a fun day.
CHKK
Were there warning signs? Yes.
PROPERTY OF MORGUE

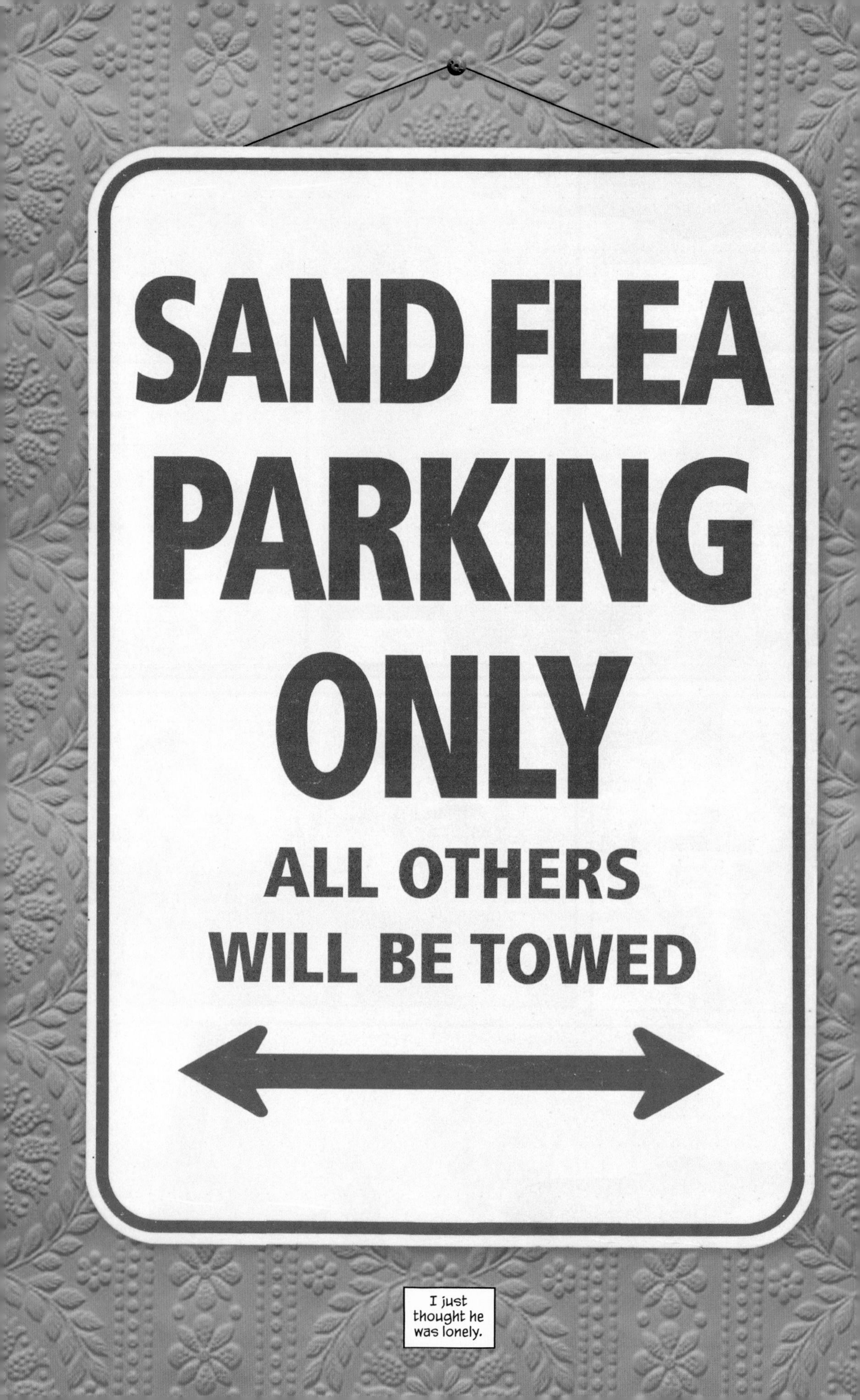
SAND FLEA
PARKING
ONLY
ALL OTHERS
WILL BE TOWED
I just thought he was lonely.

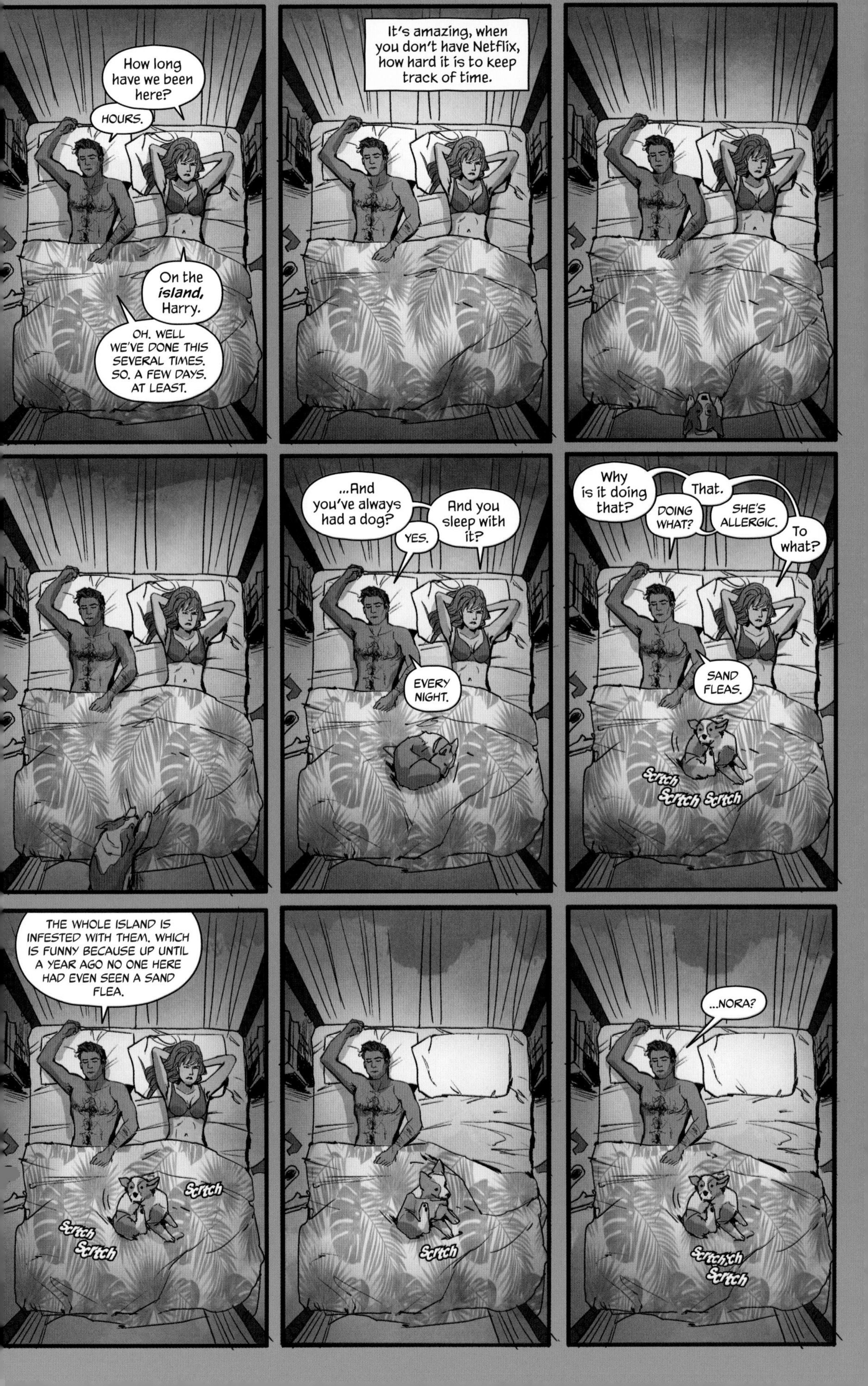

How long have we been here?
HOURS.
On the *island,* Harry.
OH. WELL WE'VE DONE THIS SEVERAL TIMES. SO. A FEW DAYS. AT LEAST.
It's amazing, when you don't have Netflix, how hard it is to keep track of time.
...And you've always had a dog?
YES.
And you sleep with it?
EVERY NIGHT.
Why is it doing that?
DOING WHAT?
That.
SHE'S ALLERGIC.
To what?
SAND FLEAS.
Scrtch
Scrtch Scrtch
THE WHOLE ISLAND IS INFESTED WITH THEM. WHICH IS FUNNY BECAUSE UP UNTIL A YEAR AGO NO ONE HERE HAD EVEN SEEN A SAND FLEA.
Scrtch
Scrtch
Scrtch
Scrtch
...NORA?
Scrtch'ch
Scrtch

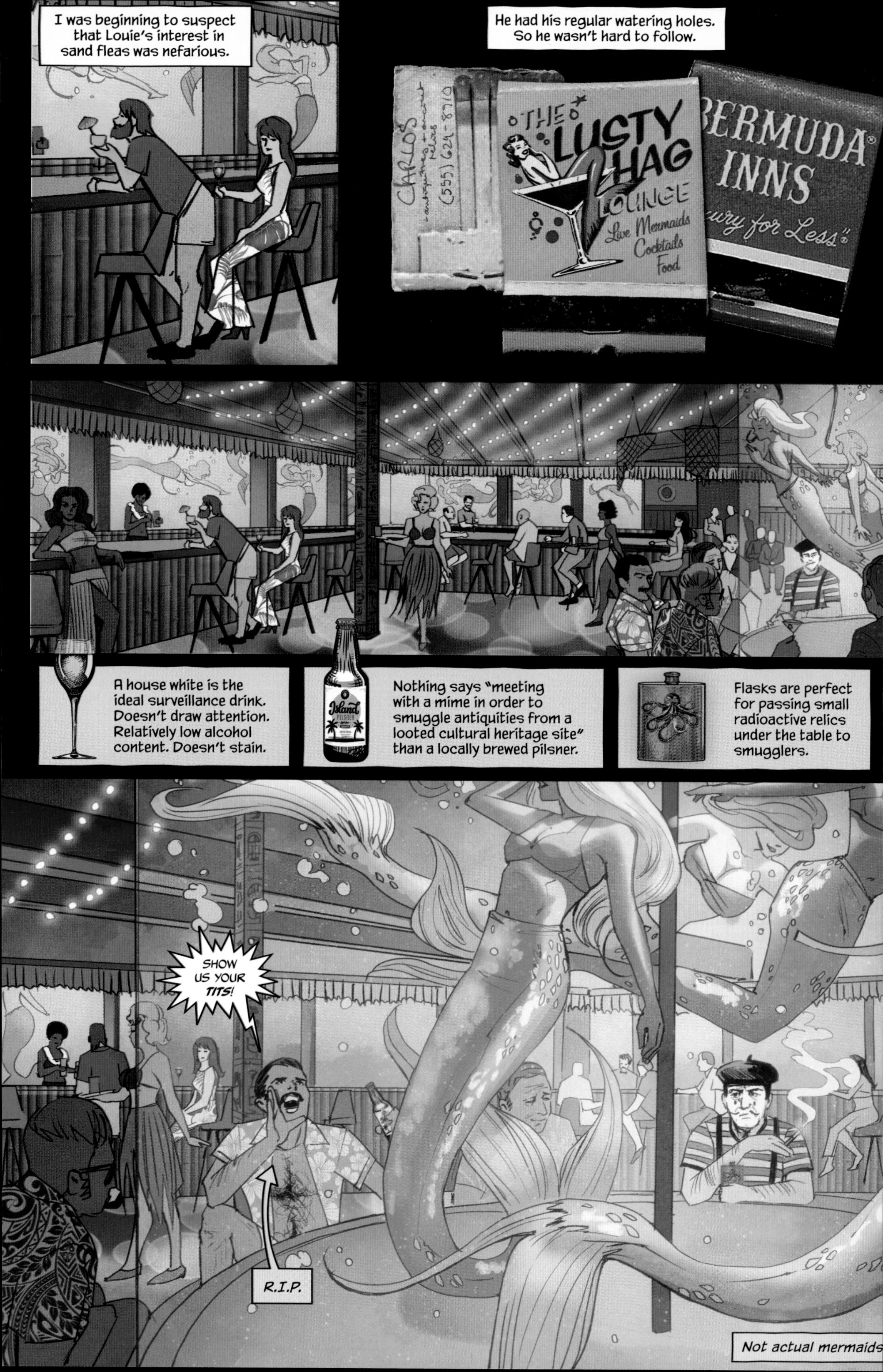

I was beginning to suspect that Louie's interest in sand fleas was nefarious.
He had his regular watering holes. So he wasn't hard to follow.
CARLOS
(555) 624-8710
THE LUSTY HAG LOUNGE
Live Mermaids
Cocktails
Food
BERMUDA® INNS
ury for Less"
A house white is the ideal surveillance drink. Doesn't draw attention. Relatively low alcohol content. Doesn't stain.
Island Pilsner
Nothing says "meeting with a mime in order to smuggle antiquities from a looted cultural heritage site" than a locally brewed pilsner.
Flasks are perfect for passing small radioactive relics under the table to smugglers.
SHOW US YOUR TITS!
R.I.P.
Not actual mermaids

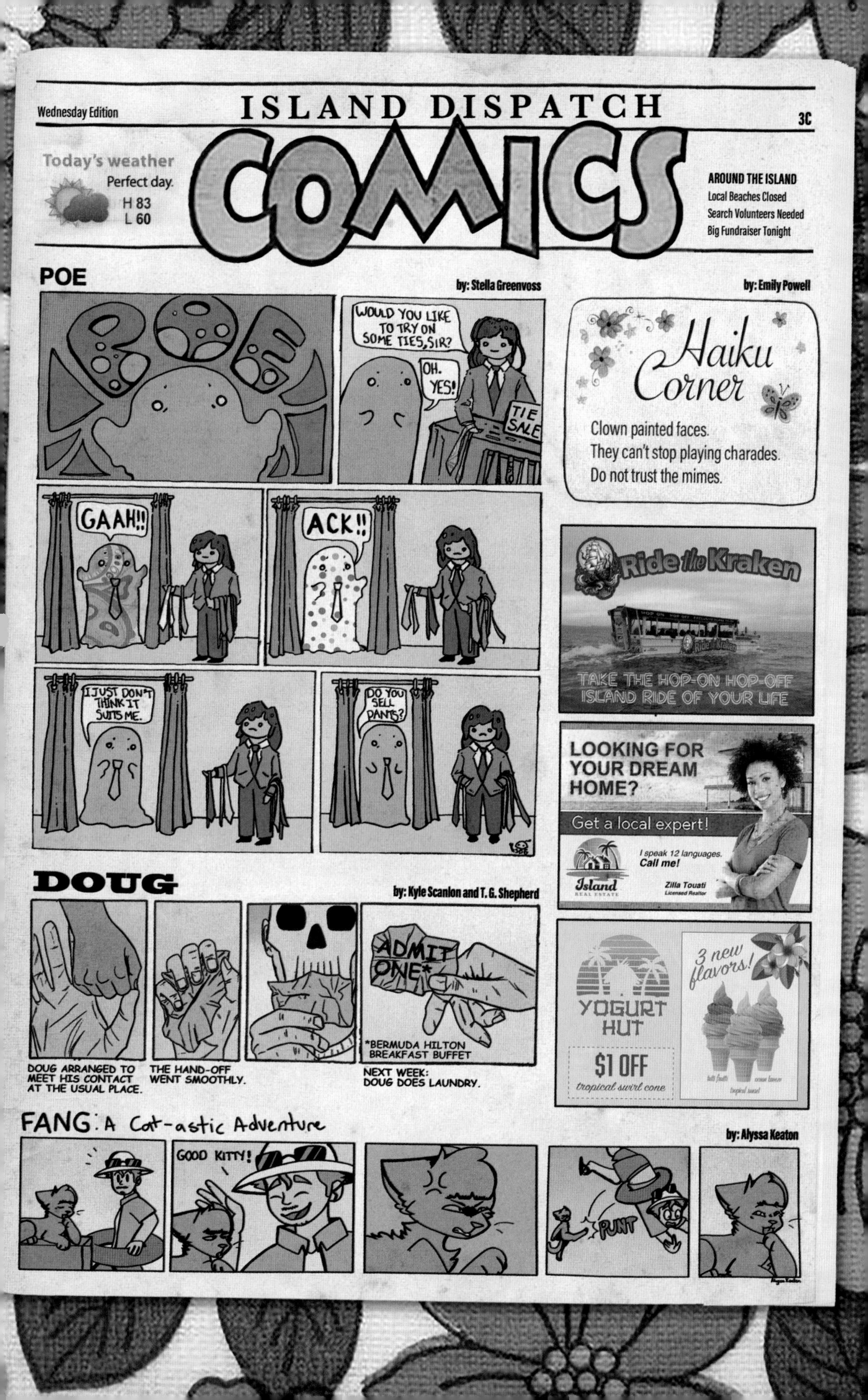

Wednesday Edition

ISLAND DISPATCH COMICS

3C

Today's weather
Perfect day.
H 83
L 60

AROUND THE ISLAND
Local Beaches Closed
Search Volunteers Needed
Big Fundraiser Tonight

POE

by: Stella Greenvoss

POE
WOULD YOU LIKE TO TRY ON SOME TIES, SIR?
OH. YES!
TIE SALE
GAAH!!
ACK!!
I JUST DON'T THINK IT SUITS ME.
DO YOU SELL PANTS?

by: Emily Powell

Haiku Corner

Clown painted faces.
They can't stop playing charades.
Do not trust the mimes.

DOUG

by: Kyle Scanlon and T. G. Shepherd

DOUG ARRANGED TO MEET HIS CONTACT AT THE USUAL PLACE.
THE HAND-OFF WENT SMOOTHLY.
ADMIT ONE*
*BERMUDA HILTON BREAKFAST BUFFET
NEXT WEEK: DOUG DOES LAUNDRY.

FANG: A Cat-astic Adventure

by: Alyssa Keaton

GOOD KITTY!
PUNT

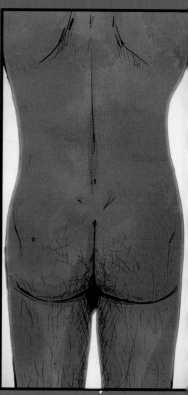

UH.

Go back to sleep, Harry.

You're dreaming.

OH. OKAY.

I DON'T THINK WE'VE MET. I'M HARRY.

I'M POE.

IS THAT FOR ME?

OH. UM. OKAY.

TERRIFIC. WELL. RIGHT THEN...

...I'M JUST GOING TO TAKE THIS GLASS OF MILK AND GO BACK TO BED.

Get the hall light, Harry.

RIGHT-O.

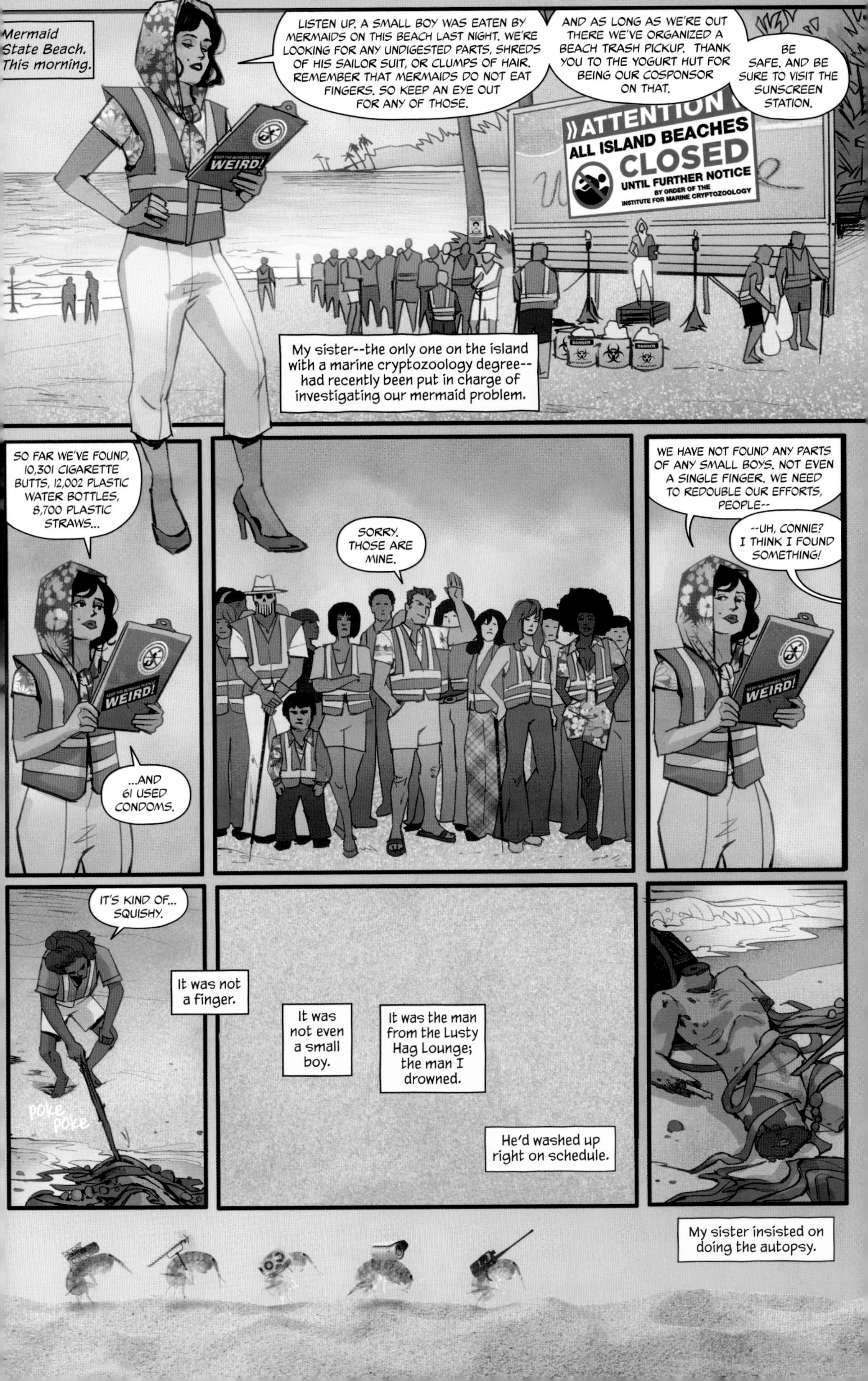
Mermaid State Beach. This morning.
LISTEN UP. A SMALL BOY WAS EATEN BY MERMAIDS ON THIS BEACH LAST NIGHT. WE'RE LOOKING FOR ANY UNDIGESTED PARTS, SHREDS OF HIS SAILOR SUIT, OR CLUMPS OF HAIR. REMEMBER THAT MERMAIDS DO NOT EAT FINGERS. SO KEEP AN EYE OUT FOR ANY OF THOSE.
AND AS LONG AS WE'RE OUT THERE WE'VE ORGANIZED A BEACH TRASH PICKUP. THANK YOU TO THE YOGURT HUT FOR BEING OUR COSPONSOR ON THAT.
BE SAFE. AND BE SURE TO VISIT THE SUNSCREEN STATION.
ATTENTION
ALL ISLAND BEACHES
CLOSED
UNTIL FURTHER NOTICE
BY ORDER OF THE INSTITUTE FOR MARINE CRYPTOZOOLOGY
WEIRD!
My sister--the only one on the island with a marine cryptozoology degree--had recently been put in charge of investigating our mermaid problem.
SO FAR WE'VE FOUND, 10,301 CIGARETTE BUTTS, 12,002 PLASTIC WATER BOTTLES, 8,700 PLASTIC STRAWS...
...AND 61 USED CONDOMS.
SORRY. THOSE ARE MINE.
WE HAVE NOT FOUND ANY PARTS OF ANY SMALL BOYS. NOT EVEN A SINGLE FINGER. WE NEED TO REDOUBLE OUR EFFORTS, PEOPLE--
--UH, CONNIE? I THINK I FOUND SOMETHING!
IT'S KIND OF... SQUISHY.
poke poke
It was not a finger.
It was not even a small boy.
It was the man from the Lusty Hag Lounge; the man I drowned.
He'd washed up right on schedule.
My sister insisted on doing the autopsy.

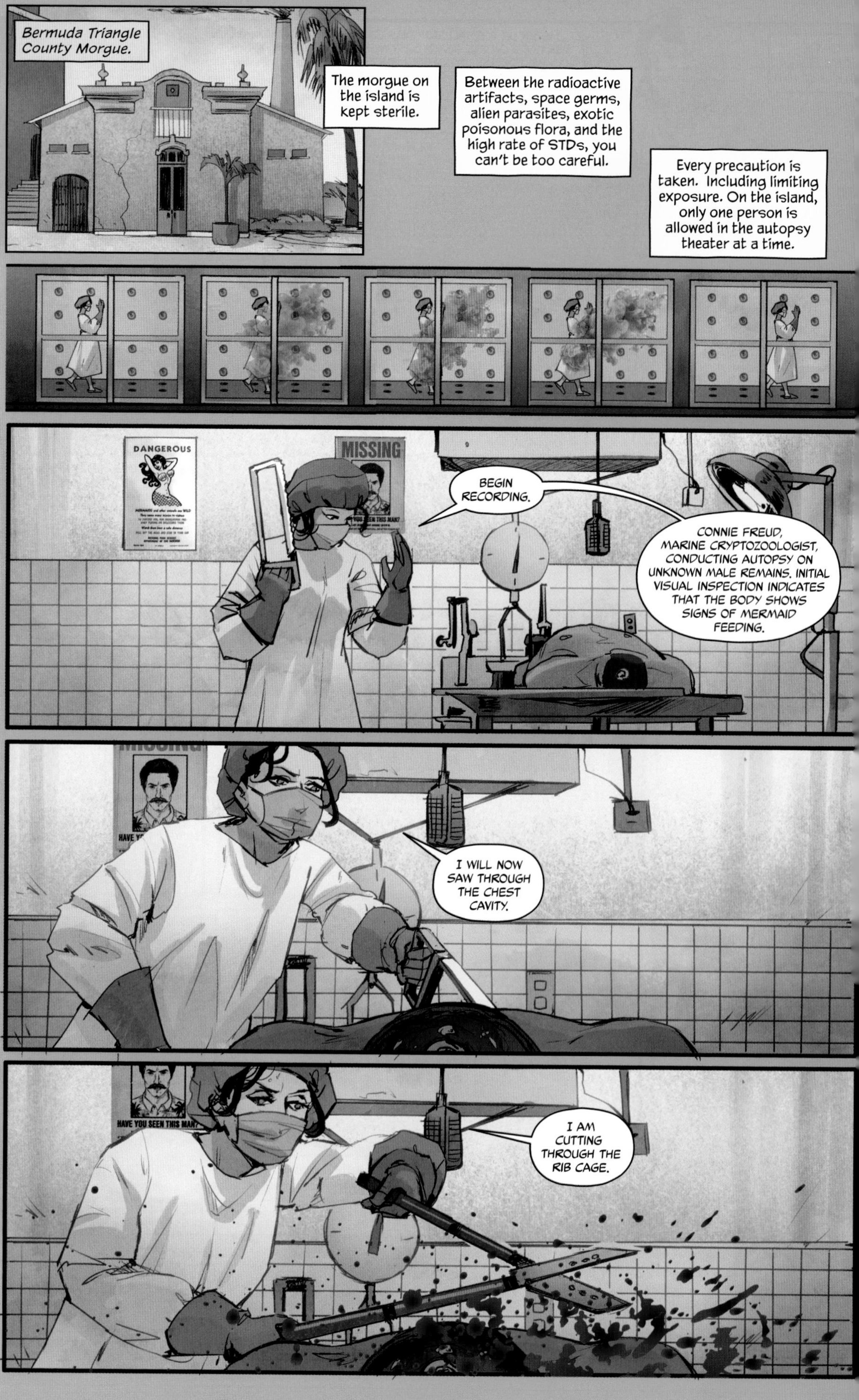
Bermuda Triangle County Morgue.
The morgue on the island is kept sterile.
Between the radioactive artifacts, space germs, alien parasites, exotic poisonous flora, and the high rate of STDs, you can't be too careful.
Every precaution is taken. Including limiting exposure. On the island, only one person is allowed in the autopsy theater at a time.
DANGEROUS
MISSING
BEGIN RECORDING.
CONNIE FREUD, MARINE CRYPTOZOOLOGIST, CONDUCTING AUTOPSY ON UNKNOWN MALE REMAINS. INITIAL VISUAL INSPECTION INDICATES THAT THE BODY SHOWS SIGNS OF MERMAID FEEDING.
I WILL NOW SAW THROUGH THE CHEST CAVITY.
HAVE YOU SEEN THIS MAN?
I AM CUTTING THROUGH THE RIB CAGE.

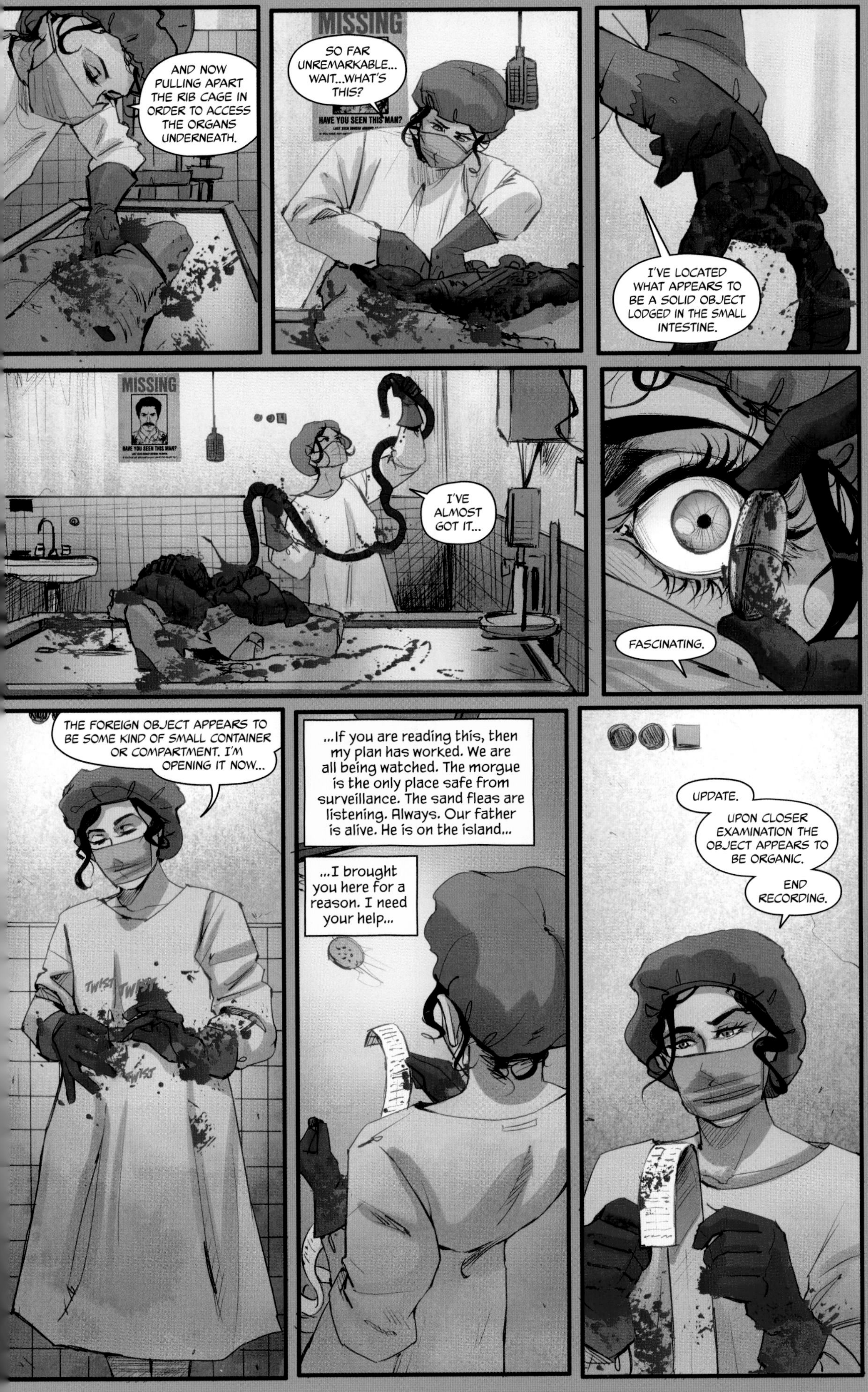
AND NOW PULLING APART THE RIB CAGE IN ORDER TO ACCESS THE ORGANS UNDERNEATH.
MISSING
HAVE YOU SEEN THIS MAN?
SO FAR UNREMARKABLE... WAIT...WHAT'S THIS?
I'VE LOCATED WHAT APPEARS TO BE A SOLID OBJECT LODGED IN THE SMALL INTESTINE.
MISSING
HAVE YOU SEEN THIS MAN?
I'VE ALMOST GOT IT...
FASCINATING.
THE FOREIGN OBJECT APPEARS TO BE SOME KIND OF SMALL CONTAINER OR COMPARTMENT. I'M OPENING IT NOW...
...If you are reading this, then my plan has worked. We are all being watched. The morgue is the only place safe from surveillance. The sand fleas are listening. Always. Our father is alive. He is on the island...
...I brought you here for a reason. I need your help...
UPDATE.
UPON CLOSER EXAMINATION THE OBJECT APPEARS TO BE ORGANIC.
END RECORDING.

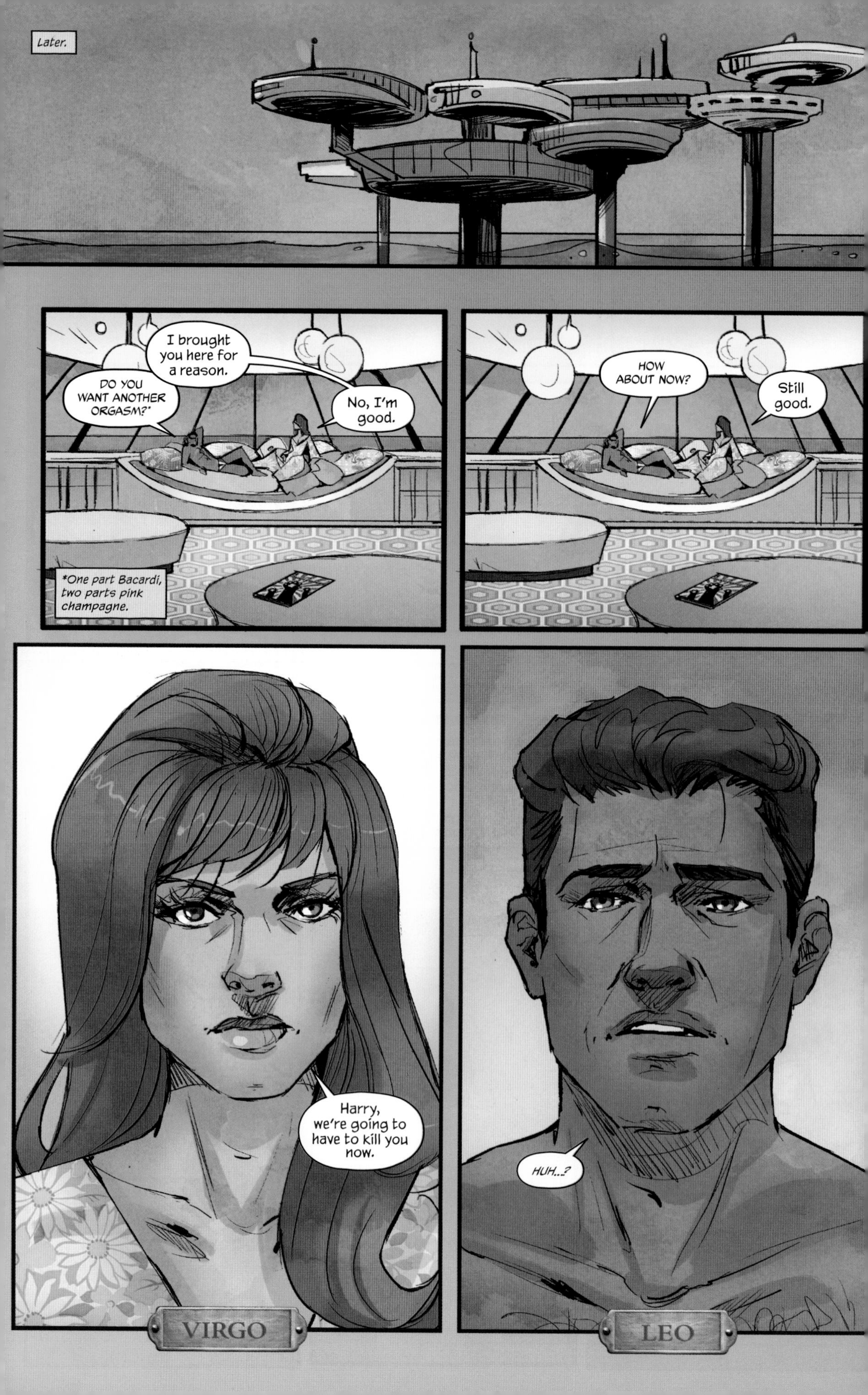
Later.
I brought you here for a reason.
DO YOU WANT ANOTHER ORGASM?*
No, I'm good.
*One part Bacardi, two parts pink champagne.
HOW ABOUT NOW?
Still good.
Harry, we're going to have to kill you now.
VIRGO
HUH...?
LEO

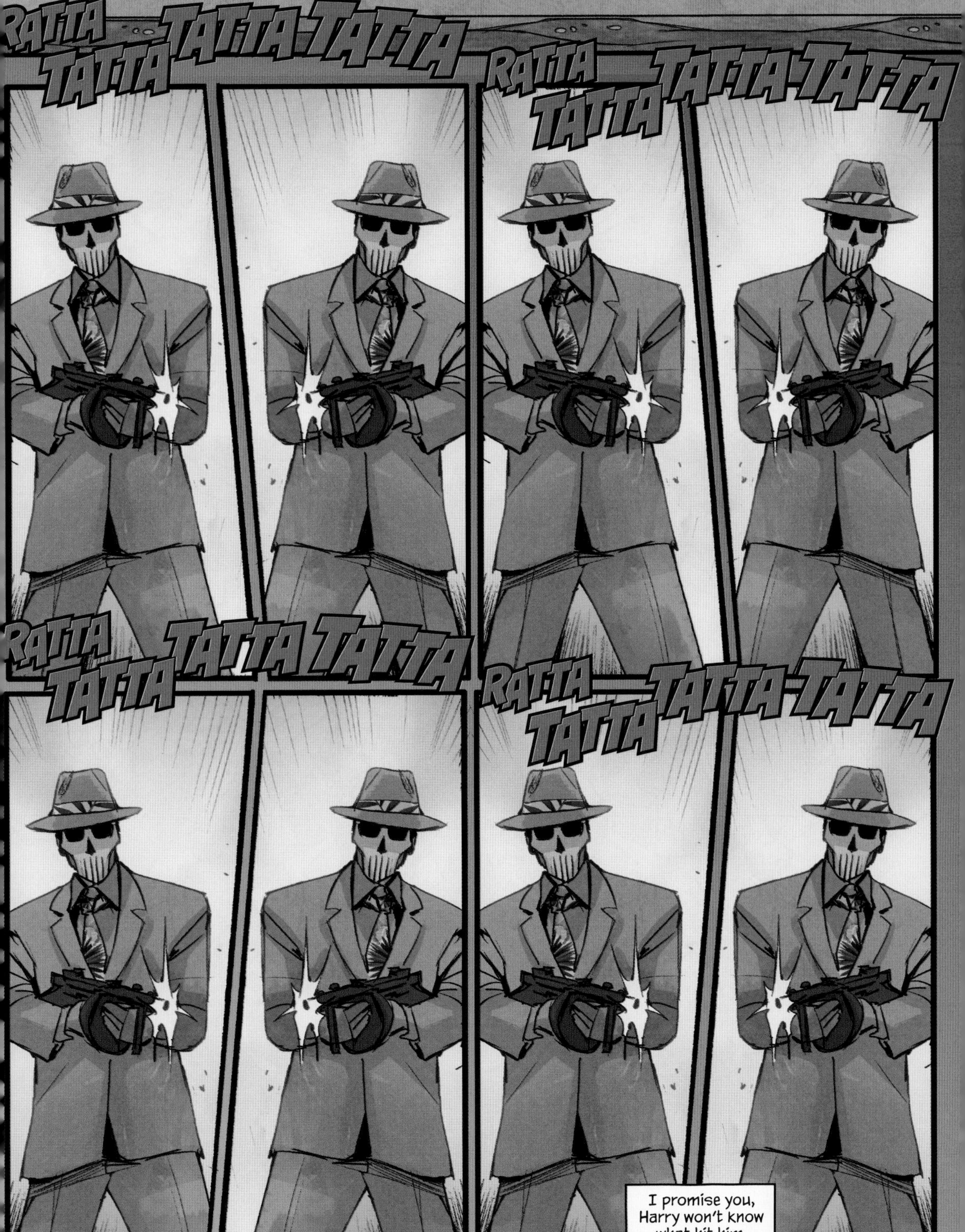
RATTA TATTA TATTA TATTA
RATTA TATTA TATTA TATTA
RATTA TATTA TATTA TATTA
RATTA TATTA TATTA TATTA
I promise you, Harry won't know what hit him.

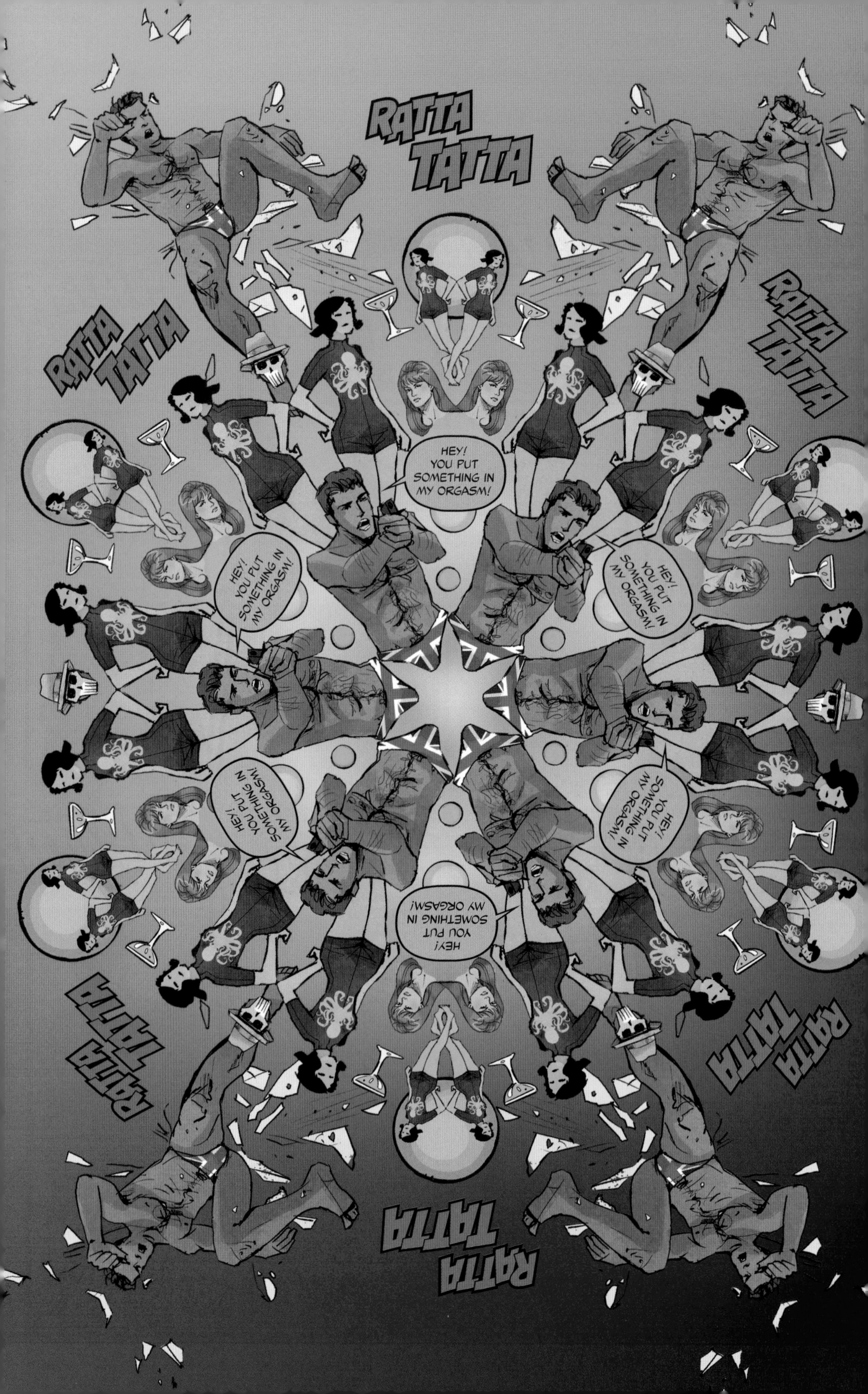
RATTA TATTA
RATTA TATTA
RATTA TATTA
HEY! YOU PUT SOMETHING IN MY ORGASM!
HEY! YOU PUT SOMETHING IN MY ORGASM!
HEY! YOU PUT SOMETHING IN MY ORGASM!
HEY! YOU PUT SOMETHING IN MY ORGASM!
HEY! YOU PUT SOMETHING IN MY ORGASM!
HEY! YOU PUT SOMETHING IN MY ORGASM!
RATTA TATTA
RATTA TATTA
RATTA TATTA

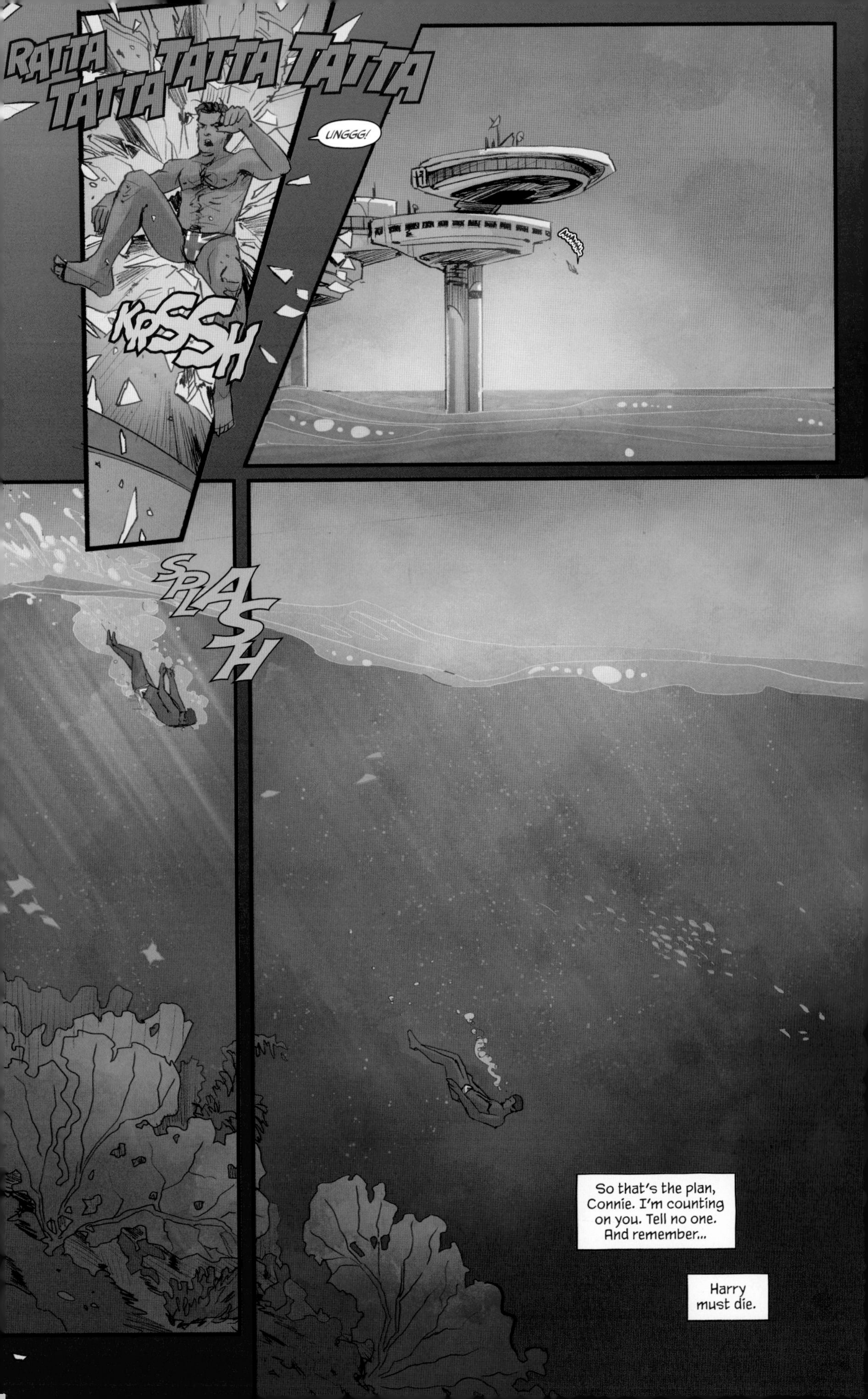
RATTA TATTA TATTA TATTA
UNGGG!
KRSSH
SPLASH
So that's the plan, Connie. I'm counting on you. Tell no one. And remember...
Harry must die.

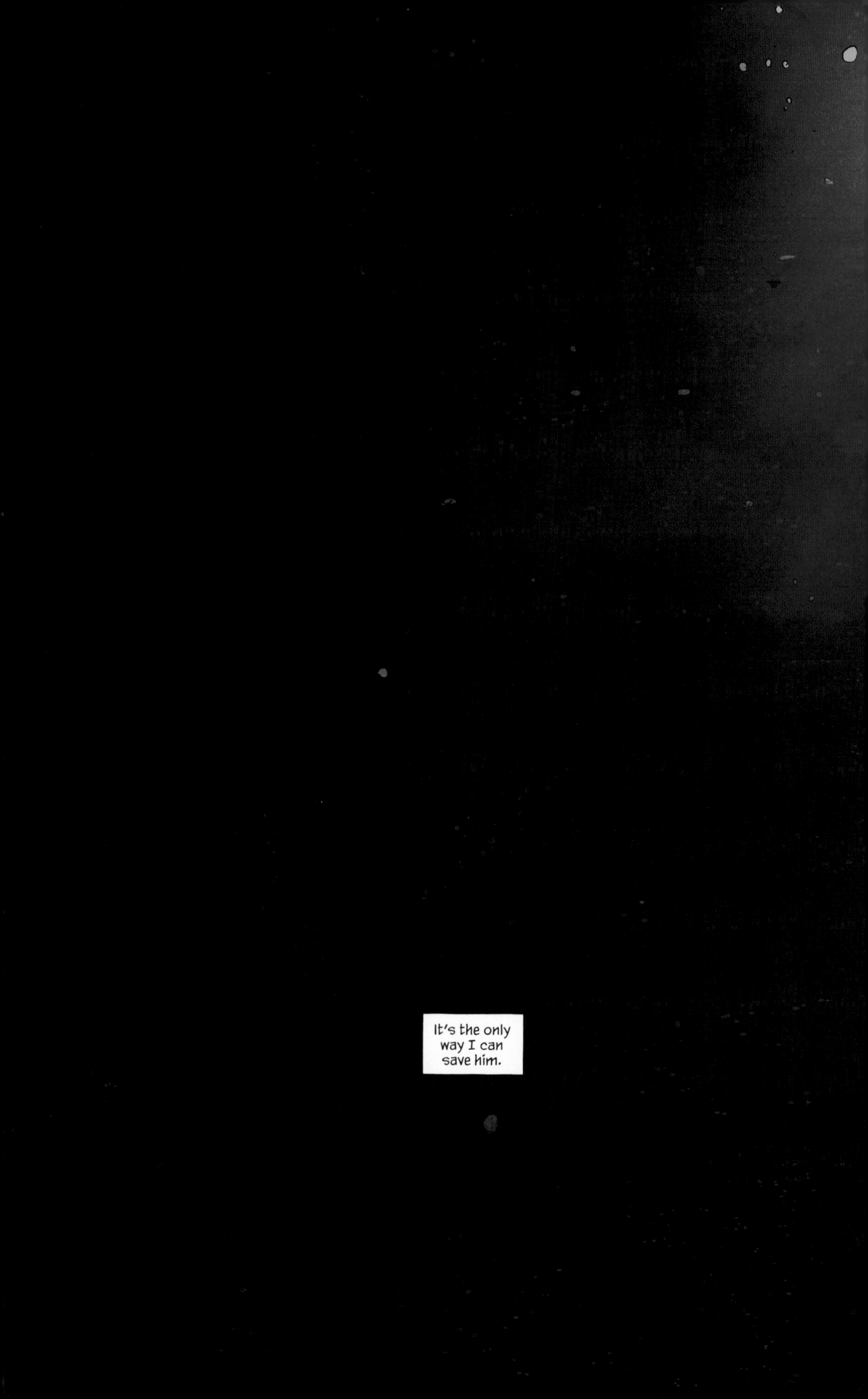
It's the only way I can save him.

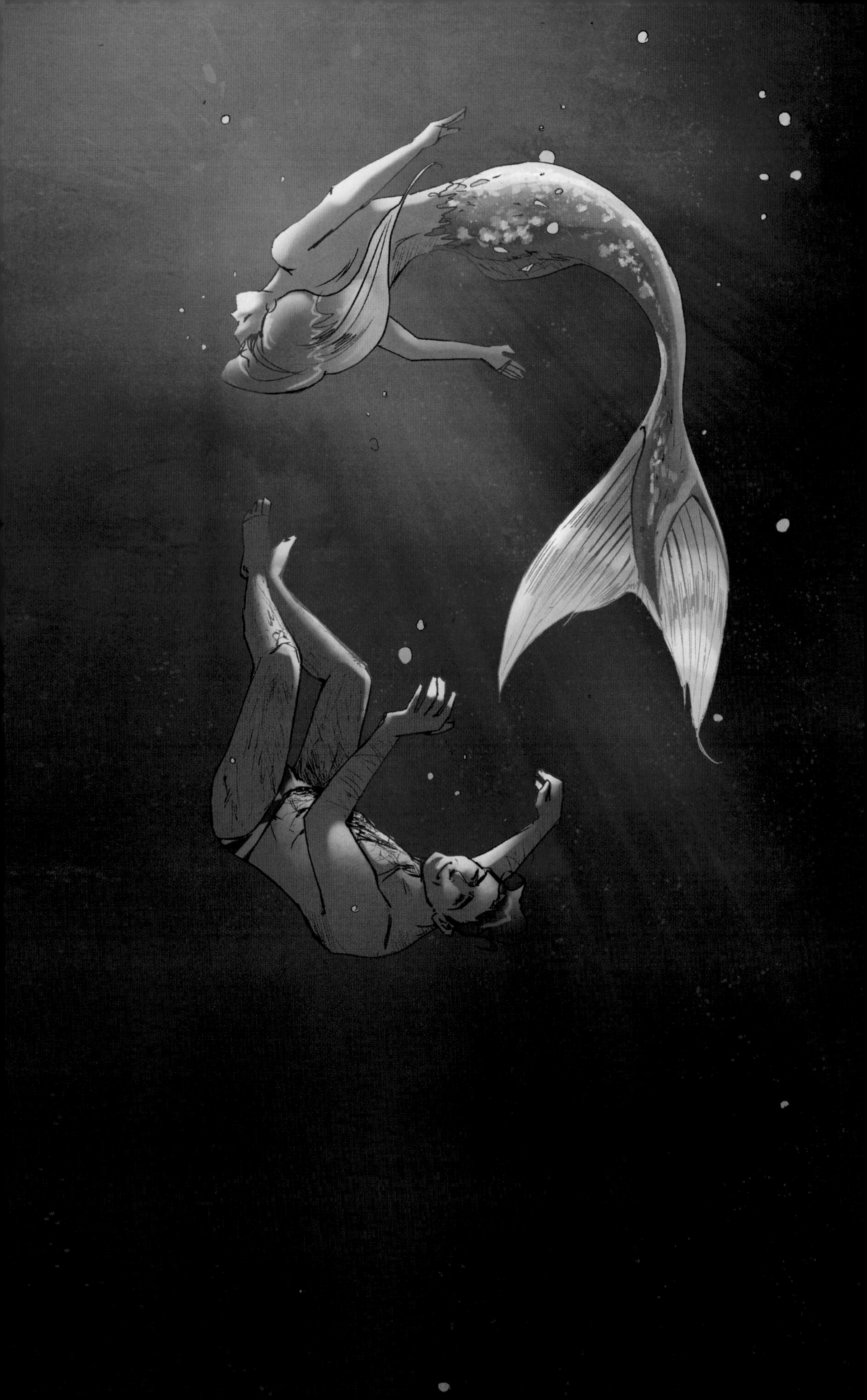

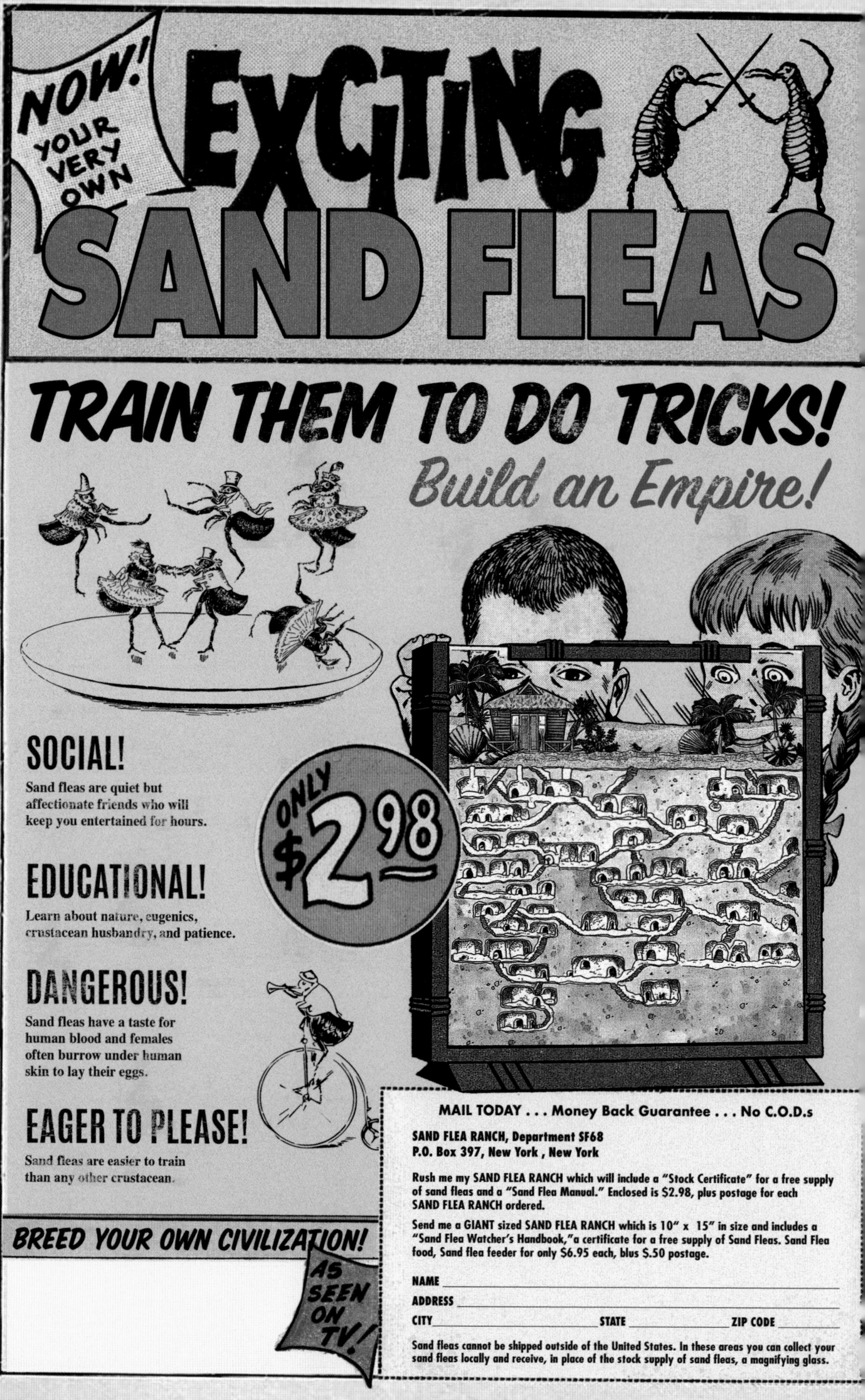
NOW! YOUR VERY OWN
EXCITING SAND FLEAS
TRAIN THEM TO DO TRICKS!
Build an Empire!
SOCIAL!
Sand fleas are quiet but affectionate friends who will keep you entertained for hours.
EDUCATIONAL!
Learn about nature, eugenics, crustacean husbandry, and patience.
DANGEROUS!
Sand fleas have a taste for human blood and females often burrow under human skin to lay their eggs.
EAGER TO PLEASE!
Sand fleas are easier to train than any other crustacean.
ONLY $2.98
BREED YOUR OWN CIVILIZATION!
AS SEEN ON TV!
MAIL TODAY . . . Money Back Guarantee . . . No C.O.D.s
SAND FLEA RANCH, Department SF68
P.O. Box 397, New York , New York
Rush me my SAND FLEA RANCH which will include a "Stock Certificate" for a free supply of sand fleas and a "Sand Flea Manual." Enclosed is $2.98, plus postage for each SAND FLEA RANCH ordered.
Send me a GIANT sized SAND FLEA RANCH which is 10" x 15" in size and includes a "Sand Flea Watcher's Handbook," a certificate for a free supply of Sand Fleas. Sand Flea food, Sand flea feeder for only $6.95 each, blus $.50 postage.
NAME
ADDRESS
CITY
STATE
ZIP CODE
Sand fleas cannot be shipped outside of the United States. In these areas you can collect your sand fleas locally and receive, in place of the stock supply of sand fleas, a magnifying glass.

THE BERMUDA TRIANGLE

A signature drink. Pink champagne and Bacardi. At the yogurt hut.

ISLAND LINES
Cruise The Bermuda Triangle

Poolside Cocktail
~ Daily Special ~

DAY 4

GIN RICKEY

Squeeze ½ lime over ice in highball glass
Add 1 jigger Gin
Fill with soda
Add squeezed lime

ISLAND LINES
Cruise The Bermuda Triangle

SPY ISLAND

A BERMUDA TRIANGLE MYSTERY

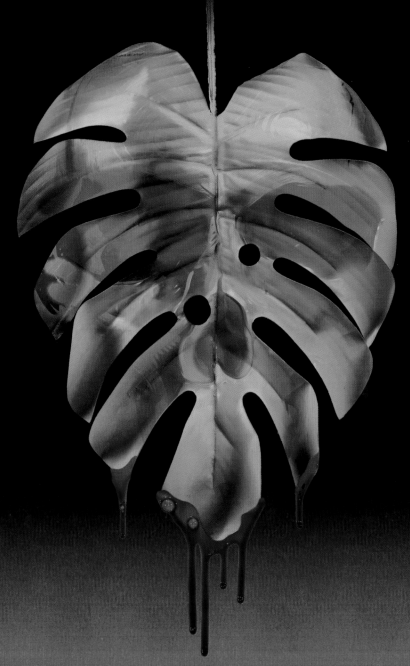

 CAIN MITERNIQUE MCCALL ROSENBERG CARAMAGNA

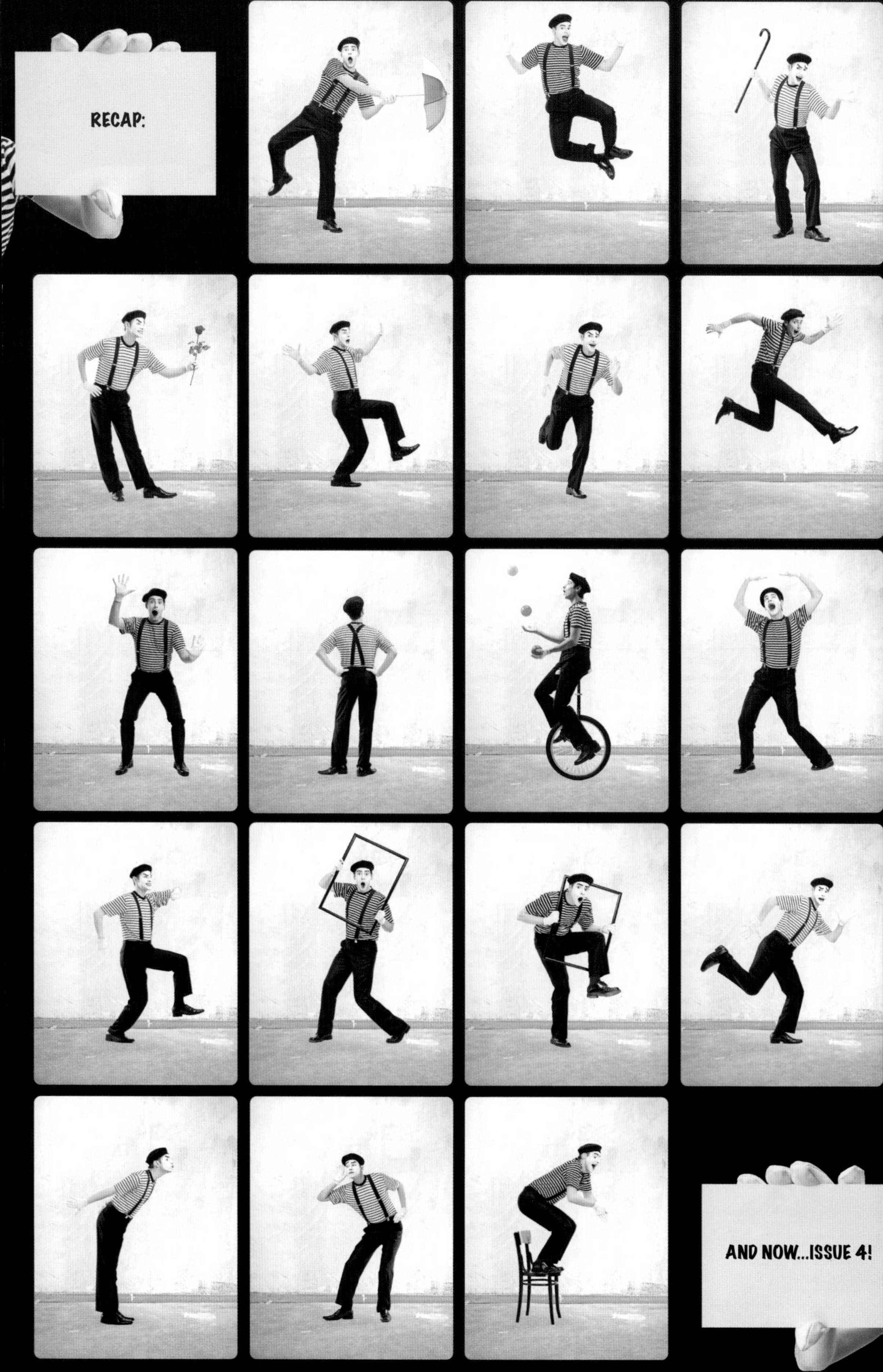
RECAP:
AND NOW...ISSUE 4!

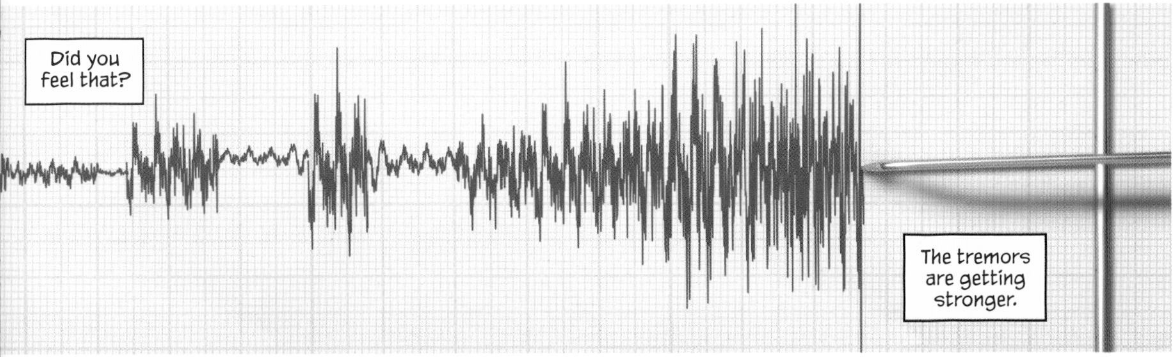
Did you feel that?
The tremors are getting stronger.

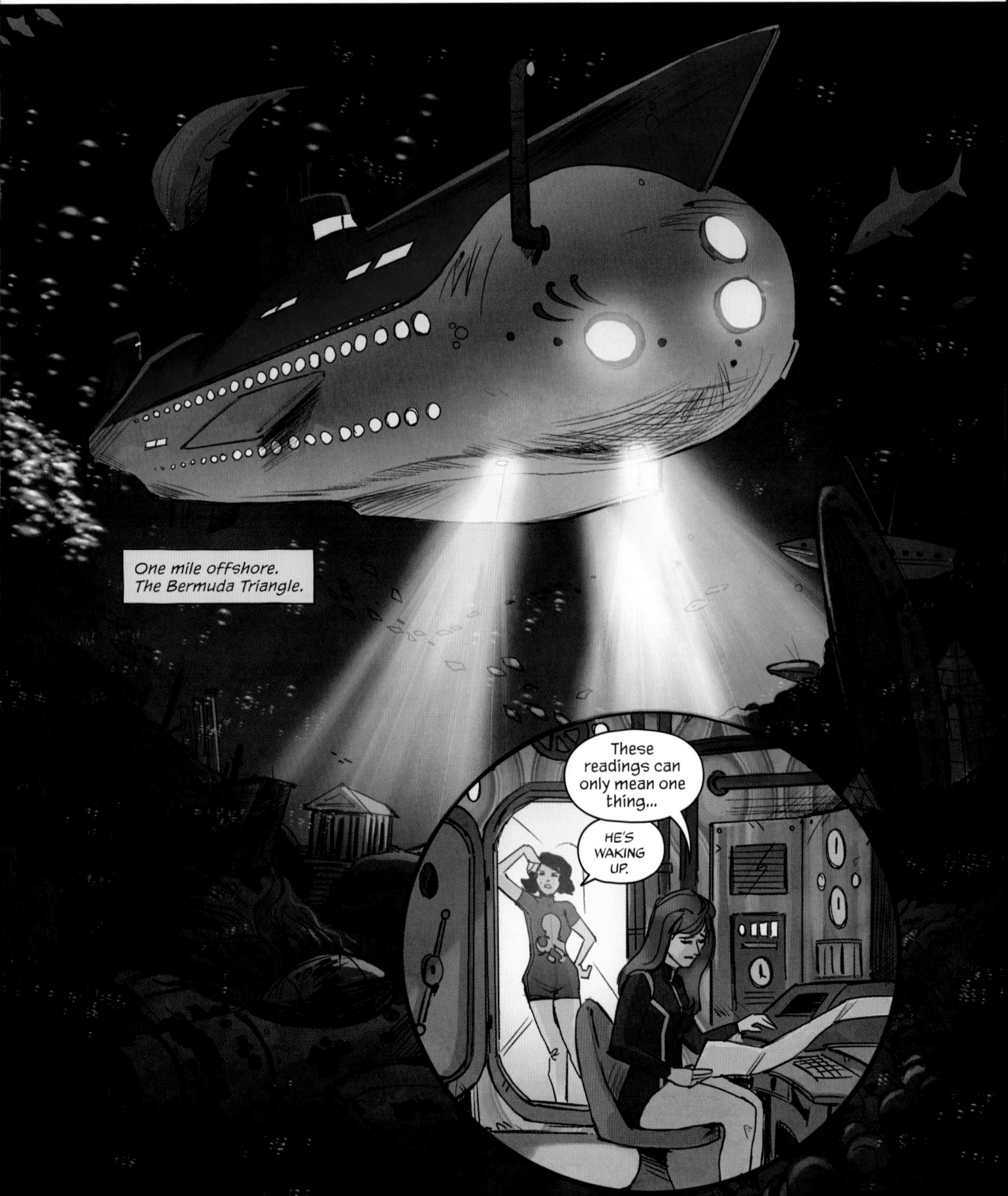
One mile offshore.
The Bermuda Triangle.
These readings can only mean one thing...
HE'S WAKING UP.

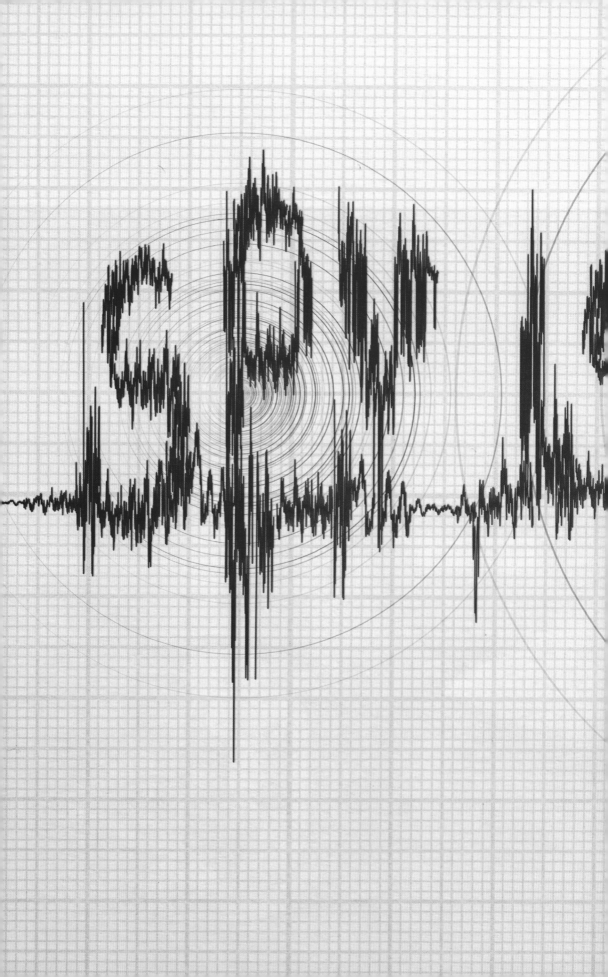

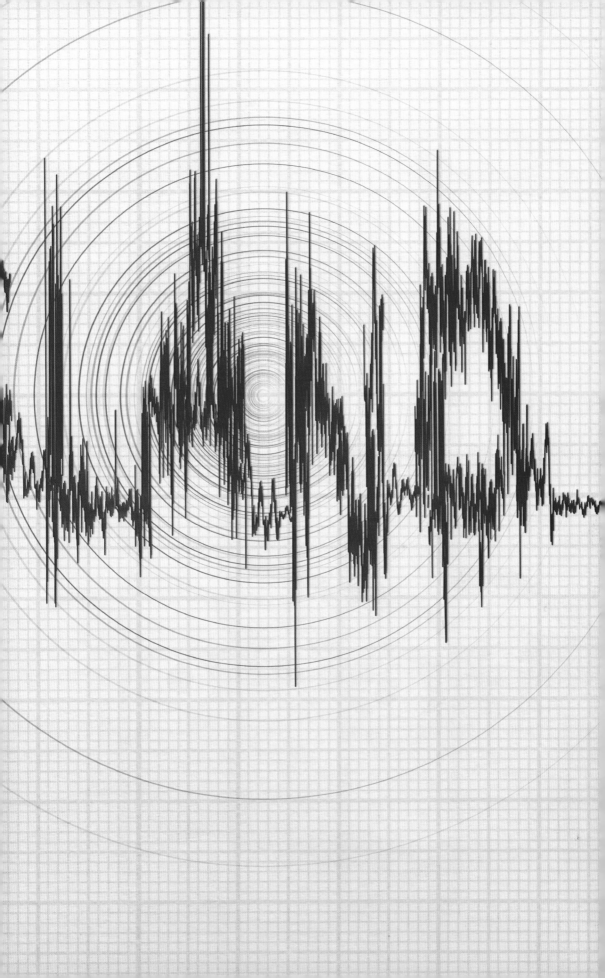

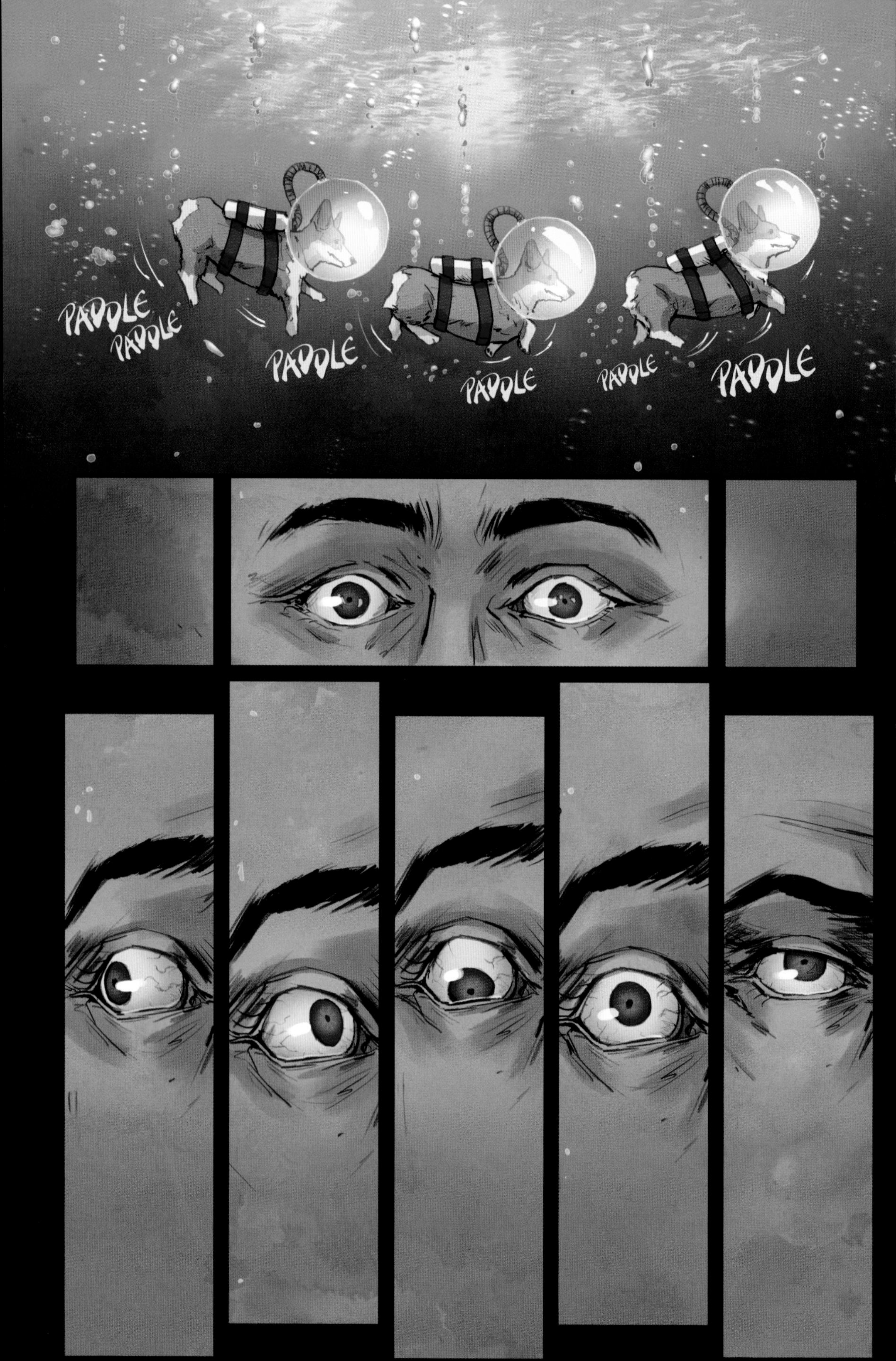
PADDLE
PADDLE
PADDLE
PADDLE
PADDLE
PADDLE

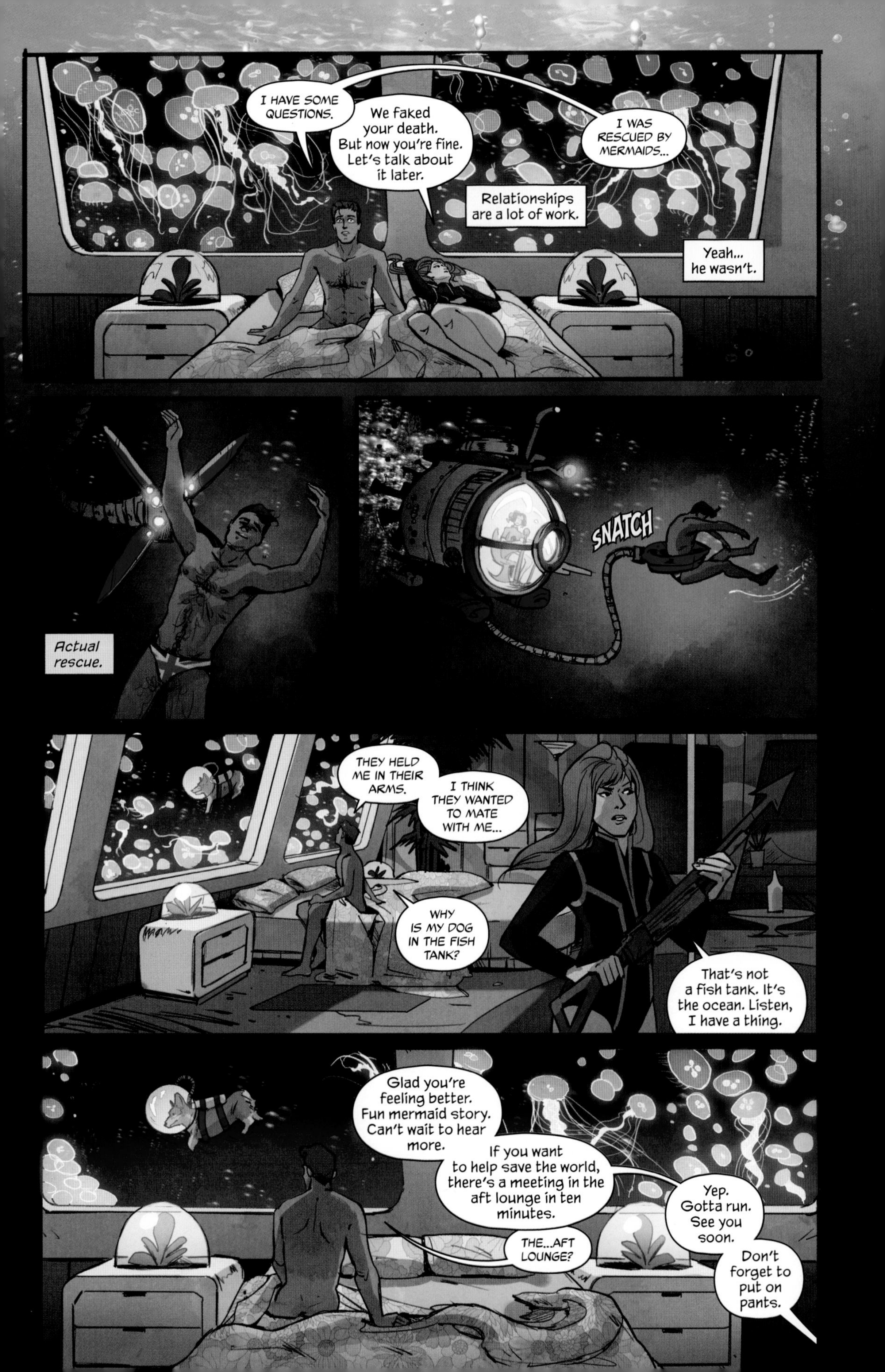

I HAVE SOME QUESTIONS.
We faked your death. But now you're fine. Let's talk about it later.
I WAS RESCUED BY MERMAIDS...
Relationships are a lot of work.
Yeah... he wasn't.
Actual rescue.
SNATCH
THEY HELD ME IN THEIR ARMS.
I THINK THEY WANTED TO MATE WITH ME...
WHY IS MY DOG IN THE FISH TANK?
That's not a fish tank. It's the ocean. Listen, I have a thing.
Glad you're feeling better. Fun mermaid story. Can't wait to hear more.
If you want to help save the world, there's a meeting in the aft lounge in ten minutes.
THE...AFT LOUNGE?
Yep. Gotta run. See you soon.
Don't forget to put on pants.

FREUD'S VIEW OF THE HUMAN MIND

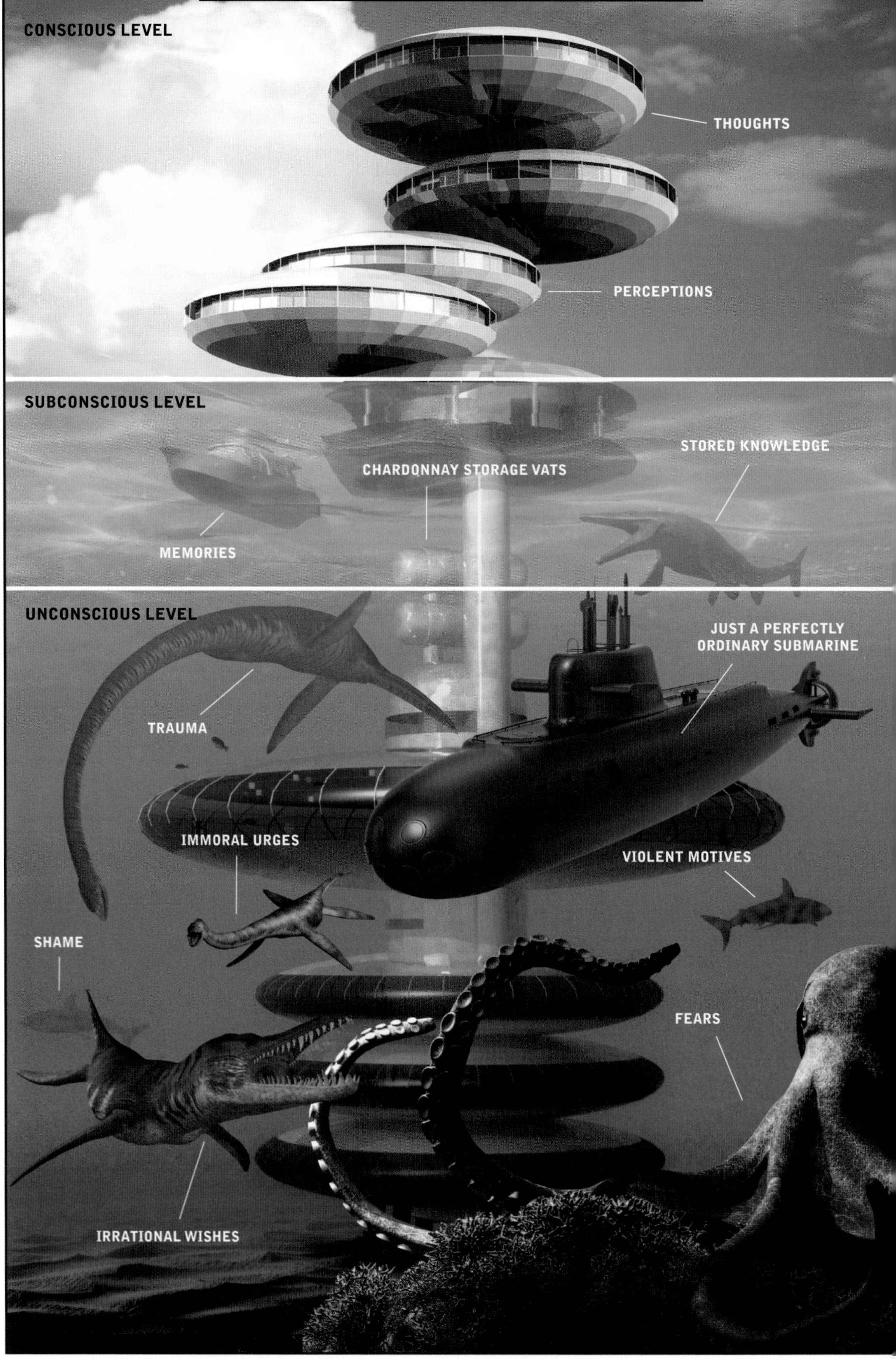

CONSCIOUS LEVEL
THOUGHTS
PERCEPTIONS
SUBCONSCIOUS LEVEL
STORED KNOWLEDGE
CHARDONNAY STORAGE VATS
MEMORIES
UNCONSCIOUS LEVEL
JUST A PERFECTLY ORDINARY SUBMARINE
TRAUMA
IMMORAL URGES
VIOLENT MOTIVES
SHAME
FEARS
IRRATIONAL WISHES

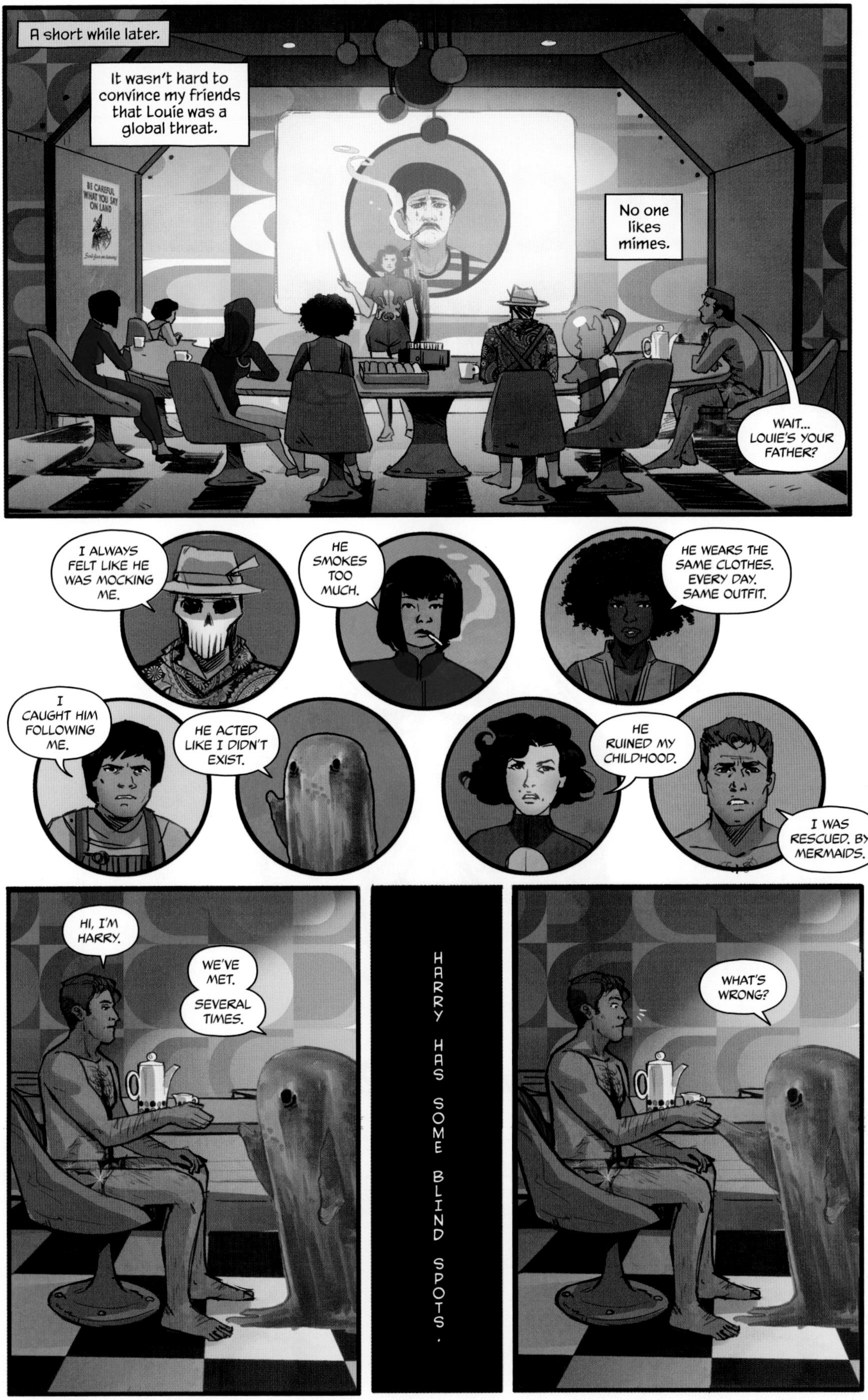

A short while later.
It wasn't hard to convince my friends that Louie was a global threat.
BE CAREFUL WHAT YOU SAY ON LAND
No one likes mimes.
WAIT... LOUIE'S YOUR FATHER?
I ALWAYS FELT LIKE HE WAS MOCKING ME.
HE SMOKES TOO MUCH.
HE WEARS THE SAME CLOTHES. EVERY DAY. SAME OUTFIT.
I CAUGHT HIM FOLLOWING ME.
HE ACTED LIKE I DIDN'T EXIST.
HE RUINED MY CHILDHOOD.
I WAS RESCUED. BY MERMAIDS.
HI, I'M HARRY.
WE'VE MET.
SEVERAL TIMES.
HARRY HAS SOME BLIND SPOTS.
WHAT'S WRONG?

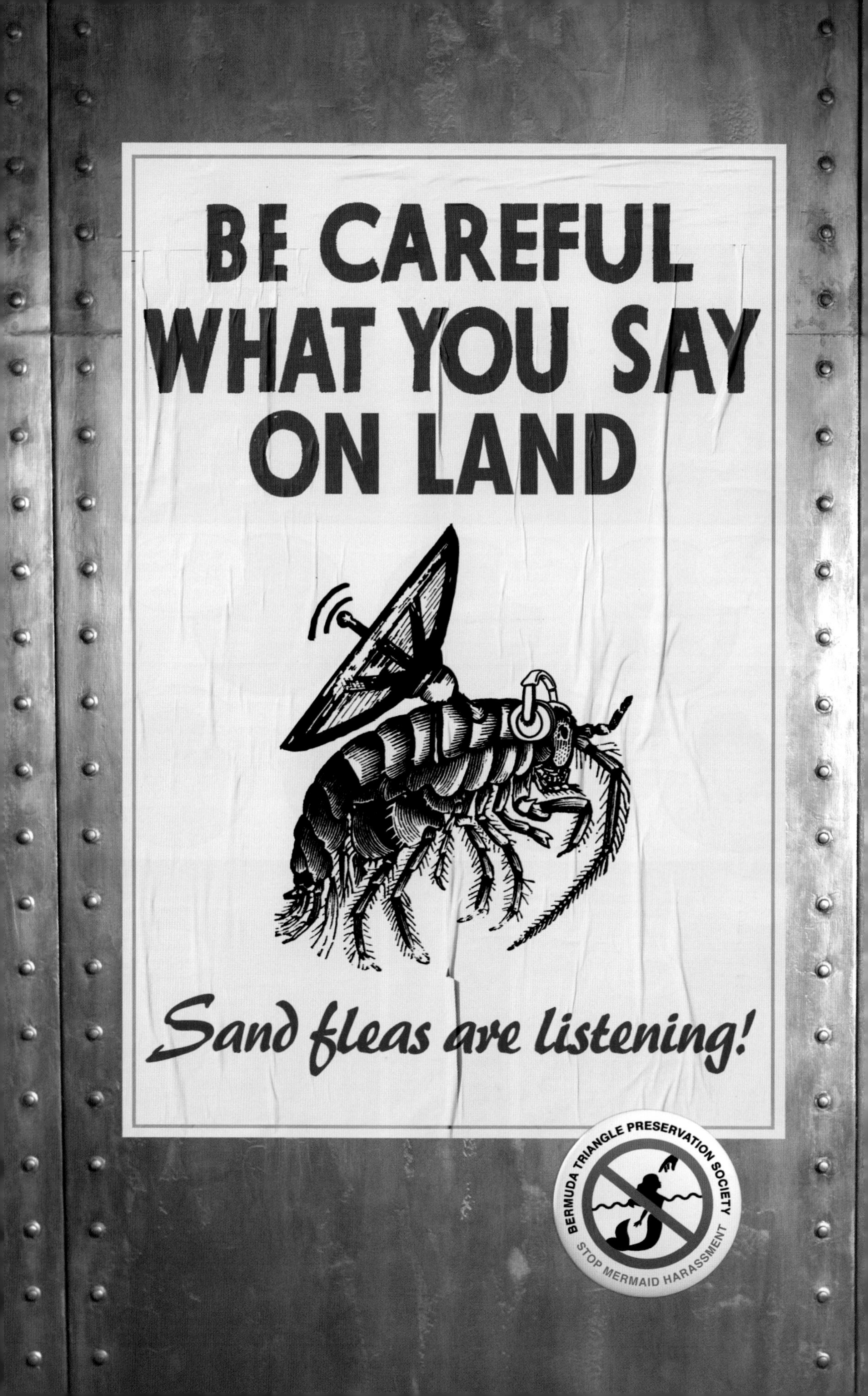
BE CAREFUL
WHAT YOU SAY
ON LAND
Sand fleas are listening!
BERMUDA TRIANGLE PRESERVATION SOCIETY
STOP MERMAID HARASSMENT

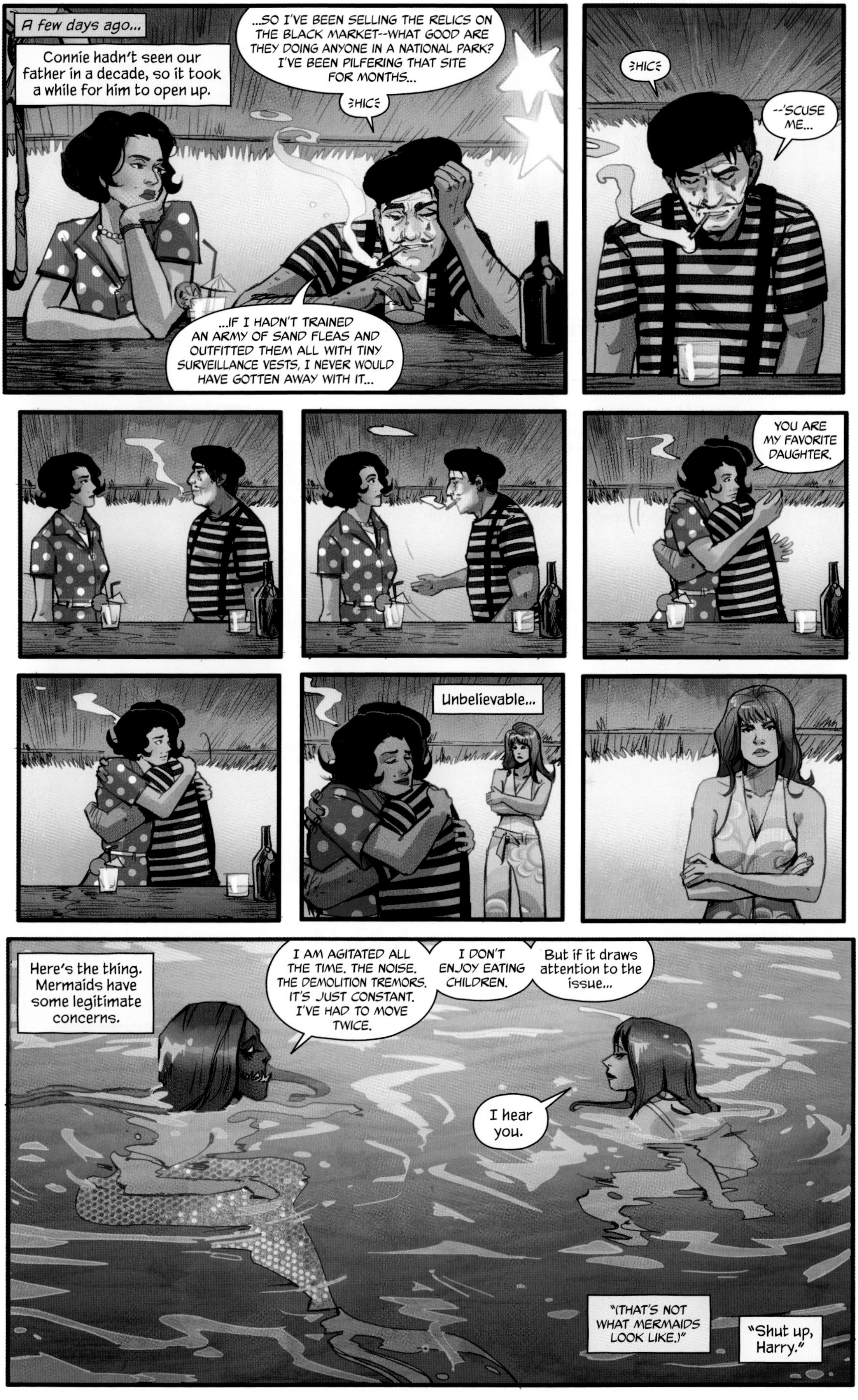
A few days ago...
Connie hadn't seen our father in a decade, so it took a while for him to open up.
...SO I'VE BEEN SELLING THE RELICS ON THE BLACK MARKET--WHAT GOOD ARE THEY DOING ANYONE IN A NATIONAL PARK? I'VE BEEN PILFERING THAT SITE FOR MONTHS...
HIC
...IF I HADN'T TRAINED AN ARMY OF SAND FLEAS AND OUTFITTED THEM ALL WITH TINY SURVEILLANCE VESTS, I NEVER WOULD HAVE GOTTEN AWAY WITH IT...
HIC
--'SCUSE ME...
YOU ARE MY FAVORITE DAUGHTER.
Unbelievable...
Here's the thing. Mermaids have some legitimate concerns.
I AM AGITATED ALL THE TIME. THE NOISE. THE DEMOLITION TREMORS. IT'S JUST CONSTANT. I'VE HAD TO MOVE TWICE.
I DON'T ENJOY EATING CHILDREN.
But if it draws attention to the issue...
I hear you.
"(THAT'S NOT WHAT MERMAIDS LOOK LIKE.)"
"Shut up, Harry."

Man & Mermaid: The definitive history

A TRUE-LIFE BOOKS series

Explore Man & Mermaid for 10 days free.

TRUE-LIFE BOOKS introduces the world's most complete facts and knowledge about mermaids, excitingly explained by leading authorities in handsome volumes delivered to your home. Learn about Exploitation, Suffering, Objectification, and more! Each volume bound in genuine leather with accents of 22kt gold!

Chapter 2:
Poaching
Despite a ban on the international trade in tails and teeth, mermaids are still being poached in large numbers. Tens of thousands of mermaids are being killed every year for their iridescent scales, which are often used to decorate high school prom dresses. The United States is the biggest consumer market for such products.
1
MAN & MERMAID:
HUNTED FOR TAIL AND TEETH

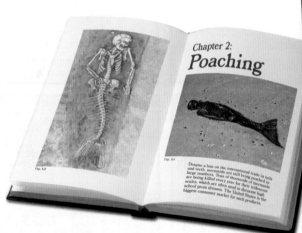

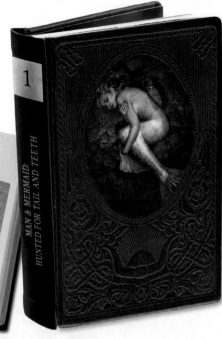

Collect All Ten.

There's no minimum purchase. You can cancel at any time and return any volume within 10 days with no further obligation.

Dive in today and start your journey through the world of Man & Mermaid.

This is the most beautiful gift you can give yourself and your family.

You will enjoy information on every subject significant to the mermaid/man relationship. Pay later! Superbly written, exquisitely illustrated and painstakingly researched by the editors of TRUE-LIFE BOOKS.

EXCLUSIVE OFFER!
Order today for your FREE Mermaid Tooth Pendant.

1
MAN & MERMAID
HUNTED FOR TAIL AND TEETH
2
MAN & MERMAID
THE TRAIL OF TEARS
3
MAN & MERMAID
FISH OR FEMALE?
4
MAN & MERMAID
SAILOR'S DELIGHT
5
MAN & MERMAID
OBJECTIFICATION
6
MAN & MERMAID
EXPLOITATION
7
MAN & MERMAID
INFANTILIZATION
8
MAN & MERMAID
CATCH AND RELEASE
9
MAN & MERMAID
THE MANATEE CONSPIRACY THEORY
10
MAN & MERMAID
SONGS AND POETRY

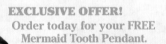

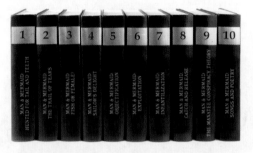

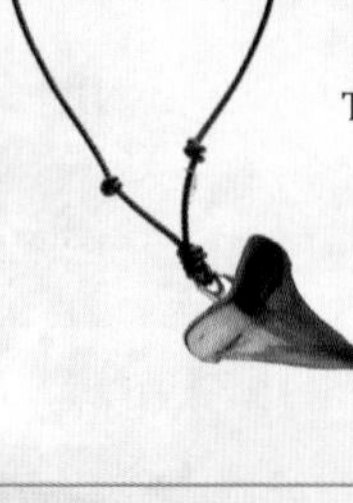

"I use these volumes as the central text of every class I teach."

– Prof. James Guy,
Dean of Marine Cryptozoology,
Denver Community College

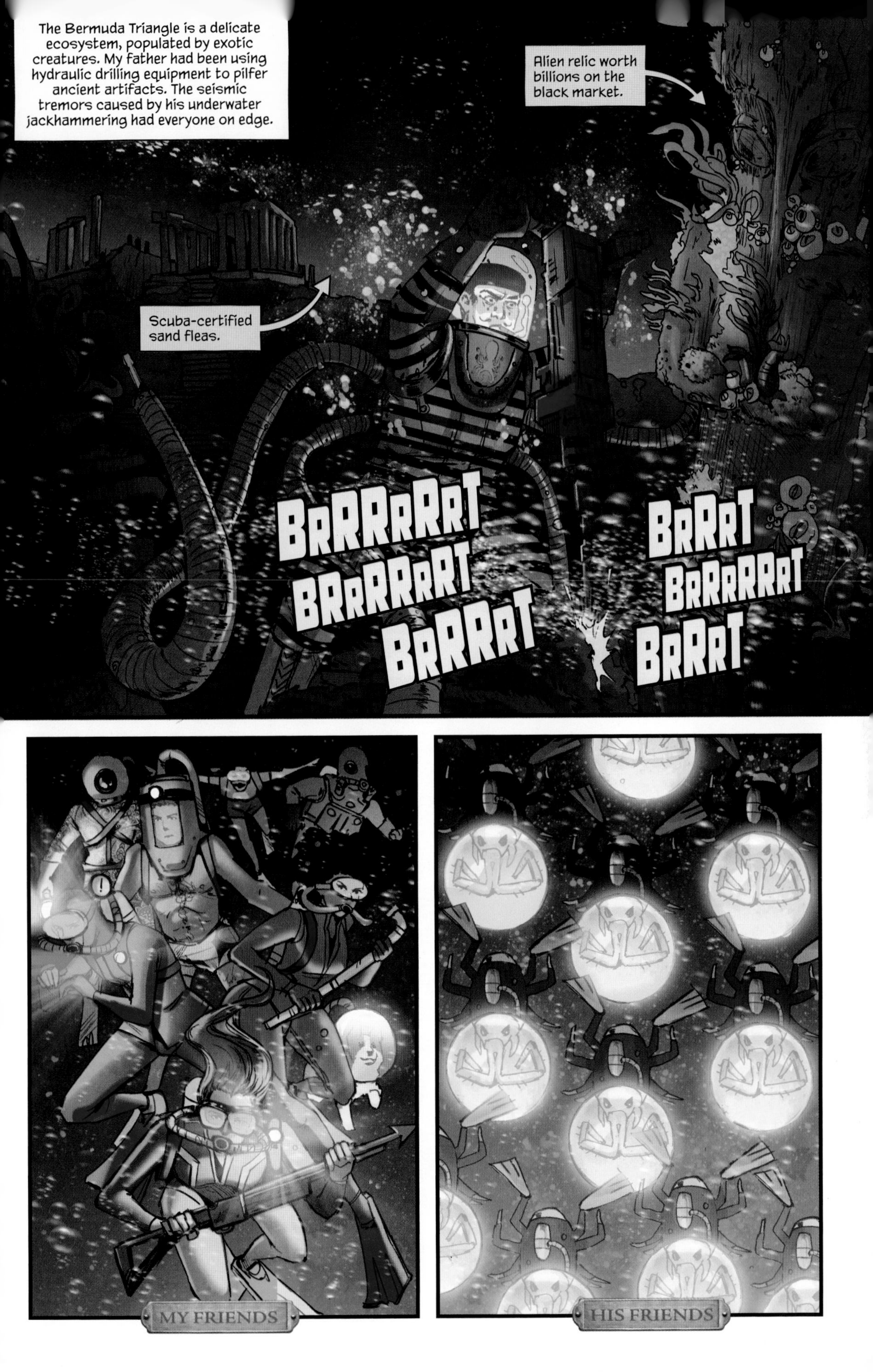
The Bermuda Triangle is a delicate ecosystem, populated by exotic creatures. My father had been using hydraulic drilling equipment to pilfer ancient artifacts. The seismic tremors caused by his underwater jackhammering had everyone on edge.
Alien relic worth billions on the black market.
Scuba-certified sand fleas.
BRRRRRRT BRRRRRRT BRRRRT
BRRRT BRRRRRRT BRRRT
MY FRIENDS
HIS FRIENDS

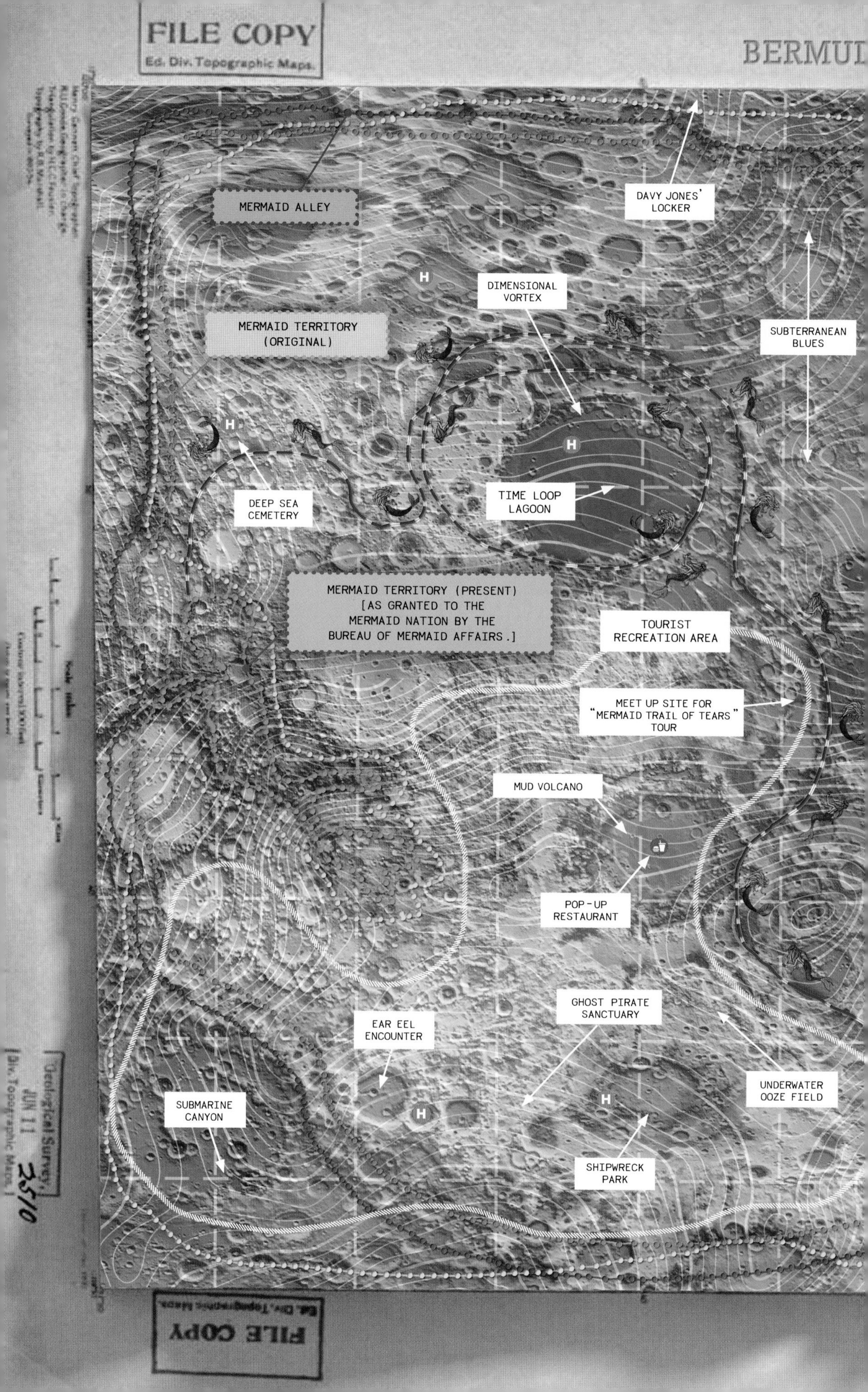
FILE COPY
Ed. Div. Topographic Maps.
MERMAID ALLEY
DAVY JONES' LOCKER
DIMENSIONAL VORTEX
MERMAID TERRITORY (ORIGINAL)
SUBTERRANEAN BLUES
DEEP SEA CEMETERY
TIME LOOP LAGOON
MERMAID TERRITORY (PRESENT) [AS GRANTED TO THE MERMAID NATION BY THE BUREAU OF MERMAID AFFAIRS.]
TOURIST RECREATION AREA
MEET UP SITE FOR "MERMAID TRAIL OF TEARS" TOUR
MUD VOLCANO
POP-UP RESTAURANT
GHOST PIRATE SANCTUARY
EAR EEL ENCOUNTER
UNDERWATER OOZE FIELD
SUBMARINE CANYON
SHIPWRECK PARK
FILE COPY
Ed. Div. Topographic Maps.

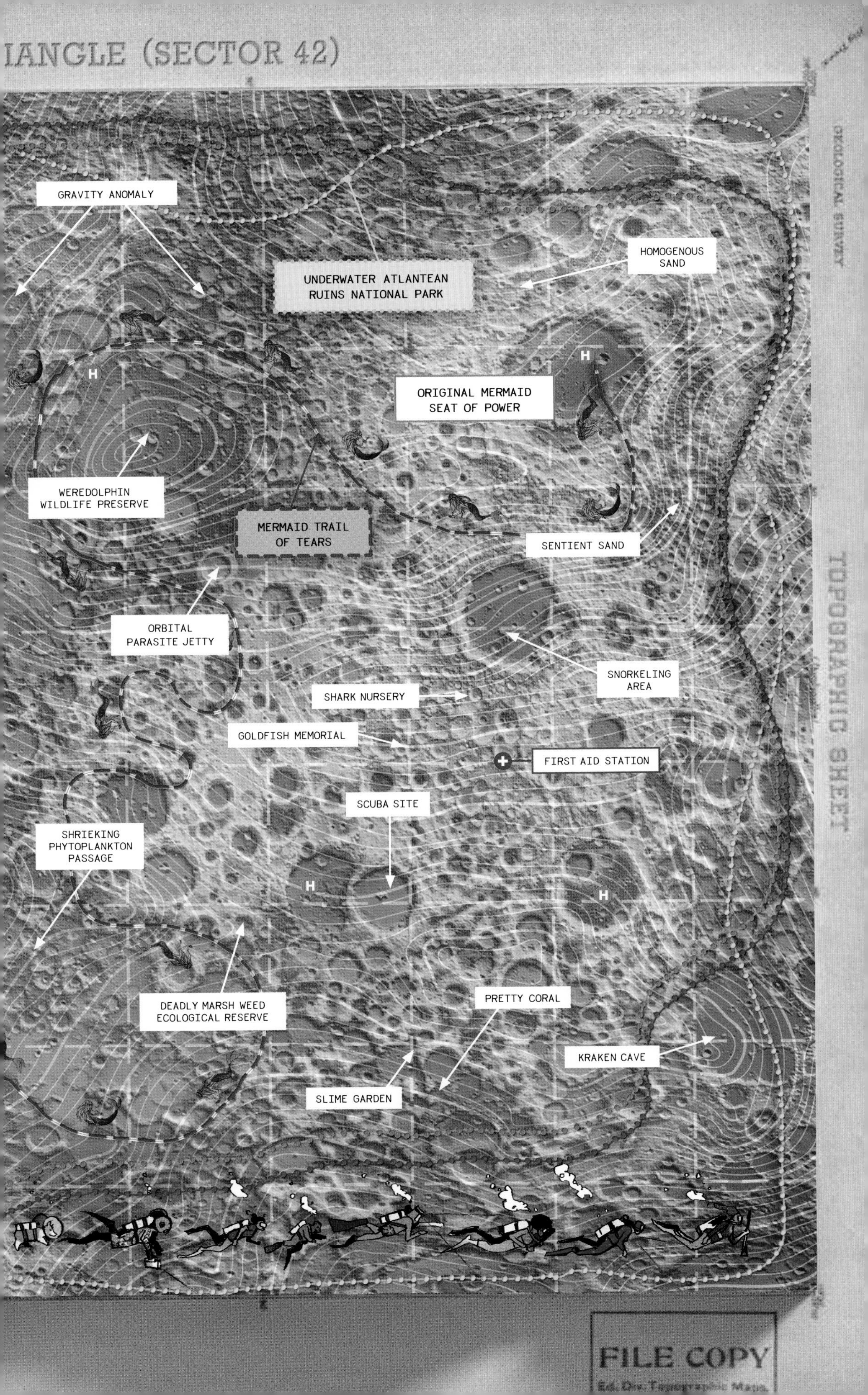
IANGLE (SECTOR 42)
GRAVITY ANOMALY
UNDERWATER ATLANTEAN RUINS NATIONAL PARK
HOMOGENOUS SAND
ORIGINAL MERMAID SEAT OF POWER
WEREDOLPHIN WILDLIFE PRESERVE
MERMAID TRAIL OF TEARS
SENTIENT SAND
ORBITAL PARASITE JETTY
SNORKELING AREA
SHARK NURSERY
GOLDFISH MEMORIAL
FIRST AID STATION
SCUBA SITE
SHRIEKING PHYTOPLANKTON PASSAGE
DEADLY MARSH WEED ECOLOGICAL RESERVE
PRETTY CORAL
KRAKEN CAVE
SLIME GARDEN
GEOLOGICAL SURVEY
TOPOGRAPHIC SHEET
FILE COPY
Ed. Div. Topographic Maps.

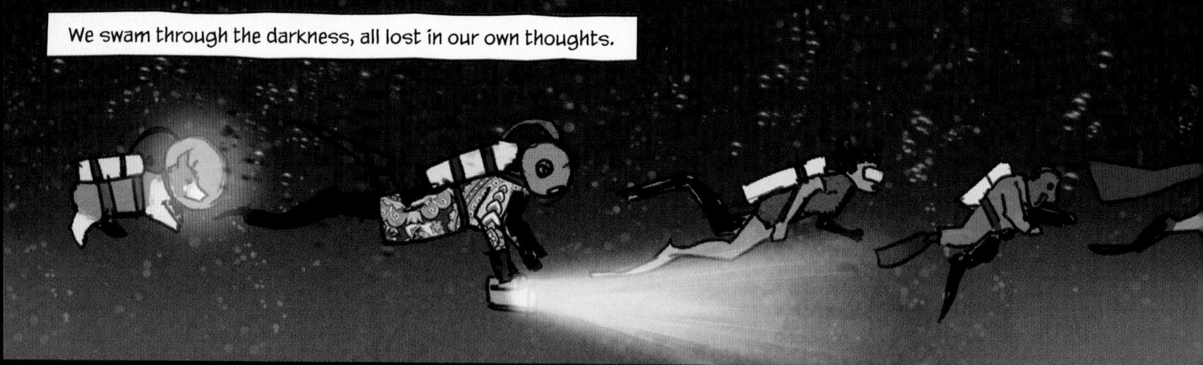
We swam through the darkness, all lost in our own thoughts.

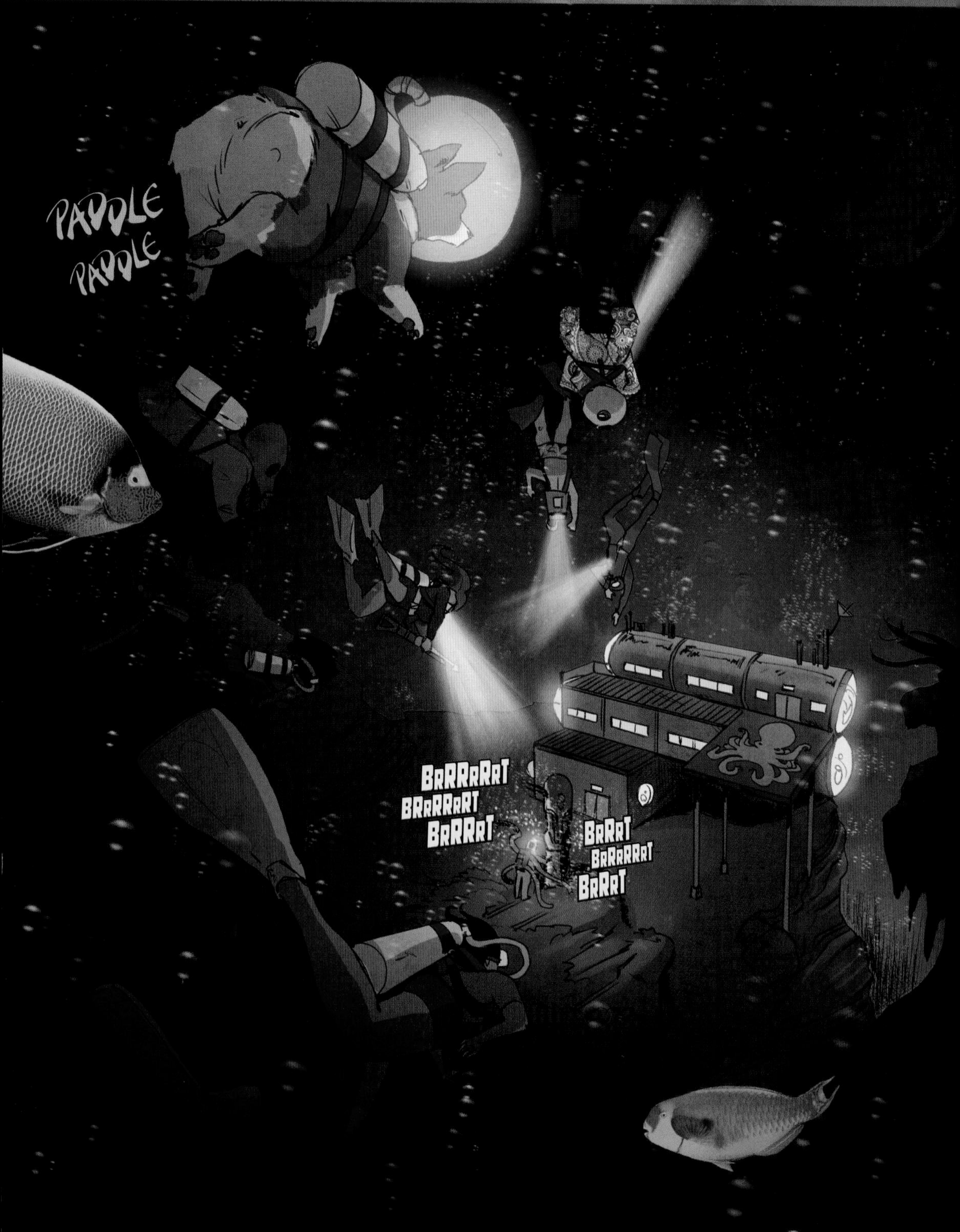
PADDLE
PADDLE
BRRRRRRT
BRRRRRRT
BRRRRT
BRRRT
BRRRRRRT
BRRRT

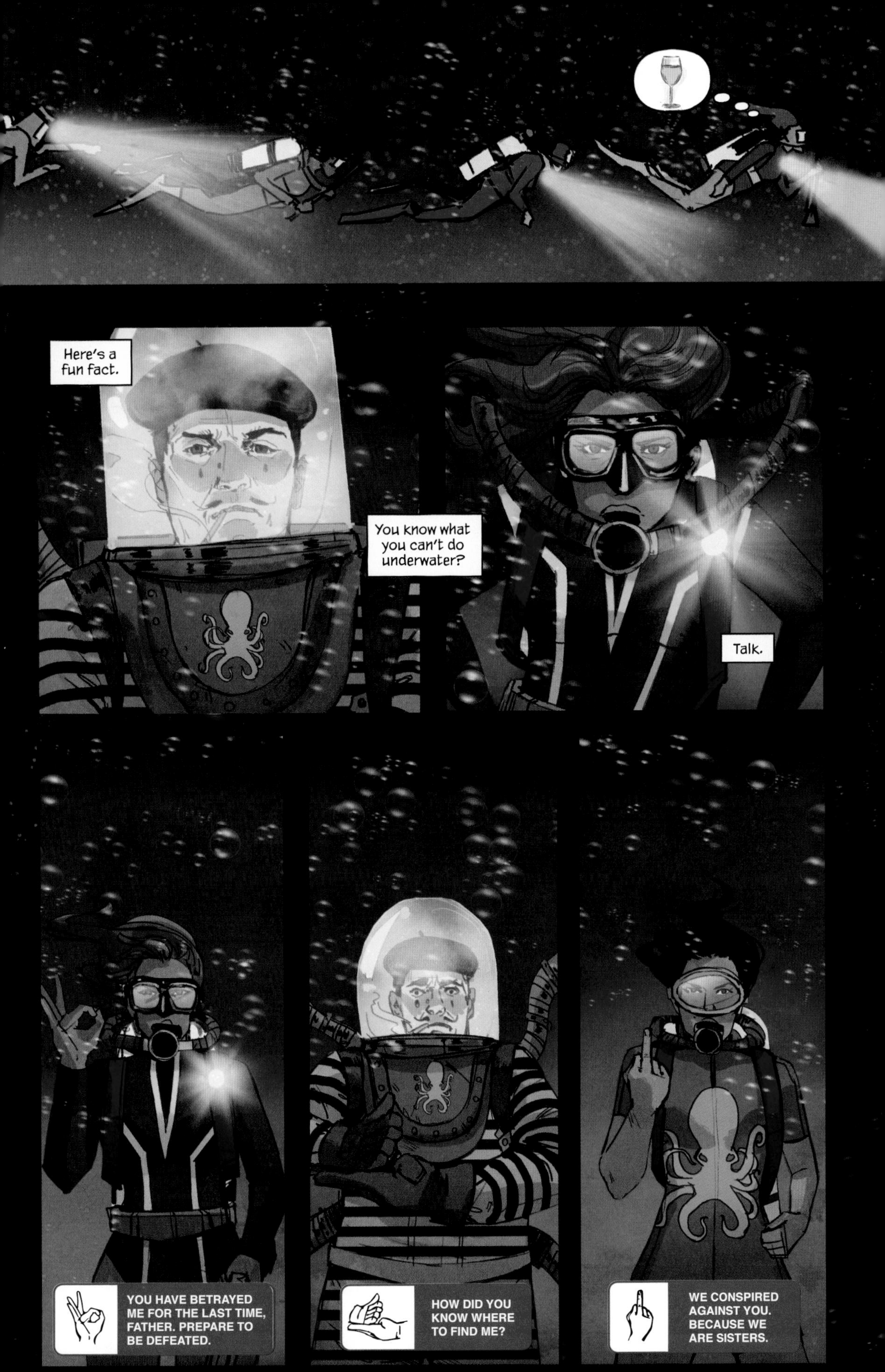
Here's a fun fact.
You know what you can't do underwater?
Talk.
YOU HAVE BETRAYED ME FOR THE LAST TIME, FATHER. PREPARE TO BE DEFEATED.
HOW DID YOU KNOW WHERE TO FIND ME?
WE CONSPIRED AGAINST YOU. BECAUSE WE ARE SISTERS.

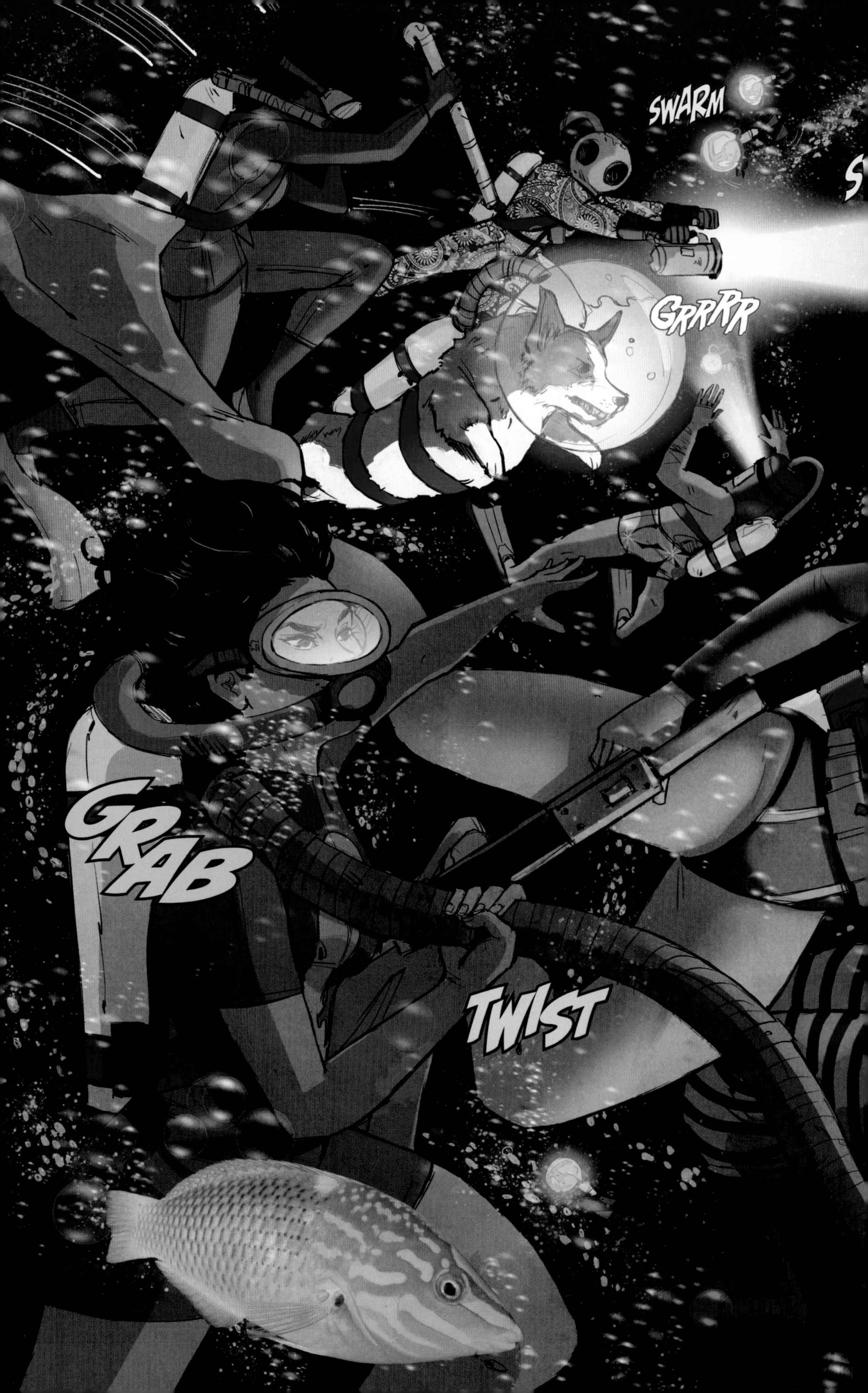
SWARM
GRRRR
GRAB
TWIST

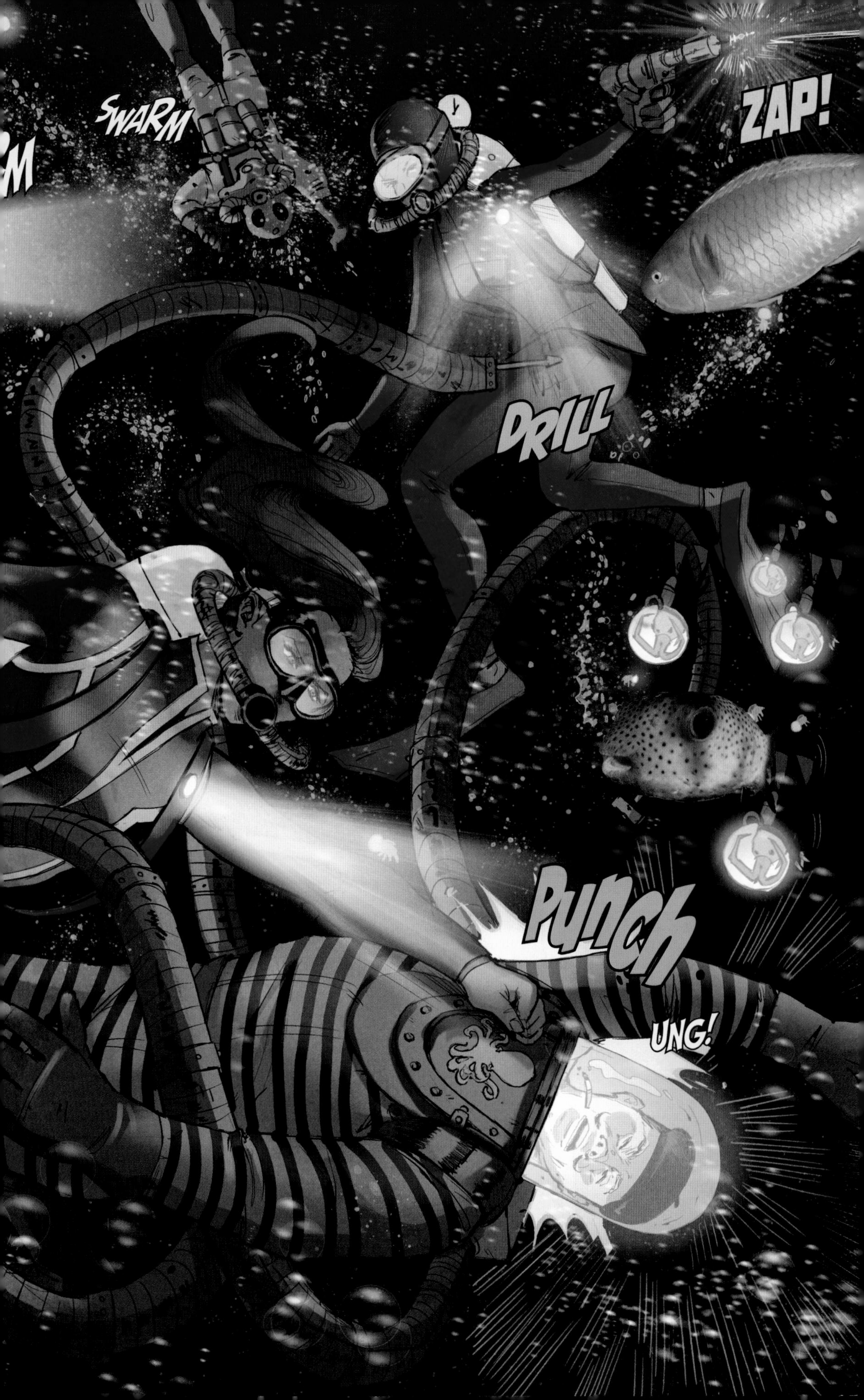
SWARM
ZAP!
DRILL
Punch
UNG!

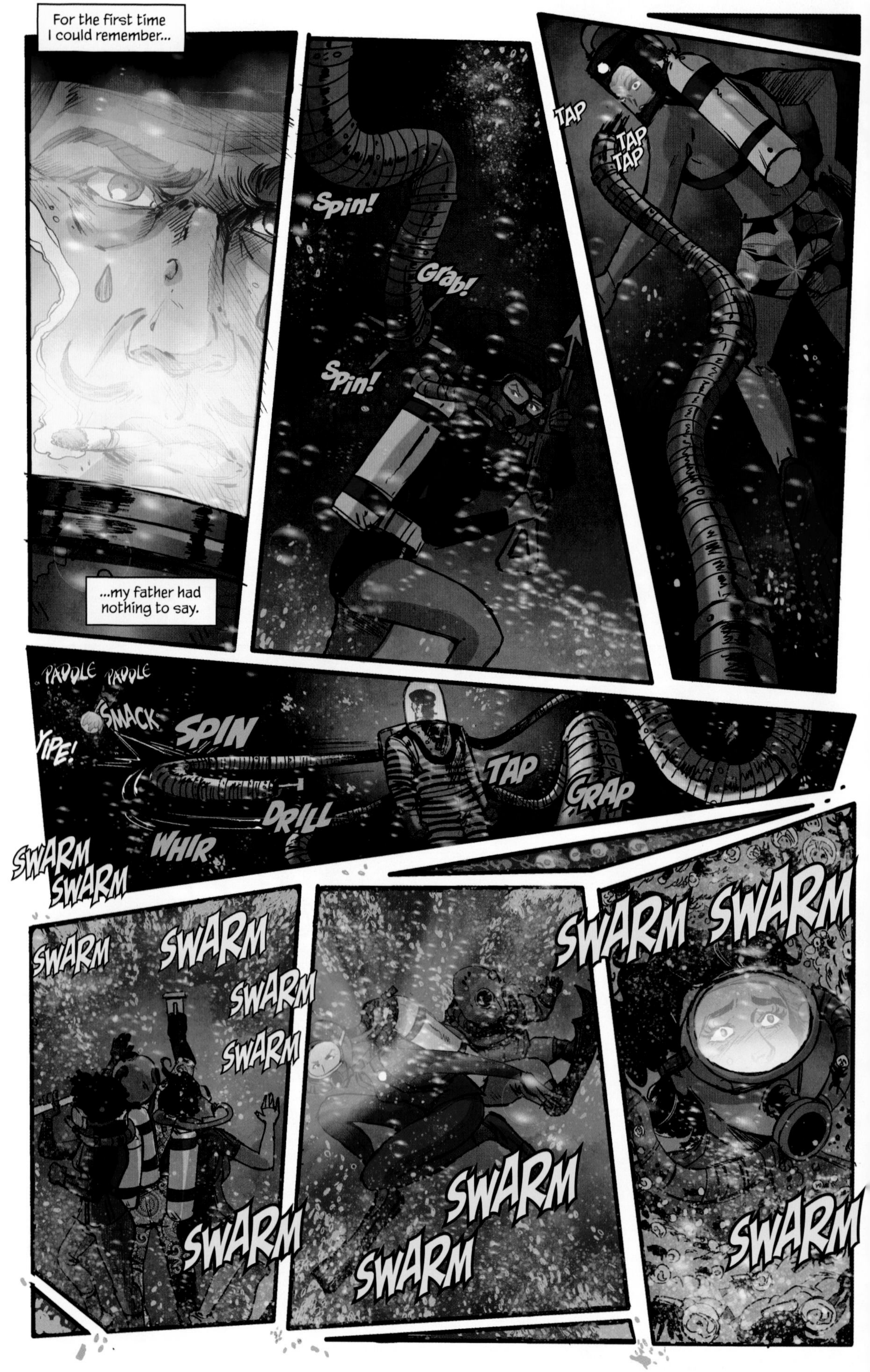
For the first time I could remember...
...my father had nothing to say.
Spin!
Grab!
Spin!
TAP
TAP TAP
PADDLE PADDLE
SMACK
YIPE!
SPIN
TAP
GRAP
DRILL
WHIR
SWARM SWARM
SWARM
SWARM
SWARM
SWARM
SWARM
SWARM
SWARM
SWARM SWARM
SWARM

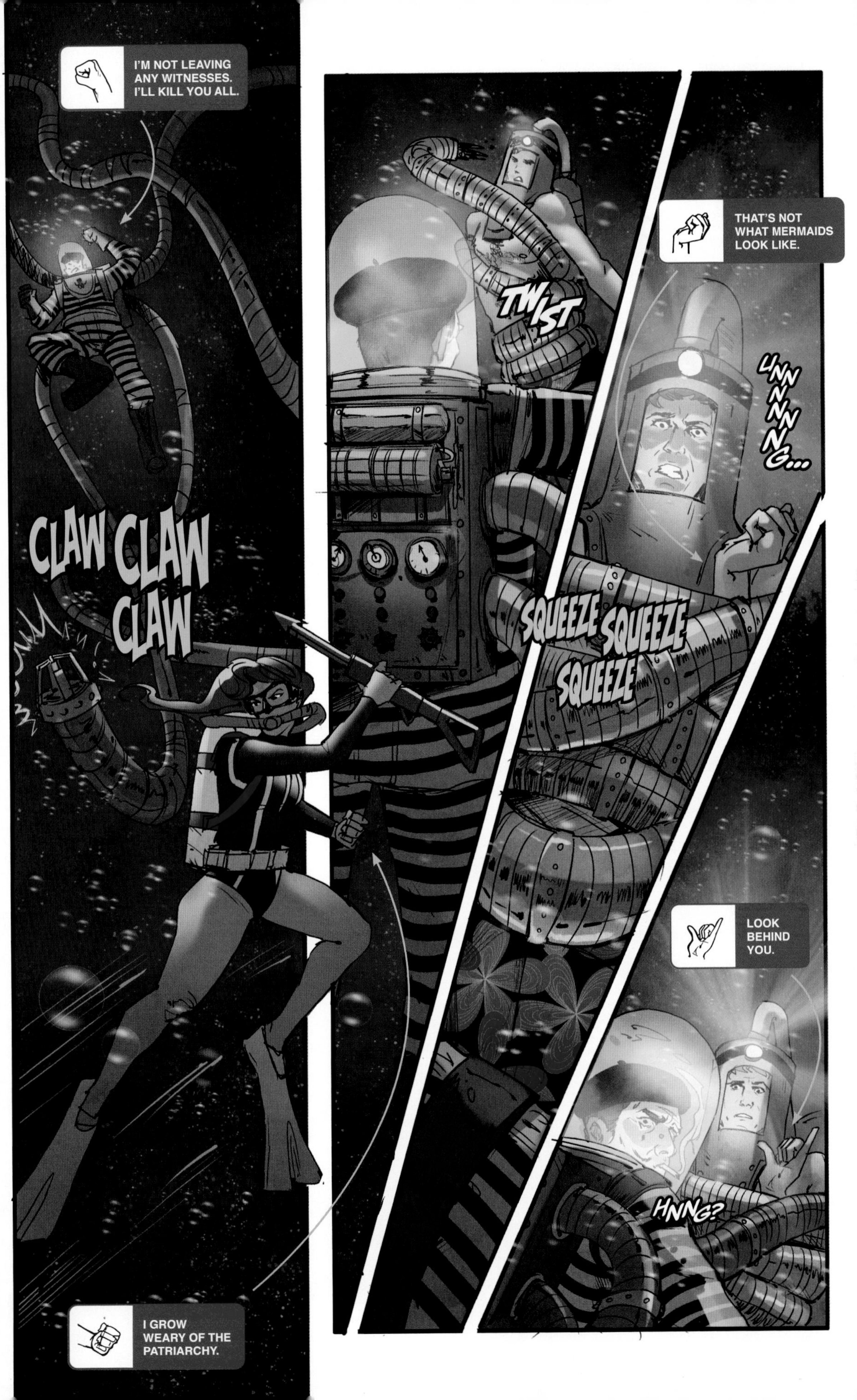

I'M NOT LEAVING ANY WITNESSES. I'LL KILL YOU ALL.
CLAW CLAW CLAW
I GROW WEARY OF THE PATRIARCHY.
TWIST
THAT'S NOT WHAT MERMAIDS LOOK LIKE.
UNNNNNG...
SQUEEZE SQUEEZE SQUEEZE
LOOK BEHIND YOU.
HNNG?

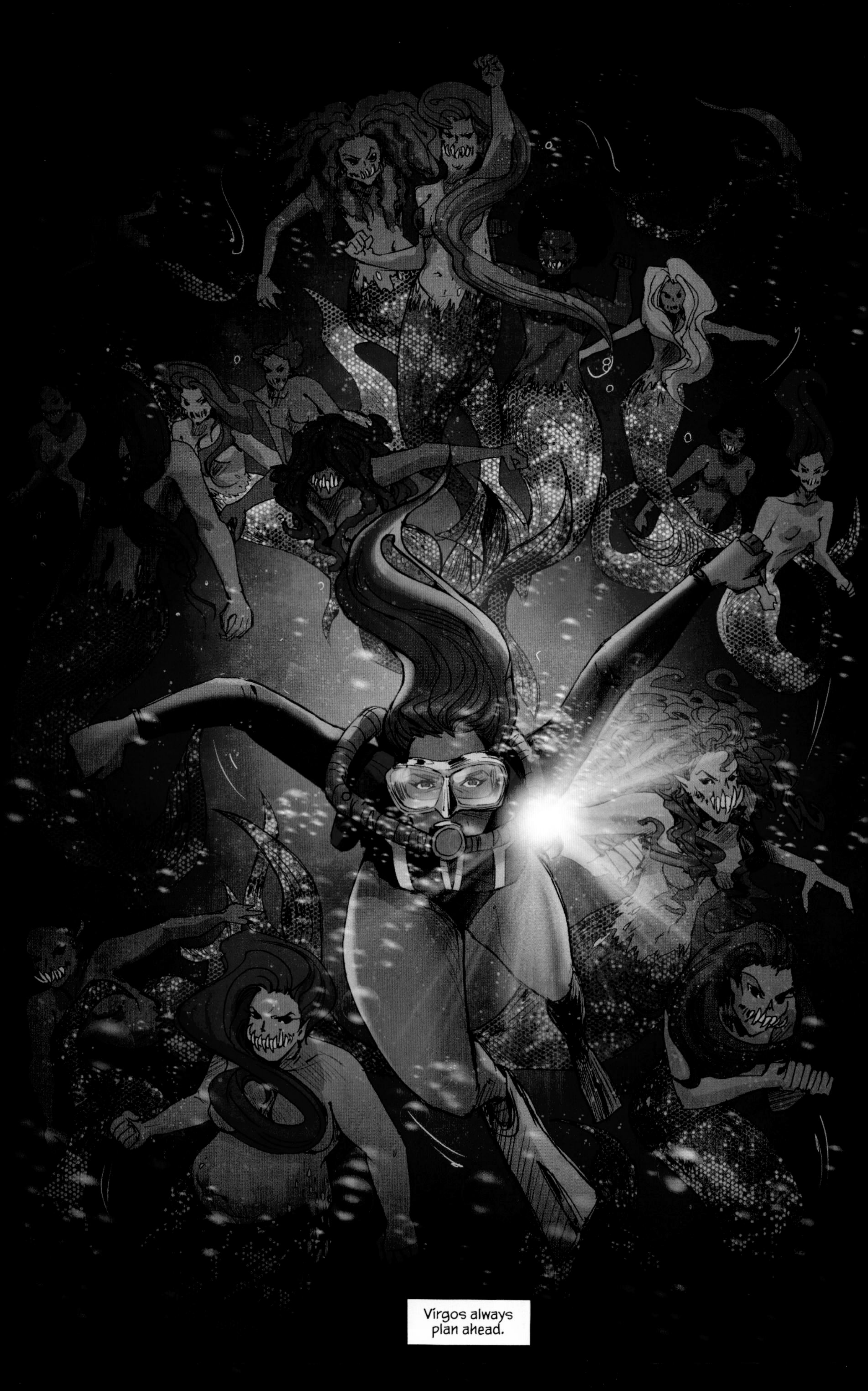
Virgos always plan ahead.

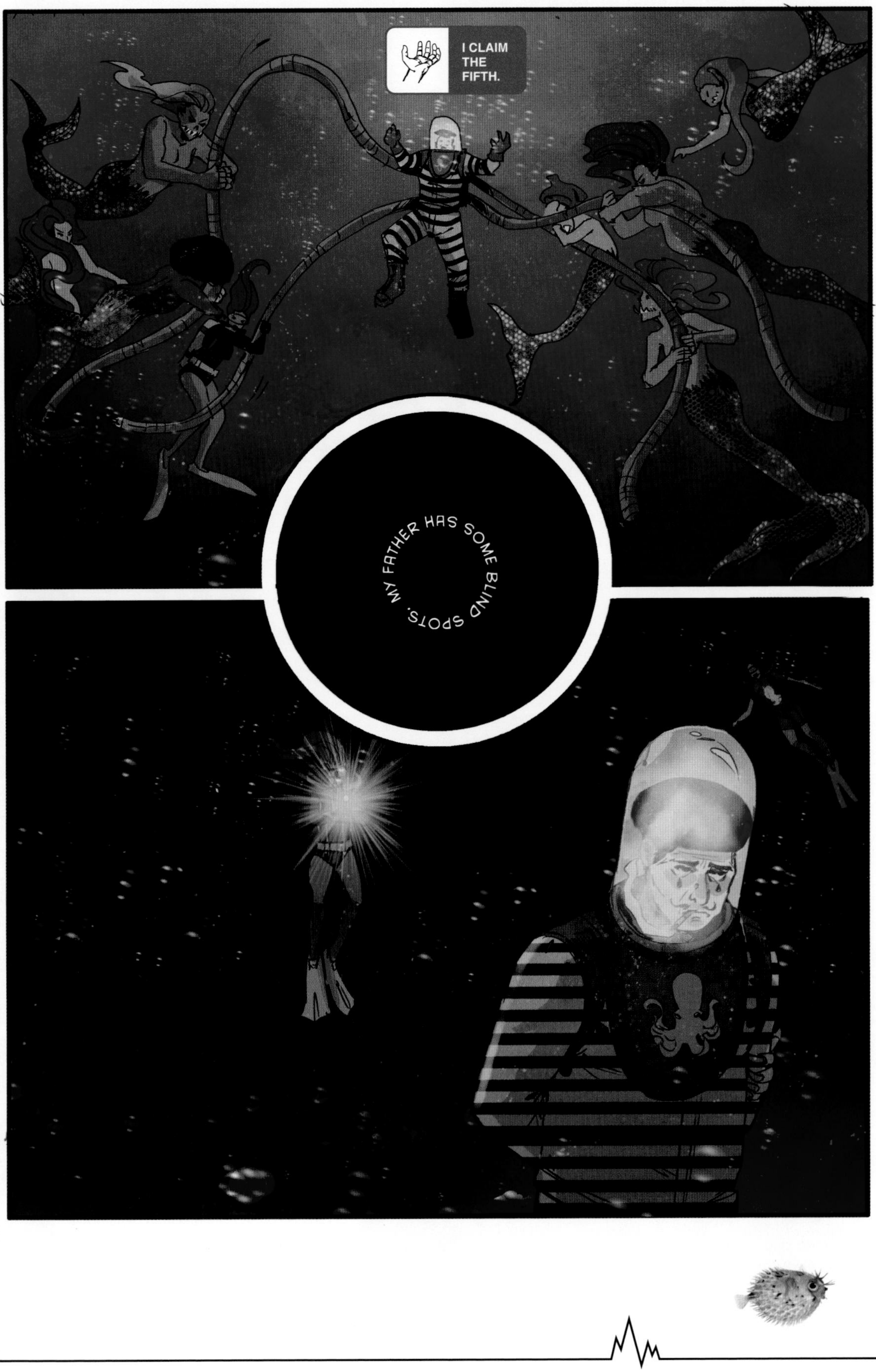
I CLAIM THE FIFTH.
MY FATHER HAS SOME BLIND SPOTS.

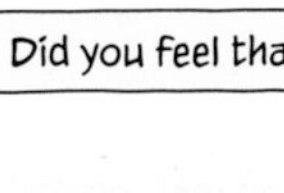

Did you feel that?

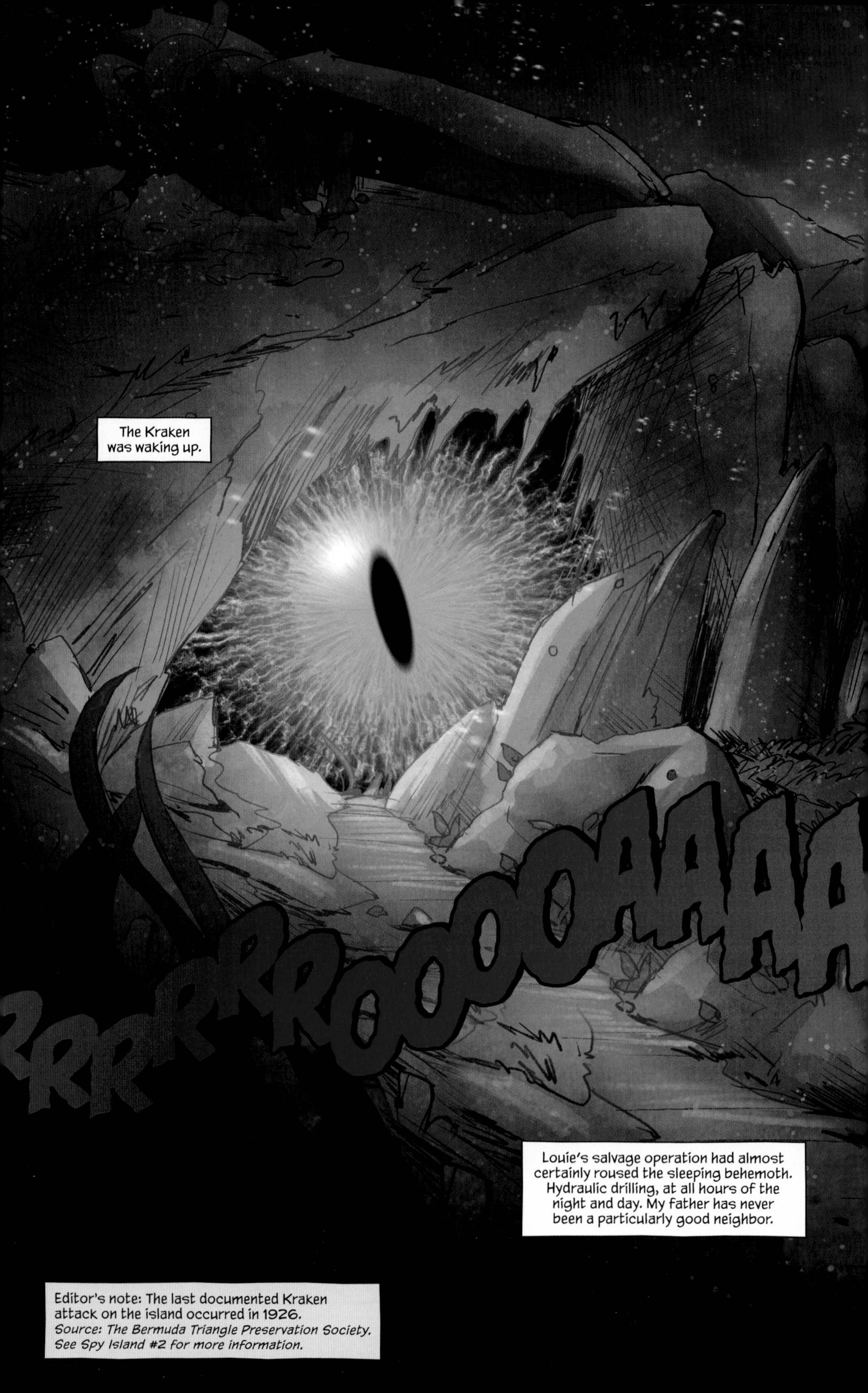
The Kraken was waking up.
RRRRROOOOOAAAAA
Louie's salvage operation had almost certainly roused the sleeping behemoth. Hydraulic drilling, at all hours of the night and day. My father has never been a particularly good neighbor.
Editor's note: The last documented Kraken attack on the island occurred in 1926.
Source: The Bermuda Triangle Preservation Society.
See Spy Island #2 for more information.

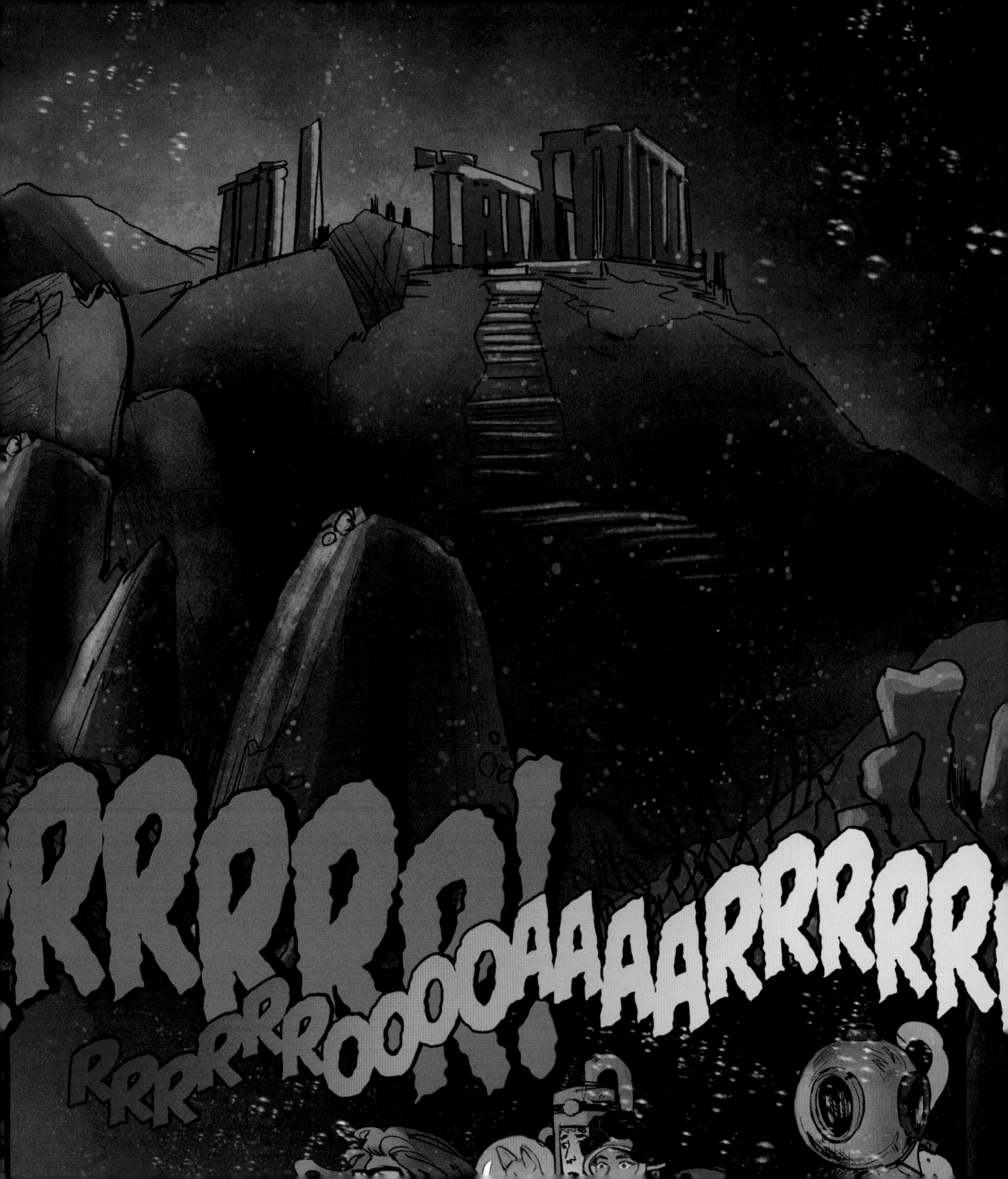
RRRRRRRROOOOOOAAAAARRRRR

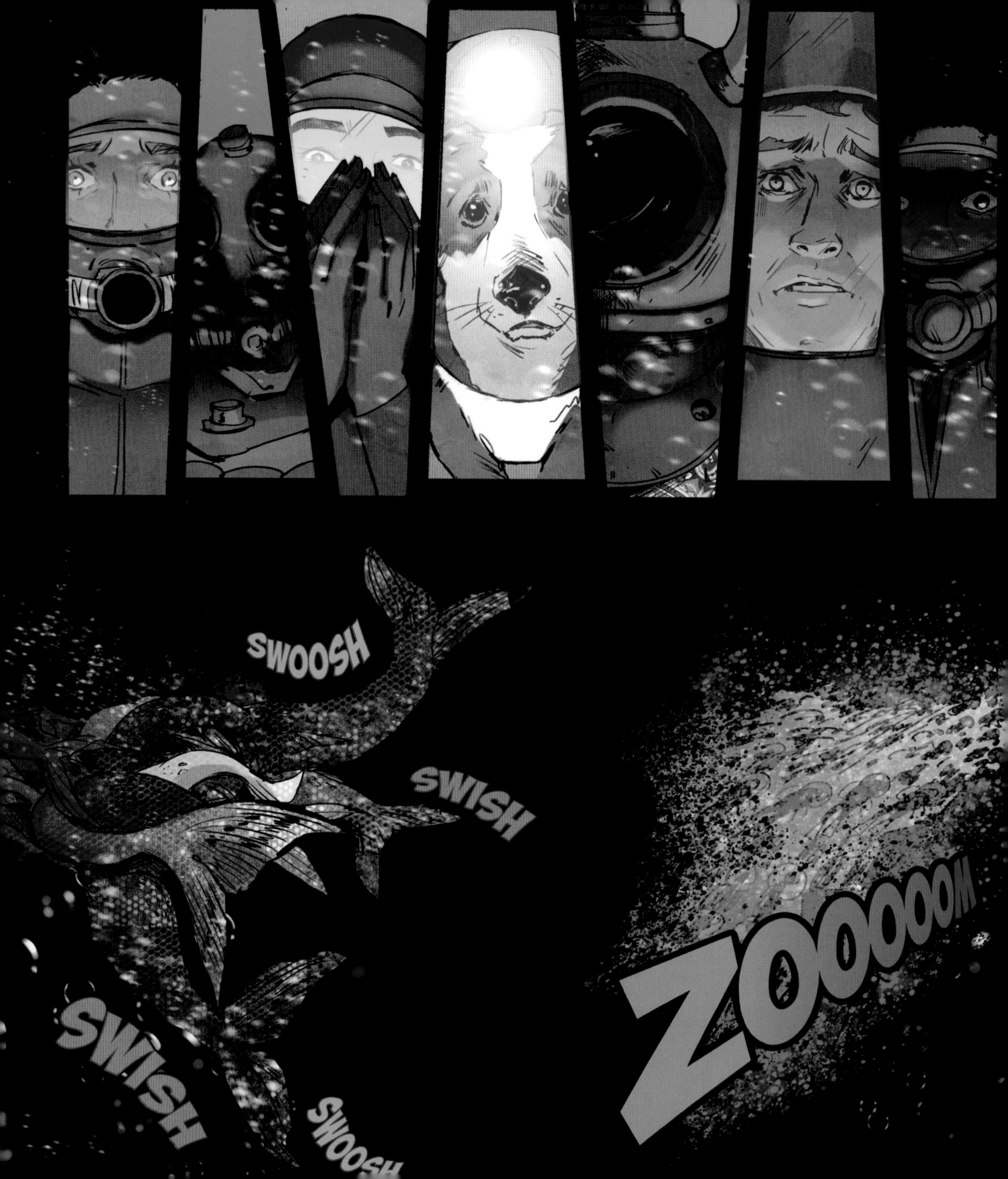
SWOOSH
SWISH
SWISH
SWOOSH
ZOOOOOM

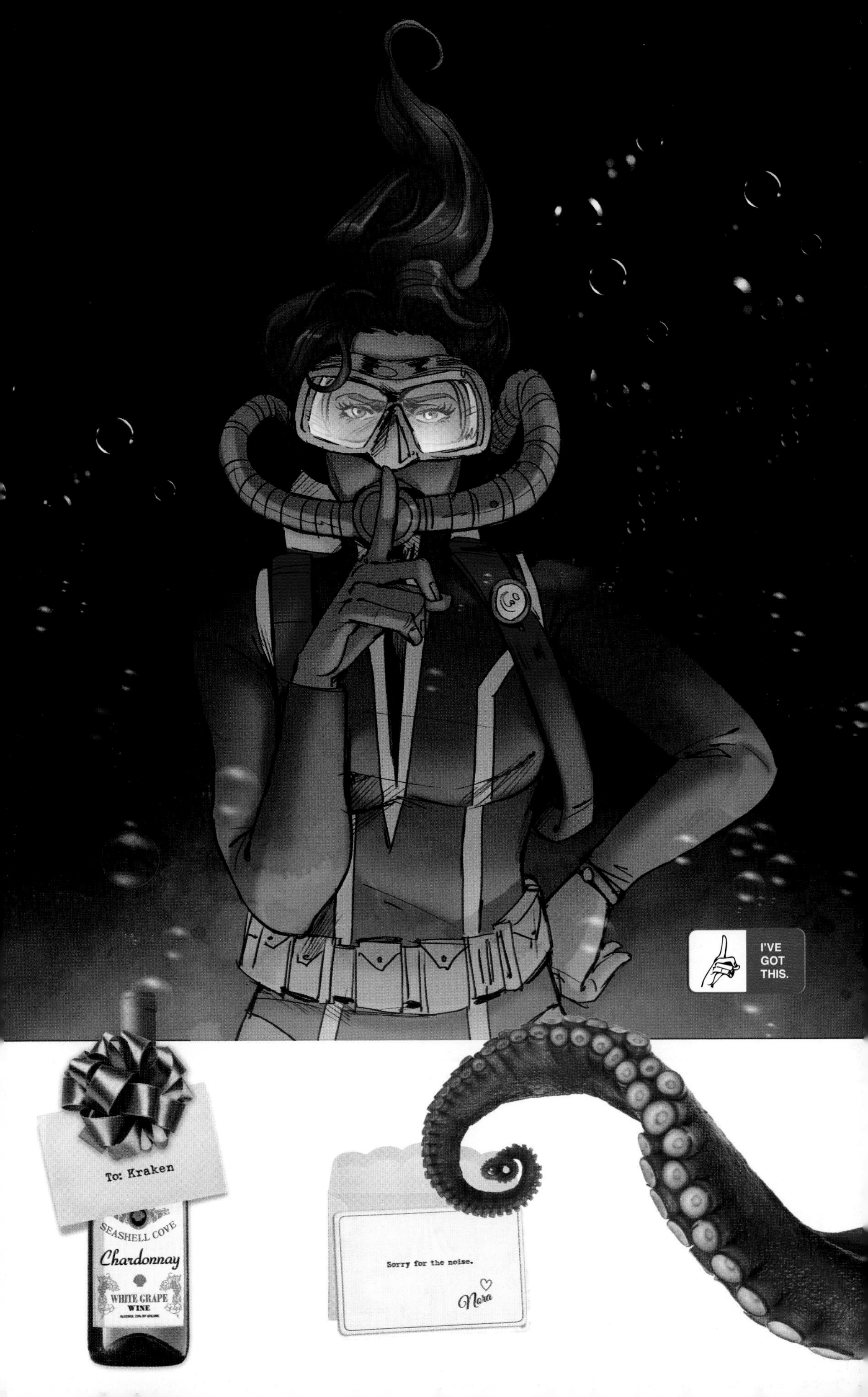
I'VE GOT THIS.
To: Kraken
SEASHELL COVE
Chardonnay
WHITE GRAPE
WINE
Sorry for the noise.
Nora

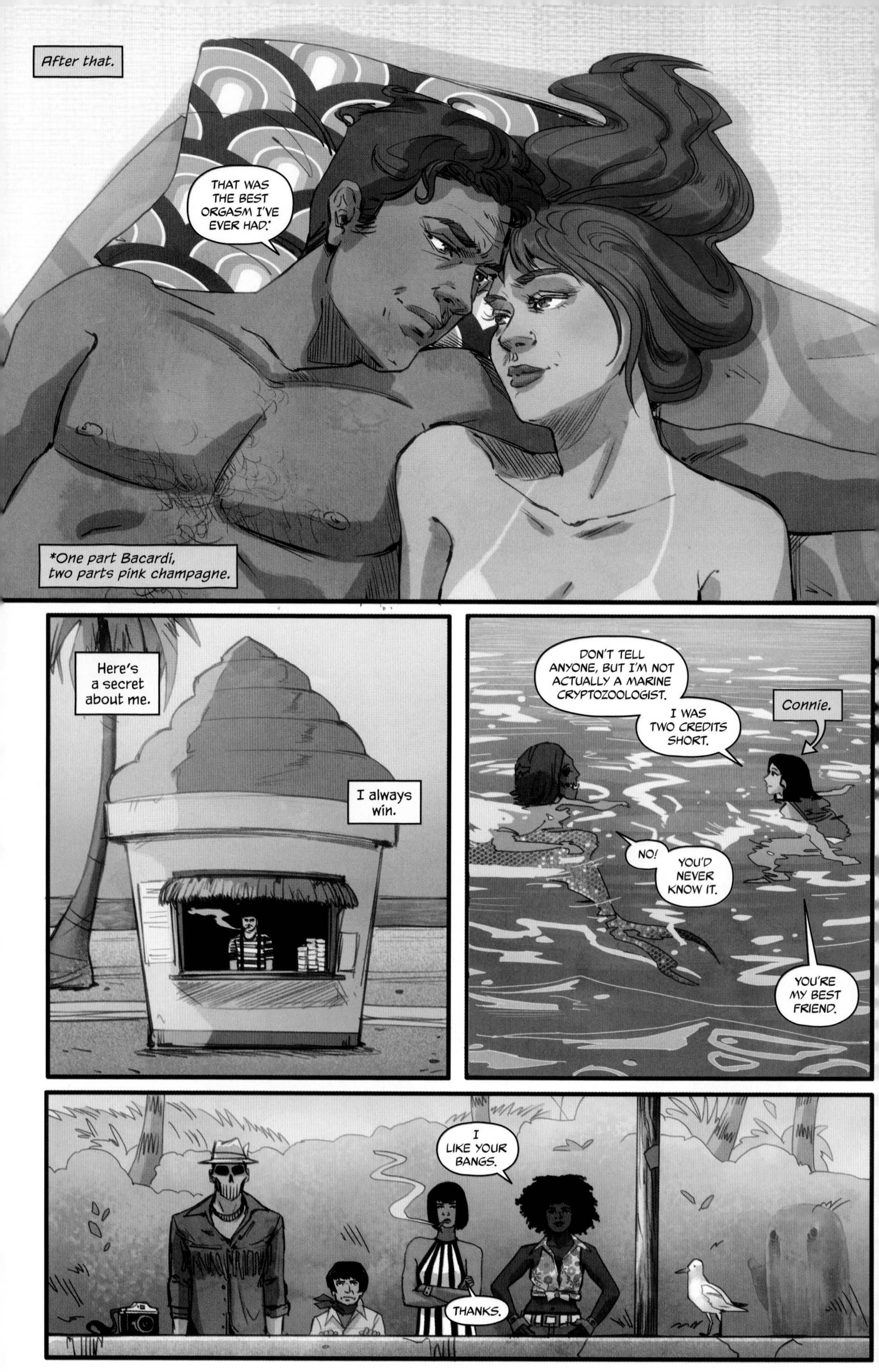

After that.
THAT WAS THE BEST ORGASM I'VE EVER HAD.*
*One part Bacardi, two parts pink champagne.
Here's a secret about me.
I always win.
DON'T TELL ANYONE, BUT I'M NOT ACTUALLY A MARINE CRYPTOZOOLOGIST.
I WAS TWO CREDITS SHORT.
Connie.
NO!
YOU'D NEVER KNOW IT.
YOU'RE MY BEST FRIEND.
I LIKE YOUR BANGS.
THANKS.

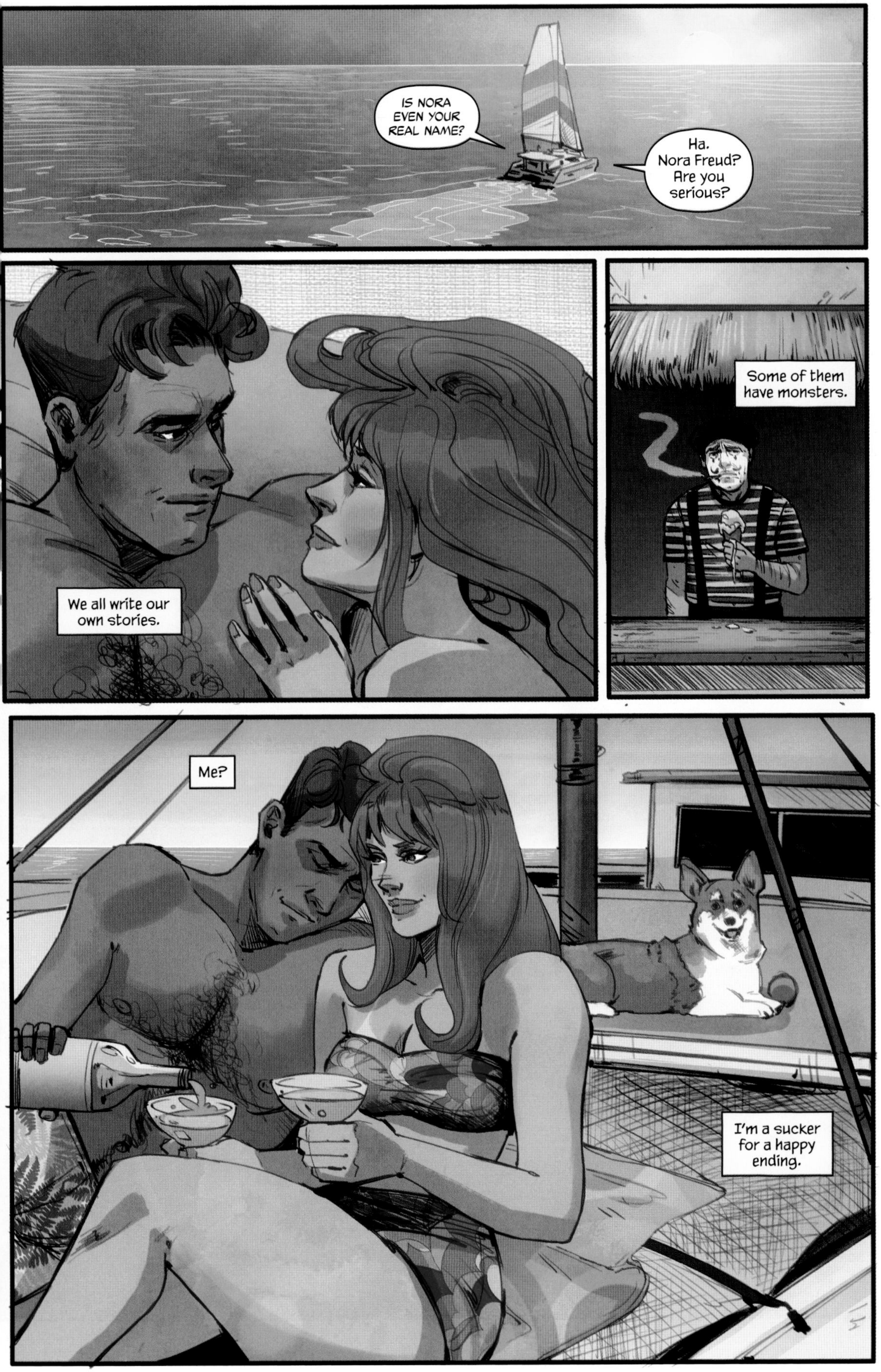
IS NORA EVEN YOUR REAL NAME?
Ha. Nora Freud? Are you serious?
We all write our own stories.
Some of them have monsters.
Me?
I'm a sucker for a happy ending.

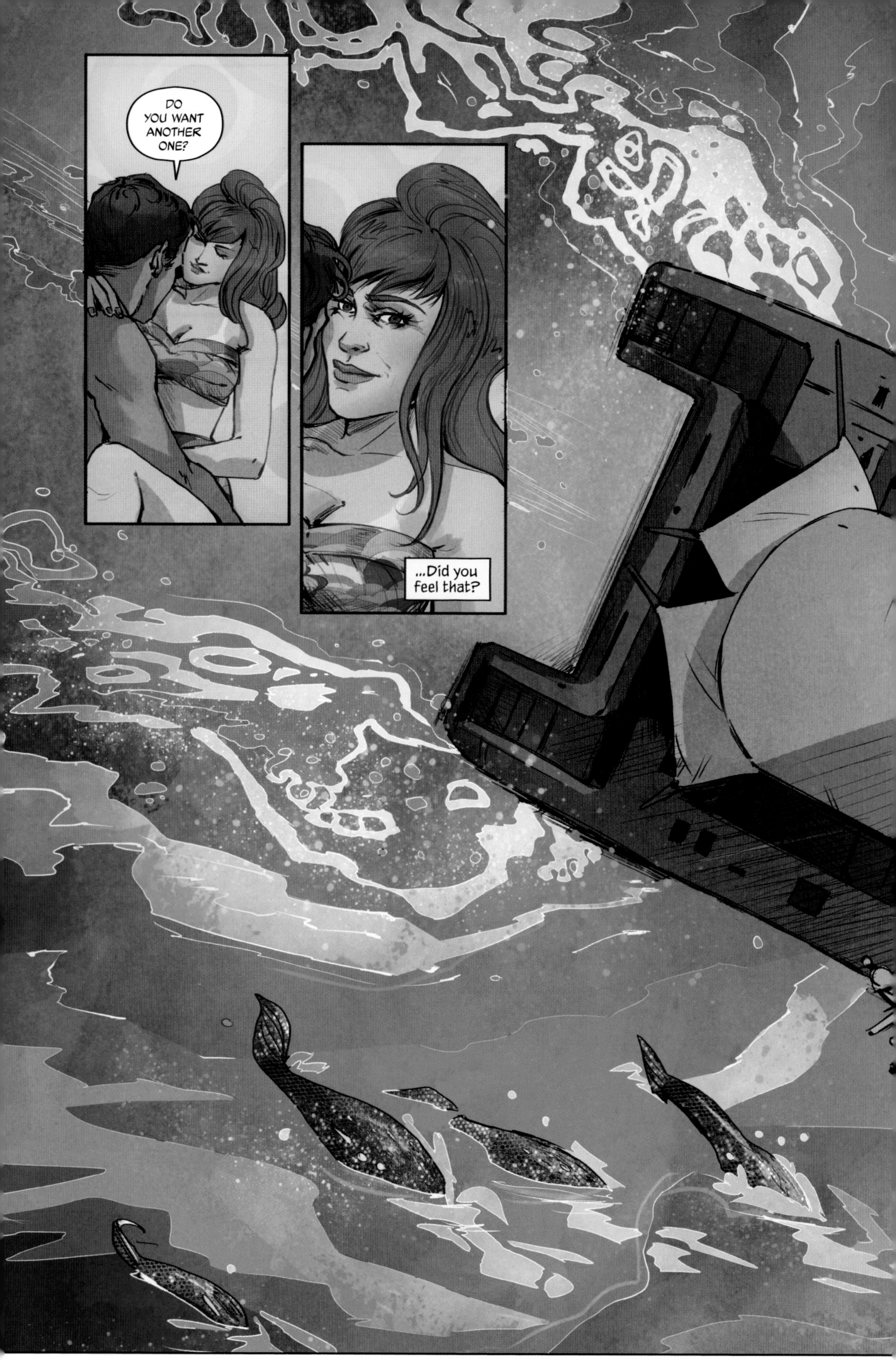
DO YOU WANT ANOTHER ONE?
...Did you feel that?

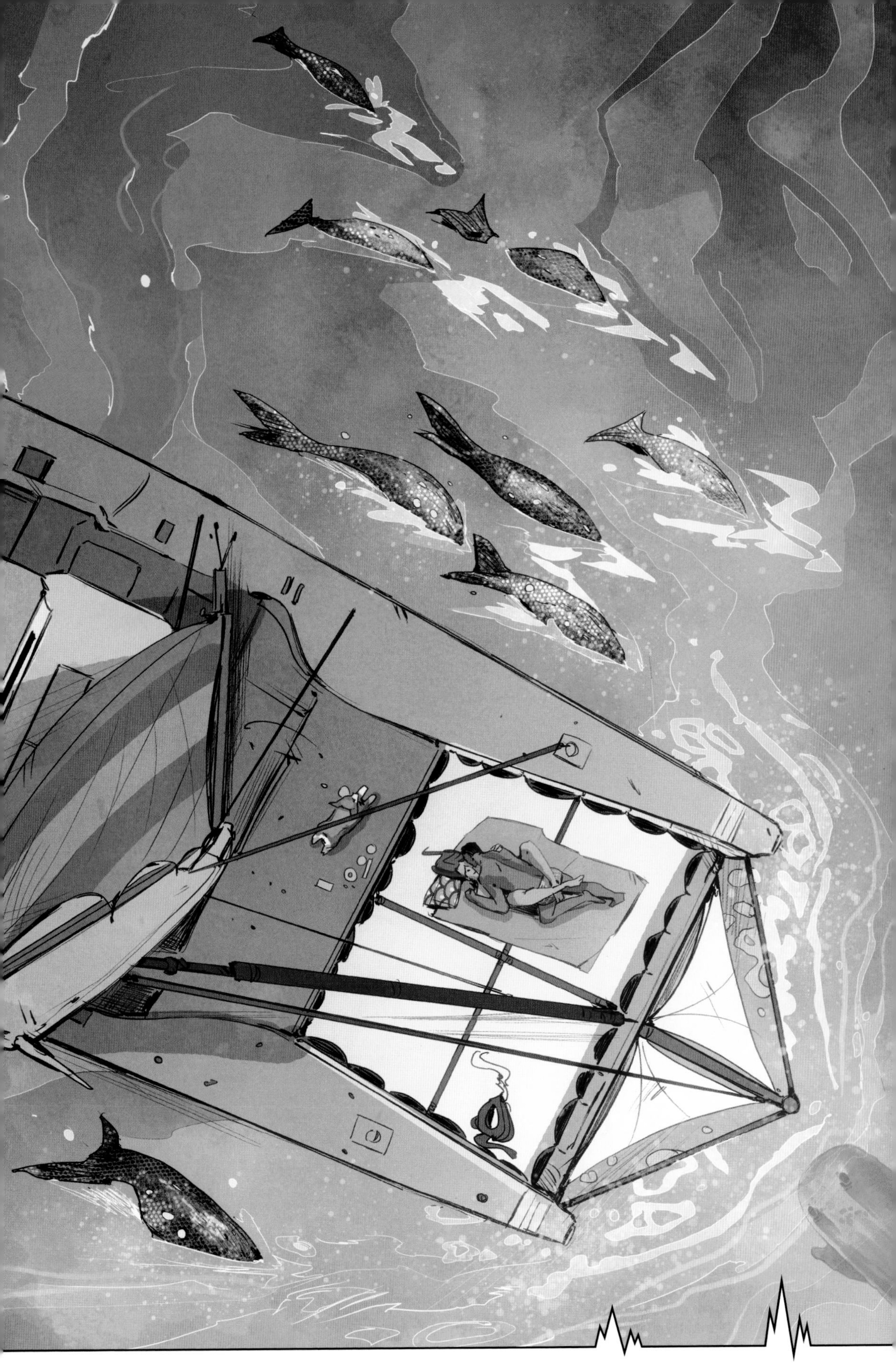

Now enjoy *Orgasms* on-the-go!

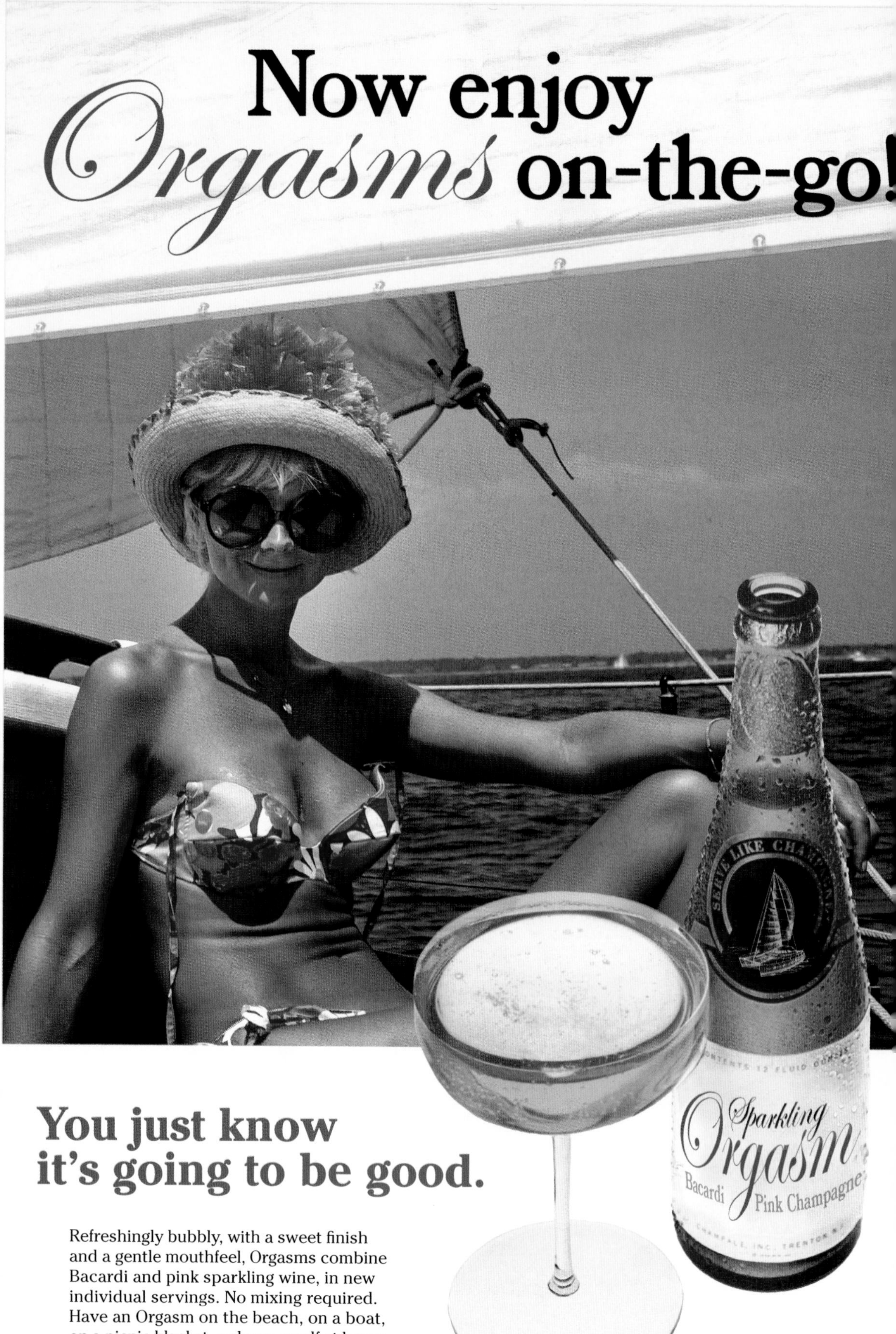
Sparkling
Orgasm
Bacardi
Pink Champagne

You just know it's going to be good.

Refreshingly bubbly, with a sweet finish and a gentle mouthfeel, Orgasms combine Bacardi and pink sparkling wine, in new individual servings. No mixing required. Have an Orgasm on the beach, on a boat, on a picnic blanket, or by yourself at home.

You're worth it.

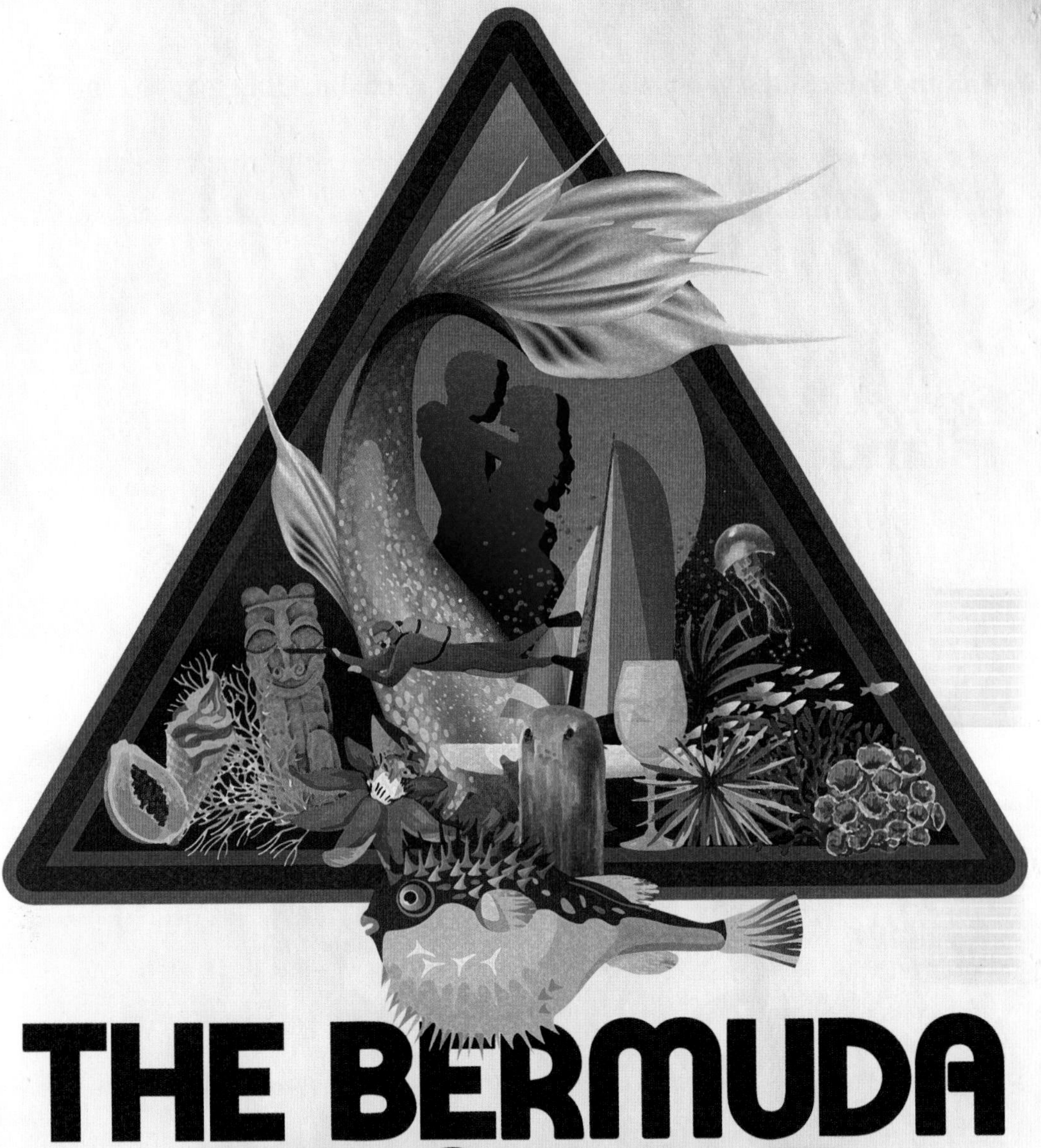

THE BERMUDA TRIANGLE

Every now and then, I feel something down below. You must feel it too.

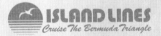

ISLAND LINES
Cruise The Bermuda Triangle

many happy returns

Revisit the excursions you have enjoyed on Spy Island. COLLECT ALL 9!

Issue #1

a

#1
Spy Island
A Bermuda Triangle Mystery

b

SPY ISLAND
BERMUDA TRIANGLE MYSTERY

c

#1
SPYISLAND
A BERMUDA TRIANGLE MYSTERY

Issue #2

a

Spy Island
A BERMUDA TRIANGLE MYSTERY
CAIN MITERNIQUE MCCALL ROSENBERG CARAMAGNA

b

#2
Spy Island
A BERMUDA TRIANGLE MYSTERY
Cain · Miternique · McCall · Rosenberg · Caramagna

Issue #3

a

#3
SPY ISLAND
A Bermuda Triangle Mystery

b

#3
Spy Island
A Bermuda Triangle Mystery
Cain Miternique McCall Rosenberg Caramagna

Issue #4

a

SPY ISLAND
A BERMUDA TRIANGLE MYSTERY

b

SPY ISLAND
T-120
A Bermuda Triangle Mystery
VHS
CHELSEA CAIN
#4

Cover Art Design by Lia Miternique, 2020

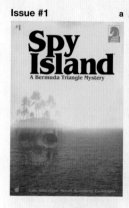

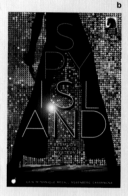

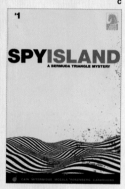

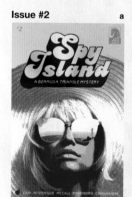

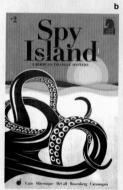

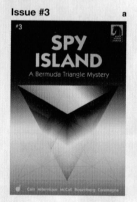

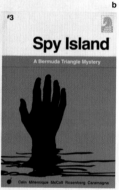

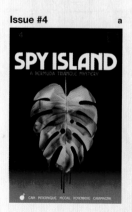

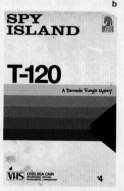